# AWACS AND HAWKEYES

★ ★ ★ THE COMPLETE HISTORY OF ★ ★ ★
AIRBORNE EARLY WARNING AIRCRAFT

# AWACS AND HAWKEYES

★ ★ ★ **THE COMPLETE HISTORY OF** ★ ★ ★
**AIRBORNE EARLY WARNING AIRCRAFT**

★ **LCDR EDWIN LEIGH ARMISTEAD** ★

MBI Publishing Company

First published in 2002 by MBI Publishing Company, Galtier Plaza, Suite 200, 380 Jackson Street, St. Paul, MN 55101-3885, USA.

MBI Publishing Company books are also available at discounts in bulk quantity for industrial or sales-promotional use. For details write to Special Sales Manager at Motorbooks International Wholesalers & Distributors, Galtier Plaza, Suite 200, 380 Jackson Street, St. Paul, MN 55101-3885, USA.

**On the front cover:** An E-2C Hawkeye. *Ted Carlson photo*

**On the back cover:** An EC-130 AWACS and an E-2C Hawkeye. *Ted Carlson photo*

Library of Congress Cataloging-in-Publication Data Available
ISBN 0-7603-1140-4


Edited by Amy Glaser
Designed by Jim Snyder


Printed in China

# Contents

# Acknowledgments

I wish to thank a number of individuals who helped make this book possible. I would like to start with my parents, Jack and Betty Armistead, who gave me an appreciation for history at an early age. I would also like to thank all of the contributors who gave me information for this book. In particular, I would like to cite Kirk Lear, Brian Vaughn, Thomas Shoaf, James Mulquin, Peter Osika, Gary Gerard, Phil Oppenheimer, Scott Stevenson, Chris Holinger, Thomas Walker, Phil Syzcimski, Art Kerr, Mike Ruszkowski, Robert Alwine, Gene Saner, Barry Fox, Michael Maurer, and Bill Richards for allowing me to include their research as part of this effort. And most of all, I would like to thank my wife, Lisa, without whose patience and fortitude to help me in this endeavor, this book would have never been completed.

# Introduction

At 0945 local on 4 May 1982, two Super Etendard Fighters of the Argentine Navy roared down the runway at Rio Grande Field on the island of Tierra Del Fuego off the southeastern coast of Argentina. Each aircraft carried a single Exocet anti-ship missile on its starboard wing as well as two external fuel tanks. Flown by Lt. Comdr. Augusto Bedacarratr and Lt. Armando Mavora, the planes headed east for a rendezvous with a single KC-130 tanker which would replace the fuel used during takeoff and the 15-minute flight. Following their refueling, the aircraft continued outbound for a short time at medium altitude and then descended to a mere 50 feet above the wave tops of the south Atlantic Ocean. Maintaining radio and radar silence, the aircraft approached the target area undetected, and at a predesignated distance from the British fleet, climbed to 120 feet and momentarily switched on their radar. Just after 1100 local, each aircraft locked on a ship, fired its Exocet missile, and then withdrew at low altitude and very high speed to the west.

The Type-42 British destroyer HMS *Sheffield* (D-80) was operating approximately 20 nautical miles west of the main British task force that had arrived off the Falkland Islands on the 29th of April. Moving south, the *Sheffield* was on radar picket duty providing air defense for the task force when her combat information center (CIC) picked up a momentary radar contact of an aircraft approaching at a very low altitude from the west, but the contact subsequently disappeared. About two minutes later, several crew members noticed a smoke trail approaching the ship from the starboard side at a high rate of speed. Shortly thereafter the ship was struck amidships by the Exocet with what was later described as a "short, sharp, unimpressive bang." The Exocet had found its target in the heart of the 4,100-ton ship where it detonated. Fire and smoke spread quickly throughout the ship, and despite a heroic effort by her crew, the fire grew out of control and by 1515 local the ship's crew had been evacuated to nearby vessels. The *Sheffield* continued to burn for some time and would ultimately sink three days later, while under tow after the fires had burned out.

How was it that in this day and age of super electronics, a relatively low-technology system was able to engage a state-of-the-art ship like the *Sheffield* and sink it? British naval forces unfortunately had come to realize perhaps their worst nightmare. They were engaged in a war, albeit a small one, thousands of miles from home, beyond the range of the shore-based Royal Air Force (RAF) Shackleton (AEW Mk.2) aircraft, and without a carrier-based deployable Airborne Early Warning (AEW) platform with which to coordinate the defense of their task force. This lack of a deployable AEW capability is at the heart of the destruction of the HMS *Sheffield*, and when combined with the lack of air superiority found throughout the Falklands War, quickly spelled disaster. Had the Royal Navy (RN) possessed an AEW capability, this attack would have certainly been detected earlier, and the fleet would have been operating under a protective umbrella, providing picket radar air defense and possibly shooting down the Argentine aircraft.

The destruction of the HMS *Sheffield* highlighted the devastating effects of these attacks. The general scenario hinged on the ability of the Argentine pilots to approach the task force undetected and close to within launch range of their air-to-surface missile. The extremely low altitudes, often less than 50 feet, made their intercept much less likely. The Argentine pilots also used an attack technique called "pecking the lobe," where they would descend each time their radar warning receiver (RWR) gear picked up RN radar transmissions. In this manner, they never flew into the heart of the defending ship's radar coverage until seconds from releasing their missiles. Thus, the HMS *Sheffield* had, at best, a capability to detect the inbound attack aircraft out to a range of 30 miles, which gave the crew of the *Sheffield* no more than a few seconds of warning of an inbound aircraft. Positioned 25 or so miles from the rest of the fleet on picket duty, she theoretically could give the main force a minute or two of warning of a direct attack by aircraft. The fact that the Argentine pilots climbed to 120 feet, and were seen by the *Sheffield* systems momentarily during the attack profile means that the attackers were somewhere between 14 and 18 miles from the ship at best when the Exocets left the rail. Therefore, in reality, the *Sheffield* never had a chance, and the rest is history. One of the most important lessons learned from this tragedy was the crucial need for AEW systems by the RN, who after this conflict quickly began to fill that void.

Revolution in warfare is, more often than not, an evolutionary process. AEW has changed the way that war is conducted, and yet the importance of these systems and platforms is often overlooked. Quiet efficiency and professionalism are the trademarks of the AEW community and it is usually only with their absence that leaders realize just how important these assets truly are. A force multiplier, AEW aircraft have become so critical to many operations that their presence is usually a go/no-go criterion. In addition, AEW aircraft are also an element of national policy, not only from a tactical air picture, but also more from a strategical context. This can be seen in the fact that a sale of one of these systems by the United States is an indication of the strength of a bilateral relationship. The purchase of an AEW aircraft can also increase a nation's military presence and prestige within a geographic region. If the United States deploys an Airborne Radar and Control System (AWACS) or other AEW aircraft to a foreign nation in times of hostilities, this movement can be seen as a sign of our nation's intentions. A good example of this, discussed later in this book, is the use of barrier patrols in the 1950s or the transfer of AWACS to Saudi Arabia during the Iran-Iraq War. In addition to a military impact, AEW platforms influence the economic power structure as well. Sales of AEW platforms (or systems or technology) can be a tool of economic trade by the United States to offset imbalances of deficits. All of these factors are huge indicators of the role of AEW as a component of national strategy.

AEW aircraft have had a long and interesting career. Most of the development and operational service of these specialized aircraft have been in the U. S. Navy and the U. S. Air Force. In fact, as early as 1942, U. S. naval task force leaders requested assets to give their fleets earlier warning of incoming threats. Experiments using land- and carrier-based patrol aircraft to search visually for enemy aircraft and ships clearly demonstrated their inadequacy for defending the fleet. In addition, ship-borne, mast-mounted radars could not detect low-flying aircraft or hostile shipping because the line of sight distance to the radar horizon is normally only 30 nautical miles, which does not give the ship defenses enough time to react. Airborne search radars that had been in development since the late 1930s were thought by some to be the answer to this problem. However, these early units were bulky, hard to use, and often required excessive electrical and cooling maintenance requirements. The early airborne radars were also limited in their ability to detect ships because the tremendous amount of clutter returned from the surface of the oceans tended to obscure the actual radar return. All of these factors delayed the development of the airborne search radars as a viable alternative until after World War II.

Once AEW radar units were developed by the U.S. Navy in 1945, they still did not completely solve the problem of detecting incoming enemy aircraft and ships. Without automatic tracking or height-finding capabilities, airborne operators could be quickly overloaded in their attempts to manually track all contacts. A method of stabilizing the radar, utilizing automated and height-finding features, was clearly needed to improve the capabilities of these early

AEW radars. These were, however, significant technological obstacles to overcome and it was not until the mid-1950s that some of these problems were solved. However, with the arrival of the E-2A Hawkeye in 1964, the U.S. Navy finally possessed a dedicated all-weather carrier-based AEW aircraft. The Hawkeye signified the beginning of a true explosion of growth for AEW aircraft because it established a record of excellence that continues today.

Naval development of these aircraft was watched with interest by the U.S. Air Force, and by 1951, that service was ordering production contracts for new aircraft. The development and use of AEW aircraft by the U.S. Air Force, like the U.S. Navy, also reflects an evolutional approach. The original U.S. Air Force AEW aircraft, the EC-121, was designed for specialized missions. However, during its lifetime, this aircraft and its successor, the E-3A, evolved to function as force multipliers, enhancing the capabilities of tactical and strategic aircraft operating in the continental United States (CONUS) or deployed locations throughout the world. Throughout the history of AEW aircraft, an evolutionary transition through a broad spectrum of technological advances becomes readily apparent.

The importance of AEW cannot be overstated. Acting as force multipliers, these aircraft are often seen as essential in the conduct of modern military operations, with their numbers having increased considerably over the past 50 years, and in particular over the past decade. In fact, procurement of new AEW aircraft continues today, with many nations looking to acquire this unique capability; yet there are only a few published books that deal with the production and development of AEW aircraft. Most of my information came from interviews with former AEW aircrew and program managers as well as archival sources. I also visited a number of historical agencies, including the National Archives, the Naval Historical Center, and the Air Force Historical Research Agency, which provided me with the majority of the primary material for this book. However, there is still more to be done. I have spent more than 10 years researching and writing this book, and I am still interested in continuing my research in this area. Therefore, I ask you to please give me any information that you think might help me in this effort. I can be reached at the following e-mail address for the foreseeable future.

Thanks.

— *Leigh Armistead*
armisteadconsult@aol.com

# List of Abbreviations

AACS . . . . . . .Airborne Air Control Squadron

AAW . . . . . . . .Anti-Air Warfare

ACC . . . . . . . .Air Component Commander
or Air Combat Command

ACE . . . . . . . .Airborne Command Element

ACO . . . . . . . .Air Control Officer

AD-5W . . . . . .Douglas-Configured
AEW Skyraider

ADC . . . . . . . .Air Defense Command

AEGIS . . . . . . .Airborne Early Warning Ground
Integration Segment

AETACS . . . . .Airborne Element of the Theater
Air Control System

AEW . . . . . . . .Airborne Early Warning

AEW&C . . . . . .Airborne Early Warning
and Control

AEW&CS . . . . .Airborne Early Warning and
Control Squadron

AEW/AIC . . . .Airborne Early Warning/
Air Intercept Control

AEWACG . . . . .Airborne Early Warning and
Control Group

AF-2W . . . . . .Grumman-Configured
AEW Guardian

AFTEC . . . . . .Air Force Test
and Evaluation Center

AIC . . . . . . . . .Air Intercept Control

ALRI . . . . . . . .Airborne Long-Range Input

AMTI . . . . . . . .Airborne Moving Target
Indicator

APS . . . . . . . . .Airborne Search Radar

ASACS . . . . . .Airborne Surveillance and
Control System

ASW . . . . . . . .Anti-Submarine Warfare

ASWAC . . . . . .Airborne Surveillance
Warning and Control

AW&CS . . . . . .Airborne Warning
and Control System

AWACS . . . . . .Airborne Warning
and Control System

AWACW . . . . .Airborne Warning
Air Control Wing

BDA . . . . . . . .Battle Damage Assessment

BuAer . . . . . . .Bureau of Aeronautics

C3 . . . . . . . . .Command, Control,
and Communications

CAEWWL . . . .Carrier Airborne Early Warning
Wing Atlantic

CAEWWP . . . .Carrier Airborne Early Warning
Wing Pacific

CAEWWS . . . .Carrier Airborne Early Warning
Weapons School

CAP . . . . . . . .Combat Air Patrol

CATCC . . . . . .Carrier Air Traffic Control Center

CETF . . . . . . . .College Eye Task Force

CGAS . . . . . . .Coast Guard Air Station

CGAW . . . . . . .Coast Guard AEW Squadron

CIC . . . . . . . . .Combat Information Center

CICO . . . . . . . .Combat Information
Center Officer

CINCHAN . . . .Commander in Chief Channel

CNO . . . . . . .Chief of Naval Operations

COD . . . . . . .Carrier On-Board Delivery

CONUS . . . . .Continental United States

CQ . . . . . . . .Carrier Qualification

CUSNC . . . . . .Commander U.S. Naval Forces
Central Command

CV . . . . . . . .Aircraft Carrier

CVA . . . . . . .Aircraft Carrier (Attack)

CVBG . . . . . .Carrier Battle Group

CVN . . . . . . .Aircraft Carrier (Nuclear)

CVS . . . . . . .Aircraft Carrier (Anti-Submarine)

CVW . . . . . . .Aircraft Carrier Air Wing

DEFCON . . . . .Defense Condition

DOD . . . . . . .Department of Defense

DPFG . . . . . .Data-Processing Functional Group

DTE . . . . . . .Development Test and Evaluation

E-3 . . . . . . . .AWACS (Sentry)

EA-1E . . . . . .Douglas AEW–Configured AD-5W

EADF . . . . . .Eastern Air Defense Force

ECM . . . . . . .Electronic Countermeasures

ELF . . . . . . . .European Liaison Force

ELINT . . . . . .Electronic Intelligence

ES . . . . . . . . .Electronic Support

ESD . . . . . . .Electronic Systems Division

ESM . . . . . . .Electronic Support Measures

EW . . . . . . . .Electronic Warfare

FAA . . . . . . . .Federal Aviation Administration

FAETULANT . .Fleet Aviation Electronic
Training Unit Atlantic

FAETUPAC . . . .Fleet Aviation Electronic
Training Unit Pacific

FAF . . . . . . . .French Air Force

FASS . . . . . . .Fore and Aft Scanner System

FOB . . . . . . .Forward Operating Base

FON . . . . . . .Freedom of Navigation

FN . . . . . . . . .French Navy

GAO . . . . . . .General Accounting Office

GCA . . . . . . .Guppy (Ground)
Controlled Approach

GCI . . . . . . . .Ground Controlled Intercept

GP . . . . . . . .General Purpose

HARM . . . . . .High-Speed
Anti-Radiation Missile

HCA . . . . . . .Hawkeye (Hummer)
Controlled Approach

HF . . . . . . . .High Frequency

HVAA . . . . . .High Value Airborne Asset

IAF . . . . . . . .Israeli Air Force

IFF . . . . . . . .Identification, Friend or Foe

IIAF . . . . . . . .Imperial Iranian Air Force

IOT&E . . . . . .Initial Operational Test
and Evaluation

IQAF . . . . . . .Iraqi Air Force

JFACC . . . . . .Joint Forces
Air Component Commander

JTIDS . . . . . .Joint Tactical Information
Distribution System

KAF . . . . . . .Kuwaiti Air Force

LAAF . . . . . . .Libyan Air Force

LAST . . . . . . .Low-Altitude Surveillance Task

MCC . . . . . . .Mission Crew Commander

SAGE ....... Semi-Automatic Ground Environment

SAM ........ Surface-to-Air Missile

SAR ........ Search and Rescue

SAU ........ Selective Augmentee Unit

SD ......... Senior Director

SEA ........ Southeast Asia

SEAD ....... Suppression of Enemy Air Defenses

SEADEW ..... Seaward Extension of the DEW Line

SHAPE ...... Supreme Headquarters Allied Powers Europe

SID ........ System Integration Demonstration

SOCC ....... Sector Operations Command Center

SSC ........ Surface, Search, and Control

SUAWACS .... Soviet Union AWACS

TAC ........ Tactical Air Command

TACC ....... Tactical Air Command Center

TACS ....... Theater Air Control System

TAC-X ...... Tactical Test

TAO ........ Tactical Action Officer

TARPS ...... Tactical Airborne Reconnaissance Pod System

TBM-3W ..... General Motors-Configured AEW Avenger Torpedo Bomber

UAE ........ United Arab Emirates

UAV ........ Unmanned Aerial Vehicle

UHF ........ Ultra High Frequency

USAF ....... United States Air Force

USCG ....... United States Coast Guard

USCS ....... United States Customs Service

USMC ....... United States Marine Corps

USN ........ United States Navy

USSR ....... Union of Soviet Socialist Republics

VAQ ........ Tactical Electronic Squadrons

VAW ........ Carrier Airborne Early Warning Squadron

VB ......... Bomber Squadron

VBF ........ Fighter-Bomber Squadron

VC ......... Fleet Composite Squadron

VF ......... Fighter Squadron

VP ......... Patrol Squadron

VPB ........ Patrol Bomber Squadron

VQ ......... Fleet Air Reconnaissance Squadron

VS ......... Carrier Anti-Submarine Warfare Squadron

VT ......... Torpedo Squadron (WWII era)

VT ......... Training Squadron

VTOL ....... Vertical Takeoff and Landing

VW ......... Airborne Early Warning Squadron

VX ......... Aircraft Development Squadron

W2F-1 ...... Grumman E-2A Hawkeye

WADF ....... Western Air Defense Force

WD ......... Weapons Director

WF-2 ....... Grumman E-1B Tracer

WV-2 ....... Lockheed AEW-Configured Super Constellation

CHAPTER ONE

# The Development of Airborne Early Warning (AEW) Aircraft

A EW aircraft changed the nature of warfare. These platforms give their commanders early warning and information on approaching aircraft and ships that were not normally available. By giving decision makers a picture of enemy threats, AEW aircraft have drastically extended the battle space and allowed commanders more time to plan their operations. It has become true in modern warfare that no U. S. military leader will go into battle without the information afforded by modern AEW aircraft. Recent examples include Operations Deny Flight, Desert Storm, Allied Force, and Enduring Freedom where U.S. Navy and U.S. Air Force AEW aircraft have manned stations around the clock, providing key information of enemy aircraft and ship movements. It is this detailed real-time information that has made these operations successful. The development of AEW aircraft proceeded from an amalgamation of many different scientific disciplines that came together during World War II. Although this book is a history of all AEW aircraft and operations, it will tend to concentrate on the U. S. Navy in the first chapter. This is because the Navy had the lead in the development of AEW aircraft, and it was this service that conducted the majority of the early research and development efforts into AEW aircraft. This was due to the enormous pressure exerted by the U.S. Navy fleet task force commanders. They desperately needed a method to combat the low-flying attacks by Japanese aircraft, whose pilots often approached the U. S. fleet at wave top level. Because of the curvature of

1

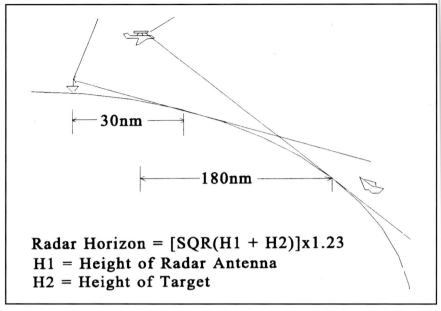

**Radar Horizon = [SQR(H1 + H2)]x1.23**
**H1 = Height of Radar Antenna**
**H2 = Height of Target**

**Line of Sight Constraints for Surface-Based Radar Systems**
Due to the curvature of the earth, a radar based on either a ship- or a
land-based platform will typically be limited to tracking low-flying aircraft
out to the radar horizon, which is approximately 30 nautical miles, and even
less for ground-based or maritime targets. As shown in this diagram, the
radar line of sight for a typical airborne radar is about 180 nautical miles.

the earth, mast-mounted radars could only detect these aircraft at ranges
of 30 to 35 miles. Early reconnaissance methods involving patrol and
scout aircraft trying to identify these units by visual detection often failed,
because it wasn't only low-flying aircraft that threatened the task force but
all incoming bogies, including hostile shipping. However, hostile aircraft
tended to receive the most attention since they were the most difficult to
detect and engage prior to releasing their weapons. This was especially
true after October 1944, with the advent of the kamikaze attacks. AEW aircraft, however, could theoretically detect an aircraft or ship at distances
far superior to earlier systems and were viewed as the answer to this complex problem. A search radar flown high in the air can extend the detection range of its radar system. If AEW aircraft could detect and target low-
flying aircraft at a safe distance from the task force, fighter aircraft from

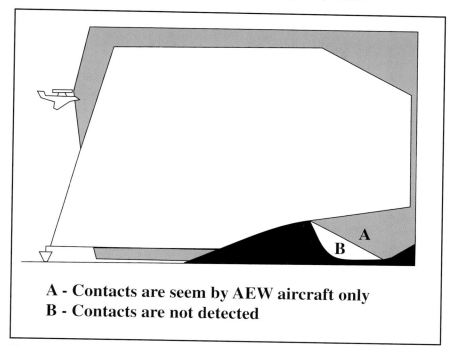

**A - Contacts are seem by AEW aircraft only**
**B - Contacts are not detected**

## Expanded Radar Coverage with AEW Aircraft

By simply raising the radar into the air, the coverage of the AEW system is extended greatly. An aircraft flying at 15,000 feet can typically detect contacts at least 150 nautical miles away, and this can be extended to 250 nautical miles by elevating the radar to 25,000 feet. An airborne system can often see over terrain obstacles as shown in this diagram.

an aircraft carrier could then be launched to engage the inbound Japanese pilots. Although this was the basic premise of the development of AEW aircraft, the technological problems encountered were very severe, and it took over 20 years to develop a dedicated all-weather AEW aircraft. Yet the research and development completed from 1942 to 1964 by the U. S. Navy was essential in the successful completion of a true AEW platform.

### The Origins of Naval AEW Aircraft

The true impetus of AEW dates to the spring of 1942, when Adm. Ernest J. King, commander in chief of the U.S. Navy, asked Dr. Vannevar Bush, the director of the Office of Scientific Research and Development

(OSRD) for the National Defense Research Committee (NDRC) to develop a radar-relay system that would allow his task force commanders to pass information beyond the present limits of their ships' radars. A radar-relay link would allow the combat systems of these different ships to combine their radar pictures to give each commanding officer a better awareness of the tactical situation. This was important because one of the most critical stages of a naval battle is the detection and targeting phase of an operation. Dirigibles, blimps, and patrol and scout aircraft have been used for decades to help in detecting enemy forces, whether hostile shipping or aircraft. However, they were normally limited to visual detection methods. Radar had been developed in the 1930s, but units in production were still very crude. Radar and a radar-relay system between ships would allow task force commanders to better understand the threats that faced their task group.

From this original tasking came the radar-relay project NA-112, established in June 1942. Much of the research was conducted at Division D of the Massachusetts Institute of Technology-Radiation Laboratory (MIT-RL). The idea of this radar-relay link was that several ships could tie their radar pictures together, thereby giving each ship a better detection capability. Throughout World War II there was continuous research and development into this radar-relay link project. However, substantial progress was not forthcoming due to technical difficulties. Early in 1944 the direction of this project changed when representatives from the Bureau of Aeronautics (BuAer), including Capt. Frank Akers, head of the electronics section, and his subordinate, Comdr. Lloyd V. Berkner, head of research and development of electronics material, held a series of conferences to review the progress of the radar-relay work. These conferences revealed that the development of radar-relay project NA-112 was progressing very slowly. Therefore, BuAer officials decided to switch the focus of the developmental research of the radar-relay link project to an AEW radar set that could be used by carrier aircraft. Commander Berkner thought that an airborne radar could achieve more success than the radar-relay project because it could theoretically detect an enemy force well before they would be able to launch an attack. In essence it could change the nature of naval warfare by drastically extending the battle space of a task force.

These conferences led by representatives from BuAer basically established the AEW program within the Navy. Commander Berkner and other BuAer officials believed that a tactical requirement existed, and procurement proceedings were begun immediately. Project NA-178, a joint Bureau of Aeronautics–Bureau of Ships project, was the ultimate outcome of these conferences. These changes infused new enthusiasm into this project with accelerated research work conducted on the radar systems that had been progressing at the MIT-RL facility. In fact, the first production system of an AEW radar was delivered to the Navy less than 13 months after the start of Project NA-178! Research on Project NA-178 was undertaken by Division D and later Division 14 of the MIT-RL facility. Even when the focus of the project changed in 1944, many of the same scientists remained on the staff. Reorganized again during February 1945 into Project Cadillac (named after Cadillac Mountain in Maine, where much of the early avionics testing occurred), the staff at MIT-RL was enlarged to facilitate development and accelerated production of the AEW aircraft. By the summer of 1945, Project Cadillac was so large that it involved nearly 20 percent of the staff personnel at MIT-RL. Headed by J. B. Wiesner, these scientists were chosen from a wide variety of backgrounds and disciplines across the spectrum of sciences to handle the complexity of this airborne radar.

The early aircraft used by MIT-RL to conduct these AEW experiments were variations of the naval aircraft available at that time. Desired qualities included roomy and robust airframes that could handle the electronic equipment and personnel needed to operate it. The primary test aircraft was the TBM-3W, which was a modification of the three-seat General Motors TBM Avenger medium carrier torpedo bomber, whose roomy interior could accommodate the bulky radar equipment. Available in large quantities, the TBM was combat tested, and perhaps more important, it was readily available. During 1944 TBMs were modified into the TBM-3W as the first AEW aircraft to undergo testing.

An airborne radar, known as the APS-20, was designed for Project NA-178 by MIT-RL scientists. The designation APS is standard military nomenclature for an airborne search radar. Without getting too technical, an airborne search radar is usually composed of five basic components: A transmitter converts electrical energy to electromagnetic energy and sends out high-powered pulses (i.e., radar). These pulses are sent out through and returned via the antenna. The returning radar signals are then sent to a receiver, where they are amplified. The signal then flows to a computer or processor that converts the signal to a video, which is then routed to a display unit, often a scope. These five basic components make

**TBM-3W (Cadillac I)**
The Grumman Avenger was the first AEW aircraft, and it housed the APS-20 radar in a ventral dome. Manned by a pilot and systems operator, these aircraft were flown by the U.S. Navy in the immediate post–World War II period. This photo shows the comparison between a standard TBM-3 and the AEW version in the foreground. *Department of U.S. Navy*

up any radar system and are common throughout the AEW aircraft that are presented in this book.

The reason that the development of an AEW radar is so difficult is because of the unique environment in which this aircraft operates. AEW radar was developed to overcome the inherent range limitations of a ground-based system. By lifting a search radar into the air, you can vastly increase the range of the system, but you also quickly encounter a number of difficult technical problems that must be overcome in order for the AEW radar to perform correctly. These include clutter from the surface of the earth, compensating for ownship motion, power-out/cooling requirements, and adequate computer-processing capability. While these problems are not insurmountable, design difficulties led to delays that took a number of years to overcome. However, for its time, the original APS-20 radar, designed in 1945, was a truly marvelous technological development.

This system was an S-band (the old military frequency designation that covered the spectrum from 1,500 to 5,000 megahertz) radar that used an 8-by-3-foot paraboloid dish antenna. Housed in a plastic fairing attached to the bottom of the aircraft, this radar had a 360-degree sweep. The original APS-20 radar developed under Project Cadillac operated at a 10-centimeter wavelength with a peak power output of 1 megawatt and used a 2-microsecond pulse. The heart of the airborne section was a complex synchronizer and a radar receiver with numerous technologically advanced features such as an identification, friend or foe (IFF) receiver. A relay transmitter was used to transmit both radar and IFF information to the shipborne receiver station, where the transmissions were synchronized and coded for decreased interference and vulnerability to jamming. The system was operated by two individuals who served primarily to correlate and relay the information. The airborne part of the system was but half the equation, as the ship-related avionics worked to bring the data into a useable format. Any ship with the necessary equipment aboard and within relay range of the aircraft could receive the data. A complex and precision-adjusted decoder was used to receive and relay the information to a number of screens within the ship's combat information center (CIC). Labeled "Bellhop," this radar-relay service enabled surface units equipped with CICs to receive the location and relative positions of various units of the task force and any unidentified targets. The displays could be expanded and sectored for detailed examination and correlation by the scope operators in a number of methods. Systems were devised in the ships' CICs whereby the AEW aircraft's motion would be eliminated and the picture centered on the receiver's location.

Likewise, in the TBM-3W, system usage depended on scope setup and layout. The APS-20 console consisted of three scans or scopes. The first was an "A" scan for monitoring system performance, monitoring Bellhop, and determining raid size of small targets. The center scope on the console was a 4-inch scope with 20/50/100/200-mile ranges. The third scan was another 4-inch scope that offered a 20-mile delayed presentation, which solved the course and speed problem, since the

7

motion was neither relative nor true. However, even with these three scopes, there was still a problem associated with the APS-20 radar during this period due to the lack of symbology. Returns were marked by fluorescent yellow "bananas" and the operator used a grease pencil to track these contacts, to develop a course and speed. Still, for all of these deficiencies, the APS-20 was a fairly advanced piece of engineering.

To test the radar in many environments, early avionics equipment was set up on Cadillac Mountain in Maine until the airframe modifications were complete. Forty sets of the APS-20 radar were simultaneously ordered for production in July 1944; so not only did research and development take place during the summer of 1944, but, in fact, production of the TBM-3Ws had already begun. Field tests of the TBM-3W were conducted in Boston during August of 1944, with full-scale flight demonstrations following in October 1944. Throughout the winter of 1944 and spring of 1945, testing and evaluation of this project proceeded on a rapid production and testing schedule. The first production aircraft was delivered in March 1945, only 13 months after the initiation of the project, with the other 39 aircraft following by early summer.

Aircraft carrier compatibility tests were conducted on the USS *Ranger* (CV-4) in April 1945 off the coast of California. Initial results were generally successful but not without problems. All personnel involved realized that further development and refinement was needed for the system to reach its full capability. Thus, testing by MIT-RL and BuAer personnel continued, although the war ended in August 1945 before the TBM-3Ws had completed this phase. Much of the data from these early tests aboard the *Ranger* proved very promising. Single plane targets were routinely detected at ranges twice that of shipborne, mast-mounted radar. Formations of aircraft were detected at ranges two to four times greater than previously feasible, while the detection range of surface vessels was also increased by a factor of six. These improvements in radar range and detection times alone justified the further development of the AEW aircraft.

Even though the Cadillac I program using the TBM-3W aircraft was well underway by the spring of 1945, there was still tremendous demand from fleet commanders for AEW aircraft in the Pacific. Engineers at MIT-RL began a second development program, entitled Cadillac II, that used a four-engine, land-based bomber to carry this AEW equipment. The Navy chose the Army Air Force's B-17G and gave it the naval designation PB-1W. The larger aircraft was utilized with the hope that this aircraft would become an airborne CIC. It would, of course, be constrained by the need to operate near land bases. However, Cadillac II aircraft gave the Navy a greater capability in tracking aircraft. More watch-standers could fly aboard the PB-1W to analyze data rather than having to send the information back to the aircraft carrier. Fortunately, to speed up development, the avionics were similar to the Cadillac I program, and a very tight production schedule was met. The Navy produced this program in record time—from June 1945, when the program began, until October 1945, when the last of the 25 PB-1W radar aircraft was delivered—and for one-fifth of the cost of Cadillac I.

The application of Cadillac I and II aircraft eventually revolutionized naval warfare. By lifting a search radar into the air, the task force commander could now see all radar contacts within attacking radius and could pursue options to engage them. No longer was he dependent on the visual search patterns of patrol or search aircraft. A single AEW radar could track several contacts without being susceptible to weather or cloud formations. From these inauspicious beginnings, all-weather, combat-ready AEW aircraft would be developed for the U.S. Navy. Awkward and somewhat ungainly, these early naval AEW aircraft were in fact to revolutionize the way modern warfare is conducted.

## Project OP/V26/F42-1

For all of the uses of AEW aircraft in late 1945, there was still some final testing to be completed before the TBM-3W or PB-1W aircraft were released to the fleet. Cadillac II aircraft (PB-1Ws) were the first AEW aircraft to be delivered to a squadron for this evolution. The Navy on 20 July 1945 reformed VPB-101 (a former patrol bombing squadron) to act as the main squadron involved in the testing of these aircraft. Established at Willow Grove, Pennsylvania, the squadron was to shift bases three times in the next 12 months, first to Atlantic City, New Jersey; then to Floyd Bennett Field, New York City; and finally to Quonset Point, Rhode Island. Receiving its first PB-1W on 15 November 1945, the squadron did not receive its first CIC (non-pilot) officer until 8 January 1946. More aircraft and aircrew followed, with VPB-101 receiving its first TBM-3Ws and their crew on 7 February and four more PB-1W aircraft in the next two months.

Due to urgent requests from task force commanders, the Cadillac programs enjoyed continual high priority within the Navy from February 1944 to October 1945. This could have changed as World War

**PB-1W (Cadillac II)**
The U.S. Navy AEW aircraft shown here is a modified B-17 with its APS-20 radar. The Cadillac II program eventually modified 40 of these bombers for use by land-based and evaluation squadrons. Note the APS-20 radar housed in the ventral dome below the bomber. These aircraft were the forerunners of the modern AWACS that are in service today. *Department of U.S. Navy*

II came to a close, but Project Cadillac was blessed in that AEW was considered a crucial technology. The Navy continued testing AEW concepts throughout the early postwar period. Much of the impetus for this increased testing came from the chief of naval operations (CNO) in his requirement to explore and document the capabilities and limitations of Cadillac I and II aircraft.

In a letter dated 29 December 1945, the CNO suggested several problems that should be evaluated by the two types of AEW aircraft. This included the capabilities and limitations of these aircraft in a variety of situations including open ocean, near land, and overland missions. Information was also needed to see how effective the APS-20 radar was in tracking meteorological events such as hurricanes and weather fronts.

Maintenance and reliability factors were unknowns that also needed to be determined. Specifically for the PB-1W land-based aircraft of the Cadillac II program, recommendations were needed for its tactical employment with fleet units at sea. Additional questions existed as to whether these land-based aircraft could be integrated into large warning nets to protect the continental United States from a possible attack.

All of these suggestions and questions about the capability of the AEW aircraft evolved into a huge CNO-sponsored project that lasted more than three years. Assigned to the cognizant office of the Operational Development Force (OPDEVFOR), this project was known as OP/V26/F42-1. Its importance within the Navy was increased considerably when on 24 July 1946, Project OP/V26/F42-1 was raised from "D" to "AA" priority, the highest within the Navy. The impetus for this change came once again from the office of the CNO, where the emerging technologies such as AEW were seen as essential in the postwar Navy. To facilitate VPB-101 in its testing, the squadron was redesignated VX-4 on 15 May 1946. This in effect placed the squadron under the cognizance of OPDEVFOR, and allowed squadron personnel to concentrate solely on testing and evaluating the APS-20 radar. Thus, VX-4 provided the aircraft and personnel for the project, although they did not use all of the Cadillac aircraft for this operation. Some of the TBM-3Ws ended up being assigned to other training units and squadrons to prepare personnel for their eventual operational fleet use.

While the Navy began outfitting the fleet, OPDEVFOR and VX-4 remained the primary units testing these aircraft and their performance in the postwar period. The results of their evaluations consisted of 11 partial reports and a final conclusion. Following the general outline of the CNO request, all reports were delivered by the fall of 1949. Capabilities and limitations of the aircraft concerning meteorological formations, surface targets, snorkel detection, and high-altitude aircraft were all investigated. Specific differences between the two platforms were noted as was the capability of the land-based PB-1W to interact with at-sea fleet units.

The scope of this OPDEVFOR project was immense. The APS-20 radar systems and AEW aircraft were treated in a variety of environmental and operational conditions against different enemy threats. The original project led to a number of other special tests involving the APS-20 radar equipment. Following the success of project

11

**ZPG-3W**
The adaptation of the Navy blimp to an AEW role was somewhat natural. This is the ZPG-3W with its radar installed above and below the envelope. What makes the blimp a natural for the AEW role is its long on-station time. Unlike aircraft, the ZPG-3W can stay airborne for days at a time, and is only limited by crew fatigue. *Department of U.S. Navy*

OP/V26/F42-1, the Navy tested the APS-20 airborne radar on just about every type of platform available to it. Some of these included the Goodyear ZPG-2W/ZPG-3W airships (Project OP/V74/F42-5 in 1949), the Grumman AF-2W Guardian and the Douglas XAD-1W/AD-3W/AD-4W/AD-5W Skyraider attack aircraft, the Sikorsky HR2S-1W helicopter, and even the Lockheed P2V-5/P2V-7 Neptune patrol aircraft. The Navy also attempted to improve the air-to-air capability of the radar by mounting it on top of the aircraft instead of underneath. In this manner land and sea clutter were minimized and high-altitude detection ranges were increased. These experiments were conducted on the PB-1W (Cadillac II aircraft) with favorable results, but production was never authorized.

As the testing continued throughout 1947 and 1948, the operational use of TBM-3Ws was accomplished through the Fleet Aviation Electronic Training Units (Atlantic-FAETULANT and Pacific-FAETUPAC). The CNO, however, believed that there was a need for more fleet AEW units and he authorized the formation of AEW squadrons in 1948. Thus, only three years after the first flight of Cadillac test aircraft and with OP/V26/F42-1 still in evaluation, the first two Carrier Airborne Early Warning Squadrons (VAWs) were formed on 6 July 1948. VAW-1 based at Ream Field, San Diego, California, and VAW-2 based at Norfolk, Virginia, became the forerunners of the carrier-based AEW communities that exist today. Initially equipped with TBM-3Ws, these squadrons eventually numbered 400 officers and enlisted men with a complement of 15 to 25 aircraft. Each squadron was divided into detachments consisting of 3 to 6 aircraft and 90 to 140 enlisted personnel that were deployed on the various carriers of the fleet. Headed by a lieutenant or a lieutenant commander officer-in-charge (OINC), the detachments were assigned to one aircraft carrier for the duration of workups and deployments. These detachments satisfied the need for a small but very necessary element of AEW expertise on each aircraft carrier.

In reviewing the history of naval AEW, it must be remembered that there were both land- and sea-based components and often their nomenclature is confusing. Airborne Early Warning squadrons (VWs) were land-based units that operated the larger land-based AEW aircraft such as the PB-1W. (VAW) squadrons are sea-based units that operate the smaller carrier-based AEW aircraft such as the TBM-3W. Thus, at one time or another there was a VAW-11, a VW-11, and even a VAW-111. Even more confusing are some of the other changes, including the VC (Composite), VX (Experimental), VPB (Patrol Bomber), and VPW (Patrol Search) designations, all of which were used in the immediate post–World War II era to designate AEW squadrons.

Organizationally these early VAW squadrons operated as huge clearinghouses for AEW information on both coasts. VAW-1 was formed from the remnants of Fleet Electronic Training Unit Pacific. Its new charter was to administer and maintain operational readiness of AEW teams assigned to carriers with a secondary mission involving meteorological observations. Established on 6 July 1948 with an initial complement of 14 TBM-3Ws and 10 TBM-3Es (the electronic warfare version of the TBM Avenger), VAW-1 was redesignated VC-11 on 1 September 1948. The VC designation was an attempt by the Navy to align its support squadrons into a comprehensible structure. The VAW squadrons as well as many other units were all redesignated as VC aircraft squadrons. By doing this the Navy theoretically reduced the different kinds of squadrons based on the carrier, although in practice there were still 4–5 of these different kinds of VC detachments on each carrier. Composite Heavy Attack, Composite Early Warning, Composite Night Attack, Composite Night Fighter, Composite Photographic, and Carrier Anti-Submarine squadrons were all designated VC squadrons at some time in the immediate post–World War II era.

Perhaps even more confusing was the history of VAW-1's sister squadron, VAW-2. Established on 6 July 1948, VAW-2 was also a large squadron with 10 TBM-3Es, 12 TBM-3Ws and TBM-3s, and 1 SNJ (a pilot trainer) aircraft with 88 officers and 174 enlisted personnel. Located at Naval Air Station (NAS) Norfolk, Virginia, the squadron relocated to NAS Quonset Point, Rhode Island, on 23 August 1948, and was redesignated as VC-12 on 1 September 1948. Thus, some of its detachments that were at sea during the summer of 1948 came back to a new home base and a new squadron name. Much of this postwar shuffling was in order for the Navy to maximize the use of its assets in a reduced force structure. Thus, while VAW-2 transferred to Rhode Island in August 1948, it took the spaces of VX-4, the land-based AEW testing squadron, which had vacated them on 24 June 1948 for their move to NAS Patuxent River, Maryland. Redesignated again in 1948, VX-4 became VPW-1; however, it continued to conduct experiments and testing in support of OPDEVFOR AEW-related operations.

Throughout this early organizational period, the Navy VAW community continued to evolve and stabilize. Squadrons were formed and detachments of TBM-3Ws were sent to all carriers, while the service completed its testing of the capabilities and limitations of these new AEW carrier-based aircraft. The land-based aircraft were also evolving throughout this period, in an attempt to determine their capabilities by operational testing with fleet units. For everyone involved, it was a very busy time as the VAW and VW communities matured.

**Naval AEW Diversifies and Stabilizes**

The Korean War interrupted the research and development activities of the naval AEW community. This conflict saw the first operational use of these AEW aircraft in a combat environment. The TBM-3Ws and the

PB-1Ws flew support missions during the Korean War, but AEW was not their primary function. Without a direct threat from the North Korean Air Force, U.S. Navy AEW aircraft flew other missions such as anti-submarine warfare (ASW); strike attack vectoring; and surface, search, and control (SSC) operations. During this conflict, VAW and VW aircrews developed much of the current tactics used by the U. S. Navy with regard to AEW aircraft. As a result, the primary mission of these aircraft quickly evolved to warfare areas other than "pure" airborne early warning. Yet AEW aircraft would prove their worth throughout the conflict with their unique detection capabilities. Detachments from VC-11 and VC-12, flying the TBM-3W, augmented all war-bound carriers. In addition to carrier aircraft, VW-1 (formed as the first of the land-based squadrons, using PB-1Ws on 18 June 1952 and stationed at NAS Barbers Point, Hawaii) was available for AEW tasking during the latter stages of the conflict. As was the case for much of the decade, AEW was not the primary mission of these aircraft.

A unique demonstration of the capabilities of AEW aircraft in this era involved the use of TBM-3Ws to lead attack aircraft in their bombing strikes. By locating the coast in points, the TBM-3Ws would vector the bombers to their targets. This was possible because the AEW aircraft had flight characteristics similar to their attack counterparts. AEW aircraft and aircrews performed admirably during this conflict, consistently demonstrating their usefulness and flexibility in meeting emerging missions in a combat environment. This in turn ensured that these aircraft and crews held an important and useful role in meeting the U.S. Navy's missions.

## The Guardian (AF-2W)

A confusing point to anyone studying the use of VAW aircraft by the Navy during this period is that some AEW aircraft were used by and assigned to anti-submarine (VS) squadrons. This was for many reasons, not the least being that after the conclusion of World War II, there were only a certain number of naval aviation aircraft types in use on the aircraft carrier. These new AEW aircraft did not fit handily into any of the former categories, which included Fighter (VF), Fighter-Bomber (VBF), Bomber (VB), and Torpedo (VT) squadrons. As stated earlier, the VC designation covered a number of detachments that were stationed on the carrier, each with different specialized aircraft, and the VAW and VS components were often grouped together under this VC title. In addition, Navy operators found the radar of these AEW aircraft very useful in locating surfaced submarines. Thus, the AEW aircraft often operated with ASW aircraft as part of "Hunter-Killer" teams. A third and perhaps more subtle reason was that for years (in fact, well into the 1970s), the VS and VAW communities were grouped together in the Bureau of Naval Personnel files. Therefore, their aircrews tended to be viewed as somewhat interchangeable. Many benefits were derived from the use of AEW aircraft in ASW missions. AEW and ASW detachments were included on every carrier, including the attack (CVA) and anti-submarine (CVS) versions, thereby increasing the number of AEW aircraft and men needed to support these detachments. More TBM-3Ws were built and used throughout their service life than might have occurred otherwise, and in fact these aircraft could very successfully perform both ASW and AEW missions.

It was not only the TBM-3Ws that served as carrier-based AEW aircraft during the war effort in Korea, but also another aircraft, namely the AF-2W Guardian, which had a corollary mission of AEW. Developed by Grumman Aircraft Corporation, it was and still is the largest single-engine piston-driven aircraft ever to operate from a carrier deck. The highly modified Guardian was present in two forms, the AEW AF-2W and the ASW AF-2S. Together these aircraft acted as a Hunter-Killer team, with the APS-20 radar version locating and targeting surfaced submarines, and the ASW version prosecuting the contact. A total of 153 AF-2Ws were built for service between 1948 and 1957. They served in VS squadrons well into the 1950s, with most being replaced by other Grumman and Douglas aircraft, including the S2F-1 (S-2A) and the AD-5W.

### The Guppy (AD-3W/4W/5W)

The Douglas Skyraider was the third design conceived by the Douglas Aircraft Manufacturing Company to replace the SBD dive-bomber. Designated XBT2D-1 and submitted to the Navy in mid-1944, the first operational prototype flew in March of 1945 and was accepted by the U.S. Navy later that year. This aircraft subsequently went into production under the simplified Navy attack designation AD. Numerous models were fielded, resulting in 49 versions of the seven basic types of Skyraider aircraft (AD-1 through AD-7). A hardy and powerful aircraft, well suited for the rigors of carrier aviation, the Skyraider was continuously produced until February 1957, by which time a total of 3,180 aircraft of the type had been built. The AD series had superior handling characteristics and a significant speed differential over the AF-2W Guardian, and was also used in Hunter-Killer teams throughout the 1950s. Nicknamed "Able Dog" or "Spad," the AD series figured prominently in the history of naval AEW. Built in large numbers, three different sets of Skyraiders were modified for AEW use.

The first modification of the Skyraider for AEW use was the XAD-1W, which was quickly followed by the AD-3W. Produced from 1948 to 1949, 29 of these aircraft were built. The AD-3W was quickly nicknamed the "Guppy" because the aircraft looked like a fat fish with the tublike radome underneath the fuselage. The next modification to the Spad was the AD-4W, of which 168 were produced from 1950 to 1951. Not all of these aircraft were used by U. S. naval forces, as 50 airframes were sold to Great Britain under the Mutual Defense Assistance Program (MDAP), and some were also used by the U. S. Marine Corps. The AEW.1 (AD-4W), as delivered to the Royal Navy, was equipped with a 2,700-horsepower Wright R-3350-26W radial engine and incorporated many upgrades over previous models, including strengthened gear, high-visibility bulletproof canopy, and an autopilot system. Basic performance data for the AD-4 series included a maximum speed of 365 miles per hour, a service ceiling of 25,000 feet, and a combat radius of 1,500 miles. Three men composed the crew of the AD-4W, including a pilot and two radar operators, with one aircrew located in the rear of the cramped fuselage. All AEW Skyraiders in the Royal Navy served with No. 849 Squadron, at Culdrose, which continues to serve as home to the Royal Navy's AEW assets to this day.

The most radical of the Skyraider modifications was the AD-5W. Produced from 1951 to 1956, this version featured a widened cockpit, and changes to the airframe that lengthened and strengthened the aircraft. In the AD-5W, the problem of relative motion on the radar operator's scope had been solved, which greatly aided the operators in using their systems. The AD-5W also added two ultra high frequency (UHF) radios (ARC-27) that were linked together so that the Guppy could act as a "middleman" and pass communications between distant stations. This mission was very important and is still a facet of VAW operations today. All of these changes resulted from lessons learned during the Korean War. The AD-5W was the most widely produced version of the AEW Skyraider, with 218 built for AEW radar use. On active service for many years, AD-5Ws in fact served until 1965, when the last deployment was made by VAW-11 Detachment Tango on board the USS *Yorktown* (CVS-10).

Because the APS-20 was useful for other missions besides AEW, many units also used versions of the AD-5W for operations such as ASW, SSC, "Guppy"-Controlled Approach (GCA), and search and rescue (SAR). Likewise, there were ASW and electronic warfare (EW) squadrons such as VAW-33 that conducted AEW as a collateral mission using the AD-5W. A tough and durable aircraft, the AD-5W was a true workhorse of the VAW community for many years.

Throughout the evolution of AEW aircraft in the late 1940s and early 1950s, there was one constant in the naval AEW world, namely the radar used by all of these aircraft. No matter what airplane is discussed, whether carrier- or land-based, they all had a common element: they all operated some version of the venerable APS-20 S-band radar. The performance of the radar and its continued use hampered serious efforts by the AEW community to establish itself as a reliable asset. This shortcoming was only to be addressed with the advent of new AEW aircraft and radar in the early 1960s.

Throughout the 1950s, there were very few "pure" AEW exercises for these aircraft, as they were deemed too valuable in their other roles to test various theories. The Guardians and Guppies were needed for missions that were believed to be far more important than mere AEW. Whether it was vectoring a fighter for an intercept or toward a tanker aircraft, or assisting in a SAR mission or ASW, it was the unique ability of the AEW aircraft to see where no other platform could that enabled these missions to succeed. Yet the VAW and VW communities of the 1950s were not the all-weather AEW platforms that the community desired. Deficient in radar performance, specifically detection and tracking, the community was still to experience many growing pains during its continuing evolution.

### Evolution of the Naval Flight Officer (NFO)

A non-technical, common problem affecting the development of the AEW community was the lack of trained officer air controllers. This affected all aircraft communities throughout the Navy, as few trained officers were available for these highly sophisticated aircraft. The Navy did not have a career path, similar to that which pilots enjoyed, that was attractive to these non-aviator officers. For much of its history, naval aviation had relied on enlisted personnel for aircrew duties not involving piloting. By the late 1950s there was a variety of aircraft in the production stage (the E-2A, the A-6A, and the F-4A)—all requiring another highly qualified officer to operate its weapons systems. In these aircraft it was more often than not the weapons system operator rather than the pilot who actually detected the target and released the weapons to destroy it.

Originally, the Navy had used pilots and naval aviation observer officers ( NAO[C], NAO[I], and NAO[R]) in early multiseat aircraft. The NAO(R) acted as an engineer in the technical development role, the NAO(I) was the intercept controller employed in the F3D and later the F4H (Phantom), and the NAO(C) was trained in AEW and air control. The VAW community had also used chief radiomen, but only for a limited time. With the introduction of dedicated officer controllers in the late 1950s, the potential of the weapons systems in the new aircraft was fully realized. Fighter and attack pilots tended to trust the officer controllers more, thus allowing VAW aircrew to receive more respect from the senior aviators in matters concerning AEW operations. Prior to the establishment of the NFO rating, all aviation officers other than pilot were designated 135X, but only a handful of these officers were designated NAO(C). Yet the general aviation training conference in Pensacola (1964–1965) changed that status. Decisions were made to change the status of NFOs, with Basic NAO school and attendance at preflight schools all sharing in this improvement. The Airborne Tactical Data System (ATDS) course at Naval Air Facility (NAF) Glynco was a positive result of these changes and was a valuable source of training to the VAW community for many years. Long before other communities faced this manning issue, the VAW and VW squadrons were training officers (often using in-house programs) for these controller roles. Without an official status change, however, their career potential was very limited. The need for a career path and regular Navy status for these non-pilot officers ultimately became the driving force behind the NFO program. Limited promotion opportunities hampered naval flight officers and it wasn't until 1970 that all restrictions were lifted. Changes in career potential aside, interestingly enough the first officer air controller to undergo dedicated AEW training was named Lt. A.E.W. Fritz, who reported aboard VC-12 on 12 October 1951.

# CHAPTER TWO

# The Spirit
# of the Barrier

The history of AEW aircraft flying barrier operations to defend the continental United States from aerial attack is a unique chapter in the early use of military services conducting joint operations. U.S. Navy and U.S. Air Force land-based AEW aircraft flew surveillance missions off the coasts of the United States for more than a decade in an effort to give warning of a possible bomber attack from the Soviet Union. Although the barrier system was never seriously tested, many people believe that its mere presence acted as a deterrent and might have precluded a major attack by Soviet aircraft. With the standup of these barriers, the United States was issuing an important signal of its intention to protect itself from a "bolt-out-of-the-blue" attack. A component of national strategy, the movement of AEW aircraft in this case effectively telegraphed to the Soviet Union the intentions of the United States.

## Defining the Need: The Soviet Bomber Threat

The original assessment of using AEW aircraft in a barrier operation by the U.S. Navy arose from the CNO Project OP/V26/F42-1, which in 1946 began a three-year investigation into the inclusion of AEW aircraft into large early warning nets. With the introduction of long-range strategic bombers projected for the Soviet Union in the mid-1950s, the military leaders of the United States felt that there was danger of an unexpected attack. When the Communist North Koreans invaded their southern neighbor in the summer of 1950, America's leaders wondered if this war was in fact a subterfuge to mask a coming Russian invasion of Western

Europe. This understandable fear of an impending war also heightened the expectation of an atomic attack against the United States. With incomplete intelligence on Soviet atomic assets, America's air defense planners credited the Soviets with capabilities roughly equivalent to those possessed by the United States. In other words, since the United States fielded a large fleet of intercontinental, atomic bombers, we expected the Soviets to do the same. Gen. Benjamin W. Chidlaw, one of the early commanders of the joint service continental Air Defense Command (ADC), echoed this sentiment:

"We know that the Soviet Union has copied and improved upon our World War II B-29 (TU-4 Bull), and has built more than a thousand of these improved planes. We know that this airplane, except for navigation and bombing gadgetry, has the range to reach all principal targets of this country. We know the USSR has still better and still faster planes under development and test and has flown long-range jet bombers which indicate the seriousness of their intentions. We also know that the USSR has created explosions of thermonuclear devices. Today the Soviet Union has the capability to attack us through the air with weapons of great destruction."

Although the TU-4's range would permit only one-way missions, it was still reasonable to assume that it or its successors might strike along the most direct route, which was simply "over the pole." As a result, in November 1950 the United States and Canada agreed to build the first of three lines of radar stations (Pinetree) spanning the northern stretches of the continent to warn of a bomber attack. Further studies acknowledged that since the radar pickets would end on the coasts, it was possible for the Russians to flank the entire radar network and fighter interceptors, especially at low altitude. So if the Soviets were to employ air refueling, or use airborne invasions of Alaska or Iceland to secure forward airfields for their bombers, all of America could be within easy reach without radar detection. To prevent this "end-run," the radar cover had to be extended seaward, to better ensure that Strategic Air Command would have enough advance warning to avoid attack and retaliate against the Soviets. Air Force historian Kenneth Schaffel noted that every major air defense study since 1947 had urged that picket ships and early warning and control aircraft be developed and acquired. Unfortunately, progress had been thwarted by lack of money and the inability of the Air Force and Navy to agree on

**DEW Radar Ship**
Both the U.S. Navy and the U.S. Air Force utilized naval radar ships (shown here) as part of the seaward extension of the DEW line (SEADEW, U.S. Navy) and the Contiguous Extension of the Continental System (U.S. Air Force). This photo shows an example of one of these radar platforms as they were outfitted in the late 1950s.
*Department of U.S. Navy*

how and where the overwater detection forces would operate, and more importantly, who would command them.

### The Airborne Radar Picket: Navy or Air Force Jurisdiction?

To fill this gap in radar coverage, a requirement was added to extend radar coverage to sea through the use of land-based AEW squadrons and radar picket ships along the seaward extension of the Distance Early Warning (DEW) (SEADEW) line and the contiguous radar extension. Still reeling from the postwar drawdown, the Navy was hesitant to engage in a costly continental air defense program which, in fact, was the Air Force's responsibility—at the expense of its own tactical fleet operations. However, when the Navy finally saw that this was a maritime mission, it made the decision to undertake this over-the-sea picket duty. This was the beginning of the VW community's involvement in barrier operations. Although not the original intention behind its development, much of VW history is in fact firmly rooted in barrier operations.

The concept of this type of aerial defense for the United States had been tested over the preceding decade by a variety of U.S. Navy AEW aircraft and platforms. As early as 30 August 1946, tentative studies had been made on the applicability of AEW aircraft in defending the United States from a surprise attack. Originally conceived in 1946 as two parallel tracks in the Atlantic Ocean, the original U.S. Navy barrier plan ran from Iceland via the Azores to Natal, Brazil, on the outer barrier, and from Argentia, Newfoundland, via Bermuda to Roosevelt Roads, Puerto Rico, on the inner barrier. This original plan was later downgraded due to financial and material constraints. In reality, once stood up, the Atlantic Barrier ran from Newfoundland to the Azores, while the Pacific Barrier was aligned along a line from the Aleutians to Midway Island.

The U.S. Air Force and ADC realized early in the post–World War II period that they needed to extend the radar coverage of their CONUS-based systems seaward to protect the United States against attack. Studies by U.S. Air Force and civilian agencies such as the Rand Corporation argued for not only extensions of the land-based contiguous radar systems but also extensions of the new early warning radar lines (Pinetree, Mid-Canada, and DEW) to the seaward flanks. Although somewhat similar to the studies conducted by the U.S. Navy, the big differences in the ADC plans lay in the orbit areas and the method of control. ADC envisioned the AEW aircraft orbiting in a number of preset locations off each coast, tied into the ADC contiguous radar system. Supplementing this structure were a proposed number of radar ships and towers that would give endurance and stability to the whole concept. The Navy, on the other hand, proposed long, racetrack orbits acting as extensions of the early warning lines. These stations were farther seaward than the ADC proposal and also involved the use of radar ships to supplement the coverage of the AEW aircraft.

These differences in approach and philosophy caused much of the concern in the early 1950s as the various proposals were fought over in the Pentagon. Originally the U.S. Air Force wanted the U.S. Navy to supply both AEW aircraft and radar picket ships for its seaward extension of the contiguous radar system. The U.S. Navy, not wanting to lose control over these assets, counterproposed that the Navy control the whole operation using its own aircraft and ships. The Navy plan was not for a continuous barrier, but rather a mixture of assets readily available to naval forces that would conduct air defense missions in addition to ASW. Obviously, this proposed usage of AEW aircraft by the U. S. Navy to conduct air defense and ASW operations conflicted greatly with the concept envisioned by ADC officials.

The Navy believed that a slow and meticulous development of radar picket ships and planes gave the Navy a better return on its investment by equipping these ships and planes for both fleet and continental air defense. Although it approved of the Navy's developments, the Air Force perceived the Navy approach as "heel dragging." Subsequently, ADC urged headquarters USAF to petition for responsibility of the airborne picket mission using the Navy-developed aircraft and tactics.

Command and control of military assets had always been a complicated matter. The U.S. Air Force believed that the ADC was the best unit to integrate all air defense systems, including AEW aircraft, within the continental United States. Major tasking of the ADC included exercising control of all active measures and coordinating passive means of air defense. However, the U.S. Navy had similar tasking. One of the enduring strategies of the Navy is sea control, which translates in this case to defense of the United States against attack from the ocean. So you can understand how there would be conflict between these two services as to the proper use of assets.

A crucial step in coordination between the U. S. Navy and Air Force was made in 1948 at the Key West Conference wherein the CNO agreed to the following usage of naval forces:

To provide sea-based air defense and sea-based means for coordinating control for defense against air attack, coordinating with other services in matters of joint concern.

To provide naval (including naval air) forces as required for the defense of the United States against air attack, in accordance with joint doctrines and procedures approved by the Joint Chiefs of Staff.

However, these and other agreements did not soothe the objections of the Air Force and particularly the ADC, who believed that these arrangements were basically "ad hoc" in nature and did not guarantee the use of these naval forces when they were actually needed. The CNO and other senior officers in the Navy understood this concern, but in reality the Navy was still committed to other pressing operations. This is because there were few units available for air defense missions throughout the late 1940s and early 1950s. Ships and aircraft were all in various training cycles for deployment, and as such they could participate in scheduled ADC exercises only on a not-to-interfere basis. These units would not be dedicated for ADC tasking, and also would not normally be on call 24 hours a day. This was of course a realistic operational problem that did not solve the desire by ADC officials for a more permanent solution.

Although the original U.S. Navy land-based AEW aircraft were Boeing PB-1Ws, these were replaced by the Lockheed Constellation series of AEW aircraft in the early 1950s. Originally using the PO-1W (WV-1) prototype, two WV-1s were developed for testing and research. Following this phase, the Navy began to build the PO-2W (WV-2). Shouldering the majority of the "Heavy AEW" missions, 142 of these Warning Star aircraft were built for military service. Huge and ungainly in their appearance, the WV-2s housed the APS-20 radar in a circular plastic radome beneath the aircraft. Another "height-finding radar," the APS-45 (shark-fin in appearance) was added to the top of the aircraft to improve the radar's performance. This arrangement necessitated the use of two scopes where data was correlated by the operator. An awkward combination, it nevertheless proved successful in improving the detection and tracking performance of the system.

The Navy had made the decision to stand up the AEW barrier, the SEADEW line, in the early 1950s, with the sea service tasked to support the radar extension of the DEW line. Ironically, although the Navy really wanted no part of continental air defense, it too had divided the WV-2s almost equally between that mission and fleet support. The first units involved squadrons composed of aircraft that provided an AEW capability to the fleet with a collateral tasking of weather reconnaissance. This category includes VW-1, VW-2, VW-3, and VW-4. The two West Coast squadrons, VW-1 and VW-3, were involved in numerous operations throughout the Pacific theater; while on the East Coast, VW-4 became known as the Hurricane Hunters for their work in the Caribbean. The second type of AEW mission involved VW squadrons that flew the barrier patrol flights. The barrier units consisted of VW-11, VW-13, VW-15, and the AEW Training Unit in the Atlantic, and VW-12, VW-14, VW-16, and

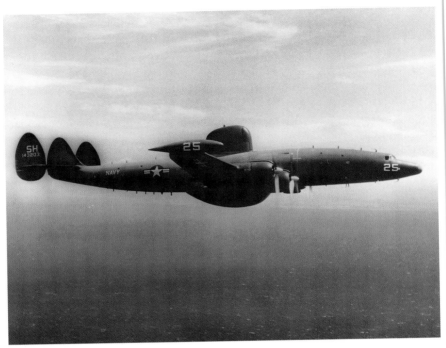

**WV-2**
The U.S. Navy built 142 of these "heavy" AEW aircraft to serve as their land-based surveillance platforms. These aircraft flew in both fleet and barrier squadrons, and were manned by large numbers of aircrew. Most Connies flew relatively low-altitude AEW orbits. The U.S. Navy typically flew at 5,000 to 8,000 feet, while the U.S. Air Force often flew higher, at 15,000 feet. *Department of U.S. Navy*

the AEW Maintenance Squadron in the Pacific. These squadrons maintained continuous radar coverage of the barriers for their entire existence.

As mentioned earlier, the original plan for the Atlantic Barrier consisted of two parallel tracks in the Atlantic, with Iceland via the Azores to Natal, Brazil, on the outer line, and tia, Newfoundland, to Puerto Rico via Bermuda on the inner one. However, the fiscal implications of this barrier proposal necessitated a less extensive program. What evolved were two barriers, one in the Pacific, the other in the Atlantic. From a home station at Barbers Point, Hawaii, the Pacific Barrier stretched north from Midway Island to the Aleutians, and in the Atlantic, the barrier ran from Argentia, Newfoundland, 1,000 miles to Lajes, Azores, and back. In both cases, the

Navy barriers were farther out to sea than the Air Force's, usually over-head the radar picket ships. While the Air Force Connies provided perhaps an hour's advance warning of intruders, studies indicated that the Navy Warning Stars might have given as much as 3.5 hours of warning for a high-altitude raid, 2.5 hours for one at low altitude, and even an hour for the Mach 3 intercontinental cruise missiles that the United States expected the Soviets to field. The WV-2s flew this mission continuously over the next decade as they patrolled the skies in search of enemy bombers and missiles en route to the continental United States.

The U.S. Air Force's use of AEW aircraft on barrier patrols differed significantly from the Navy's. While the U.S. Navy used their WV-2s on the SEADEW, the U.S. Air Force instead utilized their RC-121s and U.S. Navy radar picket ships to act as an extension of the Continental Air Defense Radar System of the United States. Called the Contiguous Extension, this would be the Air Force's first venture into the AEW arena. Since the late 1940s, the Air Force had been watching Navy progress with early warning aircraft, even participating in several tests beginning in 1950. The tests left U. S. Air Force Air Defense commanders "sufficiently impressed" to suggest that the Air Force purchase the Connies. Convinced that early warning planes could compensate for low-altitude deficiencies in their ground-based radars, in late 1951, nearly three years after the Navy ordered its first Warning Stars, the Air Force ordered 10 AEW-modified Constellation Model 749s, designating them RC-121Cs. Lockheed chose WV-2s bound for the Navy to fill the Air Force's order, but due to industry strikes, the first RC-121s did not reach their USAF units until late 1953.

The commander of the Air Force's ADC, General Chidlaw, decided to locate the AEW force at two bases, one on each coast. Sacramento's McClellan Air Force Base (AFB) was chosen as the West Coast site, while Cape Cod's Otis AFB, already home to several fighter interceptor units, would be the East Coast location. With an unprecedented mission and unfamiliar new airplanes, the Air Force had to create an organizational structure to support the RC-121s and the people who would fly and maintain them. Accordingly, on 17 September 1953, the Western Air Defense Force (WADF) at San Francisco's Hamilton AFB issued General Order 39, activating the 4701st Airborne Early Warning and Control (AEW&C) Squadron at McClellan. Intended as a temporary predecessor for an even larger organization to follow, its charter was to "man, maintain,

and operate airborne early warning and control aircraft on airborne stations as designated by headquarters for the purpose of extending radar
surveillance seaward and providing airborne intercept control stations."
With this announcement, the purpose and soon-to-be occupants of the
extensive construction along McClellan's parking aprons were no longer
a closely-guarded secret.

Pending arrival of the airplanes, ADC sent some radar operators and
technicians to train on the Warning Star's avionics at the Navy's AEW
schools. One was at San Diego's FAETUPAC, and the other in Patuxent
River, Maryland. In addition, some technicians trained under contract
with Lockheed at their Burbank, California, plant where the Connies were
being built. Despite the Air Force's apparent rush to field the Connies,
however, the delayed delivery schedule may have been to the 4701st's
benefit. At first, none of the arriving technicians was trained on the APS-
45 or APS-20 radars. Also, many of the inbound pilots and flight engineers were not current in four-engine aircraft, nor did any of the inbound
flight crews have any AEW or RC-121 flight experience. Therefore, the
information gleaned from the Navy's schools and the time spent relearn-
ing multi-engine aircraft skills on the 4701st's assigned C-47 probably
better prepared the airmen for their mission once the planes actually
arrived. The first nine aircraft the Air Force received were RC-121Cs,
which were superseded in mid-1954 by the D-model, a Model L-1049 airframe with upgraded electronics and wingtip tanks. As a result of its
ungainly appearance, the Warning Star was soon better known as the
"Pregnant Goose."

In December 1953, the organizational structure of Air Force AEW
began a series of changes to accommodate the growing number of airplanes and men. Personnel from McClellan AFB were sent to Otis AFB as
the initial cadre for the East Coast AEW effort. Meanwhile, at McClellan
AFB, the eighth Air Division stood up as one of the four West Coast divi-
sions of the WADF, and the parent organization for both the East and West
Coast wings. Early the following spring, some men returned from Otis to
form the 4712th Airborne Early Warning and Control Squadron
(AEW&CS), now a sibling to the 4701st. Otis had grown to over 2,300 men
in one year, with the 961st AEW&CS and its parent 551st AEW&C Wing
activated in December 1954, while two sister squadrons, the 960th (the
redesignated 4701st) and 962d, were activated on 8 July 1955. Within
a month, ADC stood up the 552d Wing at McClellan under provisional

status. By July, the 552d had gained permanent status, with the 963rd (built from the 4712th) and 964th squadrons underneath it. A third 552d squadron, the 965th, followed in August 1955, so in less than two years after the birth of AEW in the Air Force, there were six full squadrons of RC-121s (approaching 50 airplanes) and approximately 5,000 men in the two wings of the eighth Air Division. At the same time, the Air Force opted to make eighth Air Division directly responsible to ADC, giving it equal status with both the Western and Eastern Air Defense Forces. This arrangement lasted until mid-1957, when ADC chose to inactivate the eighth Air Division, reassigning each Airborne Early Warning and Control Wing (AEW & CW) along geographic lines to either the Western or Eastern Air Defense Force. This structure would remain essentially unchanged until the early 1960s, when new missions changed the tasking of the RC-121s and their crews.

**Flying the Barrier**

The history of the barrier operations is really quite unique. Flying a mission of deterrence, aircrews often flew from remote bases in terrible weather and on these barrier patrols over a 10-year period. Tedious in nature, the program was professionally accomplished and few sorties were ever missed. This was due to many factors, not the least being "The Spirit of the Barrier" as it was called, which came to signify the crews' pride and professionalism.

The WV-2s (RC-121) had a combat radius of nearly 1,000 miles, which permitted them to loiter on a "picket station" often in excess of 16 hours. They could cruise at 200 knots and climb to nearly 24,000 feet. Although built to be flown by a crew of 5 officers and 13 enlisted men, the Connies had room for an augmented crew of up to 31 for longer missions. Aft of the flight deck were five radar consoles which shed an "eerie, green half-light" inside the cabin as the controllers scanned their scopes for any signs of bogeys. There was no automation on these early radars, so controllers had to be constantly attentive to their scopes, marking radar "paints" or "fluorescent bananas" with a grease pencil between radar sweeps to determine the target's track and speed. It was tedious work, and the resultant fatigue invited the risk of missing a target. To compensate, the controllers usually spent less than an hour in front of their scope before another man relieved them for a short respite. The 3,000-plus vacuum tubes and complex electronics required a supporting cast, so at least two additional crewmen were trained in the in-flight maintenance of the radar. With all of the electronics gear in the aft cabin, temperatures were known to reach 100 degrees Fahrenheit, which was made even more uncomfortable by the Mae West life preservers the crew wore. Yet they persevered because the mission obviously took precedence over crew comfort.

These operations also took priority over the weather. The crews flying the barrier often experienced some of the worst flying weather in the world, with snow, high winds, and mist or fog being the norm rather than the exception. Weather conditions experienced by VW crews at Argentia, Newfoundland, were similar to what the 552d crews were encountering on Station 1, near the Aleutians. The Super Connies and their crews, however, kept flying no matter what the weather, with takeoffs and landings recorded in crosswinds up to 45 knots. One night a USAF crew made its

**WV-2**

Shown here is a picture of a Navy WV-2 on the apron at Argentia, Newfoundland, in February 1957. This would have been at the height of the barrier operations for the U.S. Navy. These aircraft would deploy from their main base at NAS Paxtuxent River for detachments, with rotations often being 30 days or more in length, while the aircrew flew their barrier missions. *Leigh Armistead collection*

**RC-121 Interior View**
The RC-121 was a very complicated aircraft. This is a picture of a young air controller who is using the radar of the RC-121 to intercept and direct a friendly fighter
toward an unknown contact. This is an important mission within the AEW aircraft,
and weapons directors are still a crucial position in modern day AWACS. *U.S.
Air Force*

departure in a wind of 92 knots! In fact, over 60 percent of the USAF missions encountered light to severe icing, with 50 percent of the flying hours
in storm-force winds! Whether it was Air Force or Navy crew and aircraft,
the weather rarely cooperated with barrier operations.

Actually, the most stressful part of the AEW missions might very well
have been the takeoffs and landings. In addition to the pressure from the
commanders to depart on time, there were serious weather considerations.
At McClellan AFB, the winter months are known to be particularly foggy.
U.S. Navy aircrew flying out of Argentia, Newfoundland, found it even
worse. As a result, in order to reach their picket station, flight crews often
took off in weather conditions so poor that an emergency return and landing were out of the question. In many cases, because the visibility on the
ground was so bad, a tug would tow an airplane out to the runway and
line it up for takeoff. Still unable to see much in front of them, the crews

would take off using what few visual cues they had. As one pilot quipped, "If you can taxi, you can fly!" It was a dangerous way of doing business, but the pressure to man the picket stations necessitated it. Quite often, when crews were heading home from the picket, the weather at the airfield would still be "below minimums," and many aircrew remember being forced to divert into more suitable airfields on numerous occasions.

While weather often hindered these operations, the actual mission of these squadrons was relatively simple. For the U.S. Air Force, the Connie and its crew would depart its base for a particular picket station, and then enter a predetermined orbit or pattern. The search operator would identify a new target on his scope, correlate it with the operator on the height-finder, and report it to the senior director and the plotter. The senior director would then radio the target's track and speed to the nearest picket ship or coastal radar and control station. Within 30 seconds of the first sighting, the ground station would, hopefully, receive and process this information and begin to question the bogey, asking the pilot to identify himself with a series of secret checks. If the coastal center was not satisfied, supersonic interceptors would race to intercept. If need be, the controllers onboard the AEW aircraft could assist in or completely assume responsibility for guiding the interceptors. Likewise, U.S. Navy Connies would fly long, rectangular racetrack patterns, looking for telltale clues of an impending Soviet attack.

The EC-121/WV-2 Connie crew consisted of the flight crew, radar techs, radio operators, and height-finder operator. Most of the mission activity was in the overwing area, with the navigator's station on the right and the navigator sitting on a portable stool in the middle of the aisle. The radio operator sat across from the navigator, and received most of his traffic while on-station via high-frequency (HF) continuous wave signal: that is, Morse code! Mounted on the radio operator's table was a Morse code key that some aircrew thought was designed by Samuel F. B. Morse himself! The radar tech's job was to keep the radar going, which in that vacuum-tube era normally meant having bits and pieces of the radar set spread up and down the aisle of the airplane, all lashed together and lit up. According to former RC-121 aircrew, these radar techs were always trouble-shooting some part of the system while on station.

A very important portion of the EC-121 was the datalink system. Known as Airborne Long-Range Input (ALRI), it allowed for automated data operations between the specially modified EC-121Hs and the

Semi-Automatic Ground Environment (SAGE) sites. The aircrew composition of the 551st squadron was different than the 552d EC-121s or Navy WV-2s because all the EC-121H radar data was digitized and transmitted to ground sites (one ground site for each airborne radar station). From the ground sites, data went via a land line mainly to the SAGE centers. There were no weapons controllers or anything like a "mission crew" on 551st EC-121s. The surveillance mission, scramble authority, and weapons control functions were all done on the ground at the SAGE centers or back-up sites. However, on the EC-121Ds (552d) and U.S. Navy WV-2s, full mission crews were flown in order to execute the mission.

Degradations of the barrier were very serious matters. For example, on the U.S. Navy Pacific Barrier, there was a location 200 nautical miles northwest of Midway termed Point "A" by which the aircraft avionics status had to be determined. If a plane was up and the radar working at Point "A," then the crew could continue on with the mission; otherwise, a relief crew and aircraft were launched. This taxing schedule necessitated extraordinary demands on the aircrew and aircraft. Extra technicians, controllers, and pilots were needed to spell each other on these long-duty days and flights.

The mission often became routine, with both services having somewhat similar flight profiles. Once airborne, the Connies began the long climb. The U.S. Air Force EC-121Hs typically orbited at 15,000 feet, while the U.S. Navy WV-2s and U.S. Air Force EC-121Ds would fly their patterns at lower altitudes, normally 5,000 to 8,000 feet. This climb-out put a lot of strain on the R-3350 turbo-compound engines, because they usually operated at maximum except take off (METO) power during the entire climb, and sometimes for up to a half hour after leveling off. (METO power was the first power reduction setting after maximum power for take off.) It often took the aircraft up to 45 minutes to climb to 15,000 feet. At about 10,000 feet, the pilots would sometimes level off briefly to build up speed for the "blower shift," during which they throttled back the inboard engines, shifted to high blower (supercharger), throttled back up, and then repeated the procedure with the outboard engines before continuing the climb. The latter part of the climb-out was where the majority of the engine problems occurred including fires, sparkplug breakdowns (shorted secondaries), and turbine failures. The R-3350 had three power-recovery turbines (PRTs) on each engine. PRTs are like the turbines on a jet engine. Engine exhaust from 6 of the 18 cylinders was collected in a common manifold and routed through one of the three PRTs, which were about a foot in diameter. The three PRT turbine shafts were geared to the engine crankshaft and contributed a significant proportion of the total power of the R-3350. Frequently, turbine blades would separate from PRTs, causing power loss and necessitating engine shutdown to preclude further damage. Sometimes the turbine blades would punch through the PRT casing, and then exhaust would exit though the holes in the casing, often causing engine fires.

Every Connie aircrew interviewed had lots of stories about faulty engine operations and engine fires. Hydraulic leaks were also common. Sometimes, depending on where the leak was, you could recover the system. However, major leaks usually forced the aircrew to abort the mission. As a precaution, Connie crews always carried several gallons of extra hydraulic fluid in quart cans, and it was routine to replenish the system several times during flight. This was done via a port in the cockpit, whereby the aircrew would punch a hole in the can, stick in a metal tube on the end of a hose connected to the system, and allow the aspirator to suck in the quart of hydraulic fluid.

Not so commonplace but equally terrifying were the mechanical failures which seemingly came from nowhere. One such "Jekyll and Hyde" flight occurred on 24 November 1958, to Crew 5 from VW-15. Led by Lt. Comdr. Robert Nelson, this aircraft was flying on a mission profile from Argentia for four hours, and everything was normal as WV-2 neared its turn point north of Lajes. The flight deck had turned over to the second shift, and Ens. Joe Kuhn was at the controls of the aircraft as they turned north and began their climb to 10,000 feet. All of a sudden, the pilot's yoke jerked sharply back and the WV-2 experienced an extreme nose-up attitude. Full forward yoke by both pilots failed to correct the problem and the nose continued to arc upwards until a 60-degree angle of attack was reached. At this time, the aircraft experienced a stall and departed controlled flight. Falling off to the right, the aircraft was in a 90-degree dive and lost 3,000 feet of altitude before control was regained. Aircrew and flight equipment were strewn about the cabin, and though panic had not set in, many aircrew wondered what had happened to the aircraft.

This calm lasted for only 2 minutes, when a second and much more violent series of maneuvers began. Once again, radical nose-up attitudes were experienced, with no amount of inputs by the pilots affecting the aircraft. Each time the aircraft would stall and then fall through in a dive before the pilots could regain control. Four more of these violent maneuvers occurred until by the last one, all aircrew thought that they were going to die. Somehow on the fifth dive, as the aircraft was heading straight down, elevator control was regained and finally the pilots managed to fly the aircraft to an emergency divert in Lajes, Azores, and recover safely. Subsequent investigation revealed that a locknut on the elevator piston rod was loose, which unscrewed the piston rod from the elevator assembly. Within several weeks, an RC-121 from the 962d experienced similar conditions, and the crew almost bailed out of the aircraft.

These incidents and others like them are shown not to exemplify how dangerous the missions were but perhaps more importantly, how critical these missions were to the defense of the United States. According to Adm. John J. Hyland (ret.) former commander of the Barrier Wing, the mission of the barrier was considered essential to the security of the United States. Dedication to duty and determined aircrews kept these planes up and flying around the clock. For example, just to maintain continuous radar coverage of the U.S. Navy Atlantic Barrier required two to four aircraft to be airborne simultaneously. An incredible task, it was accomplished professionally and in a timely manner. A young seaman who helped maintain these giant aircraft once said, "You could set your watches by their takeoffs and landings."

Likewise, in the U.S. Air Force, a wide-eyed newspaperman flying with the 4701st in 1954 related how the aircraft flew "at distances which reach several hundred miles out to sea . . . pushing back the frontiers of danger and giving our defense forces precious minutes in which to repel invaders from target areas." Memories of picket duty by the men who flew the missions, however, tend to be more mundane. In the early days of the mission, ADC wanted the Connies airborne on all picket stations, 24 hours a day, in hopes of making the AEW umbrella complete. For several years, takeoffs were made every 4 hours, with the throttles being pushed up for takeoff power exactly on time. If an aircraft was unable to make its scheduled takeoff because of maintenance problems or for other reasons, another crew and aircraft were on moment's notice standby duty to fill in. This frantic schedule was hard on both the crews and the airplanes. Fortunately, as commanders better understood the Soviet bomber threat and realized the mission might still be accomplished with fewer aircraft and less wear on the planes and their engines, the policy on manning the stations changed. At McClellan AFB, for example, there were five basic picket stations, numbered 1, 3, 5, 7, and 9. These stations stretched from north to south, with number 1 putting the planes just off Alaska's Aleutian Islands, and number 9 situated near Baja, California. The new policy allowed a high-ranking officer in the wing to make a random selection just before the crew departed on which station they would man during this shift. In this way, there was little chance of the enemy predicting where the Connie might be in order to circumvent it. One crew might be assigned to Station 1, but the plane that relieved it might well end up on Station 3. Still, it was a tiring pace, with the crews regularly flying missions averaging 16 hours every third day.

The 551st Wing's mission was to maintain "continuous random" airborne coverage of at least one "station" off the east coast of the United States. What the continuous "random manning" airborne coverage mission meant was that at least one EC-121H had to be operational on one of the four stations that the Connies from Otis AFB manned. Located about 150 miles off shore, these stations were near the ADIZ, the Air Defense Identification Zone, where aircraft were required to have ADC clearance to operate. At higher defense conditions (DEFCONs), increasing numbers of stations would be manned. The stations were basically 100-mile-long racetrack patterns, running north-south, identified as Stations 2, 4, 6, and 8. To maintain this coverage, one aircraft launched every 4 hours, starting at 0200. The six launches a day were allocated among the three squadrons (960th, 961st, and 962d). Every couple of weeks, the schedule would change between squadrons so that each squadron would get their "fair share" of the 0200 launches! If a Connie on station had a problem (radar, datalink, in-flight emergency, etc.) typically the next scheduled mission would be moved up for an immediate takeoff.

Air defense exercises were a major part of the operation for U.S. Air Force barrier operations. The general scenario was an increasing status of DEFCONs with a recall of crews. The aircrew had trailers with bunks alongside the squadron ops building to sleep in if needed. Once certain states of alert were reached, the aircrew would sit in the airplanes on alert. The Big Event was launching the fleet! Everything that was flyable would launch! Looking back, many aircrew still cannot believe that they participated in these exercises. When called away, all aircrew would rush to start engines of all operable aircraft, and taxi on their own command, falling in one behind the other as they got out to the taxiway. Usually, by the time a couple of airplanes got to the end of the runway, the pilots could expect that the Soviet raid was inbound, so it was time to "FLUSH" the fleet! The trigger for this exercise was a series of code words, just like in the movies.

Supposedly missiles were on the way, so the aircraft had to launch fast. The entire wing was cleared for takeoff to proceed out to STOPs or "strategic orbit points" to sit out the raid. Takeoff was at 15-second intervals. The first one off got the highest altitude, next one 500 feet lower, etc. The STOP was on a predetermined radial. Of course the Federal Aviation Administration (FAA) didn't want anything to do with this, so they just gave ADC a whole block of sky and the aircrew cleared themselves. Pilots would call out their positions to try to keep some spacing, but it was not uncommon for two aircraft to call out the same radial and DME while trudging along in the murk! Luckily the "ole big sky" theory was in the pilots' favor. Fortunately, as barrier operations continued, these "FLUSH" drills were eventually determined to be too dangerous and were discontinued.

With the long hours and fast tempo of operations, it was inevitable that accidents on barrier flights would occur. An example of the bravery and heroism displayed by these aviators is shown in a story about a 551st E-121H that crashed into the Atlantic Ocean on 11 July 1965. Lts. Fred Ambrosia and Tom Fiedler were the pilots, while T. Sgts. Gene Schreivogel and Gil Armstrong were the flight engineers. There was a full crew on board as well as some Reserve Officer Training Command (ROTC) instructors who were at Otis for summer training getting EC-121 mission familiarization. The emergency began about the time of level-off, with a large fire on the number 3 engine. The crew shut down and feathered that engine and discharged the fire extinguishers, but the fire burned back into the nacelle and wing, filling the fuselage with smoke. Lieutenant Ambrosia decided to put the aircraft down in the water, a nighttime ditching in zero-zero weather with an engine on fire. Very risky, but he was too far from land, and really had no other options. The pilots made a rapid descent from 15,000 feet to about a thousand feet and set up a steady slow rate of descent, nose up, on a heading aligned parallel to the forecast direction of the swells. When the Connie contacted the water, it broke up fore and aft of the wing into essentially three large sections. The nose section sank immediately. While the SAR effort continued for several days, there were only three survivors, for most of the crew were lost in the crash.

Lt. Fred Ambrosia was awarded a posthumous Distinguished Flying Cross (DFC), an award almost unheard of at the time. It was only through his skill that there were any survivors. At the memorial service, the 551st Wing flew a missing man flyby, five EC-121Hs in a "six-ship" close formation at about 300 feet. Today there is a monument at Otis Air National Guard (ANG) Base memorializing the crew. Within two years, the 551st was to lose two more EC-121Hs in similar accidents (11 November 1966 and 25 April 1967), and the last mishap involved Colonel Lyle, 551st Wing Commander who was flying as aircraft commander.

Connies were complicated aircraft, and they experienced their fair share of in-flight emergencies. Engine failures of one sort or another and hydraulic problems were not at all uncommon occurrences. Many aircrew believed that the 551st AEW&CS had more incidents than their U.S. Air Force or U.S. Navy counterparts because they were required to fly at a 15,000-foot on-station operating altitude. This altitude was needed in order to have line-of-sight ALRI radar datalink radio coverage with the ground sites for each of the four stations. U.S. Air Force Connies were always "max'd out" for takeoff on these barrier missions, and at 142,000 pounds, these aircraft carried the maximum amount of gas to fly as long a mission as possible. Many believe that this weight was pushing the basic design limit of the Connie.

Maintenance was also a large operation. The engines and radar were major items requiring constant attention. There were four large engine oil marks permanently soaked into the ramp, so there was never a need to mark the aircraft parking spots. For every launch, chances were fifty-fifty that the pilots would have to get something fixed either before or after engine start and run-up. Engine run-up prior to takeoff was a large drill in itself. It often took 20–30 minutes depending on how things looked and the engineer's proficiency and/or state of nervousness. To run up, the pilot would put the aircraft "on the step." The main landing gear rotated 15 degrees back and forth around their hinge axis, and the idea was to smoothly ease on the brakes while increasing power to get "on the step" and to keep the gear rotated back so that the airplane wouldn't jerk back and forth onto and off "the step" with power changes during run-up. It sounds strange now, but the pilots reported that this was just part of the routine. While "on the step," aircrew would check mags, props, and blowers, and take a look at every sparkplug on the engine analyzer. After run-up, pilots took the aircraft "off the step," eased off the brakes as they reduced power, and then reset the brakes. If everything was OK, the pilots checked the avionics, got their flight clearance, and began to taxi for take-off. Looking back, many aircrew have remarked about the huge effort in maintenance personnel and money that went into keeping these aircraft airborne and on schedule for barrier operations.

## The Demise of the Barrier

Tests and exercises conducted by ADC in the late 1950s indicated that Connies were not performing their missions as well as expected, mainly because of difficulties with the electronic equipment. Progress in ADC's persistent attempts to fix quirks in the system seemed excruciatingly slow, and by 1959 ADC wanted to transfer the whole AEW mission, planes included, to the Navy. Calmer heads prevailed at headquarters USAF, and the transfer did not occur. The Navy and the Air Force, however, were both examining and justifying the use of these assets. High costs for personnel and aircraft tended to make these missions vulnerable during periods of fiscal restraint. Thus, for all of the effort involved in maintaining radar coverage of the barrier, by the early 1960s, just when the United States was completing the construction of its permanently manned land radar sites, the SEADEW line was already beginning to be phased out. The first sign of this occurred on 1 February 1960, when the Navy disestablished a number of Pacific Fleet AEW units and reassigned all aircrew, technicians, and aircraft to Airborne Early Warning Squadron Pacific (AEWBARRONPAC). ADC also realized that despite some unanticipated advances in Soviet bomber technology and production, the Russians had shifted their focus from manned bombers to the new ballistic missile production. In the perpetual scuffle for defense funds, the U.S. Air Force strived to implement a cost-effective air defense system capable of defeating a combined aircraft-missile threat. The picket ships and several other air defense assets were scrapped, and although the Connies survived, the 1960 defense budget reflected an understanding that the main threat was no longer from bombers alone, but from ballistic missiles and bombers. Anticipating that the much faster ballistic missiles would be the primary strike force, with the Soviet bombers in a second-strike role, the relative importance of the USAF's Connies was also diminished, and ADC discontinued its participation in barrier operations. This same consolidation effort was undertaken by the U.S. Navy in fleet operations with the disestablishment of VW-3 on 30 June 1960 and VW-15 on 15 April 1961. Then, in August 1961, another change occurred when the Atlantic Barrier was shifted northeast to operate from Keflavick, Iceland. The North Atlantic Barrier, as it was now called, had two tracks, an eastern one that ran from Iceland to the Norwegian Sea, and a western one from Iceland to the Denmark Straits. These shifts and changes all combined to gradually close down barrier operations.

There were other changes in the early 1960s that also signaled the end of the barrier. The Navy redesignated all its aircraft in 1962 to realign their identification with the DOD-wide designation system. Thus, the WV-2s became EC-121Ks, and later, advances in avionics changed them to EC-121L/EC-121M/EC-121N/EC-121P and WC-121N. Aided and abetted by the Navy's ongoing focus of its AEW operations on fleet protection, technology and expense doomed the Navy barrier operations. The Navy saw the barriers as coming at the expense of their fleet exercises and training, and by mid-1965 the service had decommissioned the barrier squadrons and retired its "Willie Victors" or reallocated them to other missions.

Were the barrier operations successful? Were they necessary? These are difficult questions to answer. Many believe that these aircraft were a waste of money and personnel, yet deterrence is always a hard mission to quantify. Some historians believe that these barrier missions probably deterred Soviet aggression through their demonstration of national intent and perhaps more importantly, they gave the citizens of the United States a feeling that they were protected from a hostile attack. The standup of the barriers was a huge signal to the Soviet Union. The aircrew interviewed for this publication, whether U.S. Navy or U.S. Air Force, all believed that they were conducting a mission vital to the defense of the nation, and perhaps in the end, that's all that really matters.

# CHAPTER THREE

# The Desire for a Dedicated AEW Platform

The 1950s was a time of rapid change and growth in the naval VAW and VW communities. No longer were they fighting for survival, as carrier task force commanders depended on AEW services for many tasks and services. Likewise, in the U.S. Air Force, officers in the AEW&C community were increasingly aware that because of the EC-121's improving capabilities for airborne command and control, the Air Force was choosing to pull these aircraft off picket duty more and more often. Yet the biggest development was still to come. In 1955 the Navy requested the development of a carrier-based aircraft with a built-in CIC that included automatic radar tracking capability. This development would allow aircrew to track hundreds of contacts over water or land, while vectoring aircraft and acting as a radio relay for critical information to the task force commander. No longer would the controllers be forced to manually track contacts with a grease pencil. In essence, such a platform could control the battle from its station high above the task force.

## Shortcomings of the Current Aircraft

The terrible problems associated with the APS-20 radar, whether onboard the AD-5W, WV-2, or EC-121, are often very difficult to understand. An operator had no symbology (video that designates a contact) to use, only a long-pulse raw radar return (basically just pure energy reflecting from the target). This raw radar return does not contain any heading, speed, or altitude data. To determine a target's course, the operator had to laboriously track each contact individually for at least three minutes to get a roughly accurate set of data. Obviously, the aircrew could quickly become overwhelmed in a busy operating area. Because the APS-20 radar had no symbology, no corresponding altitude displays, no automatic tracking system, and only raw radar videos to track, it was considered somewhat crude and cumbersome. The APS-20 was inadequate for the many tasks, including near-land tracking, multiple engagements, and others, that were demanded of it by the mid- to late 1950s. American military officers desperately wanted new AEW aircraft and radar systems to combat the increased threat from long-range Soviet anti-ship cruise missiles and bombers that faced the United States.

Technical advances in an AEW radar, therefore, were to do more than anything else to improve the use and standing of these squadrons within the Navy and Air Force. The original APS-20 radar was adequate in the early developmental phase of this technology; however, better performance had been sought for some time. Initially this was achieved by upgrading the airframe (a faster aircraft can search more area) to ensure its compatibility with fleet anti-submarine and attack aircraft, but avionics upgrades were not forthcoming. Through a series of different AEW aircraft, from the TBM-3W Avenger, the AF-2W Guardian, the Skyraider AEW series (AD-3W/4W and most importantly the AD-5W), the PB-1W, the WV-2, and the EC-121, the U.S. military had repeatedly changed the aircraft, while only slightly updating the avionics package. The U.S. Navy also experimented with mounting the APS-20 radar system into airships, specifically the ZPG-2W and ZPG-3W. Non-rigid helium-filled envelopes, these airships supported a height-finding radar on top of the structure, and the APS-20 radar in a fairing underneath the gondola. These airships could operate continuously for over 60 hours, with some crews exceeding the 200-hour mark. However, crew performance was noted to deteriorate rapidly under the harsh, cramped, and noisy conditions. While initial experiments were promising, long-term development was never funded, and these airships were transferred to the U.S. Coast Guard in the 1950s. The Navy also experimented with modifications to the venerable Willie Victors. Lockheed developed the WV-2E, changing the radome configuration to a rotating overhead dome, and introduced it on 8 August 1956. Using an APS-82 radar fitted into a large antenna above the fuselage, the concept was that these aircraft would replace the WV-2 in operation for the U.S. Navy. Other

**ZPG-3W**
Here is another view of the ZPG-3W. As mentioned earlier, the U.S. Navy experimented with the use of blimps as AEW platforms by installing APS-20 radars. These systems are forerunners of the current aerostats in use today. There are many analysts who advocate lighter-than-air technology as the future of AEW.
*Department of U.S. Navy*

events, namely the call for a carrier-based aircraft and subsequent developments in that arena, eventually doomed the WV-2E to a testing status.

None of these approaches, however, whether it was faster, larger, or upgraded aircraft, did anything to solve the future problems of the different AEW communities. What was needed was a multi-seat aircraft with a new radar system that could simultaneously "see" in a 360 degree pattern, and one that possessed automatic tracking and height-finding capabilities. This was the aircraft and system that the U.S. military wanted.

43

Yet, while the requirements were basically the same, the two principal services took different approaches to acquire this new AEW capability.

## U.S. Navy: Bureau of Aeronautics Request

In 1955 the U.S. Navy Bureau of Aeronautics (BuAer) issued a requirement for a new carrier-based Airborne Early Warning/Air Intercept Control (AEW/AIC) aircraft that would be equipped to detect distant airborne targets and vector fighters into intercept positions. Numerous proposals were entered for this major contract, but in the end, it was Grumman and its Design 123 that won the AEW/AIC competition. Although the eventual winner of the competition was not known for many months, it was quickly recognized by BuAer that the development of this new aircraft would be a long and tedious process. In the meantime, a carrier-based replacement aircraft for the AD-5W was desperately needed; therefore, in November 1955 the BuAer issued an order for two prototypes of the Grumman E-1B (originally XWF-1 and WF-2) as an interim aircraft until the winner of the AEW/AIC competition could be introduced to the fleet. Little did the Navy and the VAW community realize the longevity of this interim aircraft, which would eventually serve until 1976.

Called the "*Willie Fudd*," "Stoof with a Roof," and other assorted names, the E-1B was a definite improvement over the AD-5W. Possessing an APS-82 Hazeltine S-band radar (the same radar used in the WV-2E) in a teardrop-shaped housing, this platform flew with a crew of two pilots and two controllers. The E-1B normally operated at an altitude of 5,000 to 7,000 feet where it could detect airborne contacts without interference from land masses or sea clutter. As good as the E-1B was in contrast to the AD-5W, it was still limited in fleet operations. With a limited height-finding capability, no symbology, and no automatic tracking, the APS-82 radar could still be overwhelmed in a multi-target environment. Yet, for all of these limitations, the APS-82 was still an improvement over the APS-20. Target heights were determined through use of an operator-controlled, tilting antenna. The radar displays were ground-stabilized, which greatly facilitated the detection and tracking of contacts. The aircraft incorporated tactical datalinks allowing the air controller to pass information to the aircraft and ship without voice communications. The ability of these nets to pass vast amounts of data and information was a great improvement over older systems, including Bellhop. Although a qualitative improvement over its predecessors, the E-1B was always viewed as a temporary solution

**E-1B**

The *Willie Fudd* was an "interim" AEW aircraft that was produced by the U.S. Navy while the Hawkeye was under development. Shown here are four E-1Bs as they fly over NAS North Island in San Diego, California. This base was home to the U.S. Navy West Coast VAW squadrons from 1962 to 1978, before they transferred to NAS Miramar. *Department of U.S. Navy*

to the AEW problem faced by the U. S. Navy. It was assumed that the ultimate AEW platform for the Navy would be the eventual winner of the BuAer competition, which would be the Grumman E-2A Hawkeye—destined to become the primary AEW aircraft of the U. S. Navy.

## Constraints Imposed by Aircraft Carrier Limitations

Based on a radical new design, the Grumman E-2A (originally W2F-1) was a tremendous breakthrough that was years ahead of its competition. With the selection of this design by BuAer on 5 March

1957, the Navy for the first time had selected an aircraft design whose sole purpose was to conduct AEW operations. The E-2A Hawkeye was not only a giant step in avionics advances for the Navy, but was also the first AEW aircraft that was not adapted from an existing airframe. The ability of the Grumman engineers to fit this technologically advanced radar package into a platform suitable for aircraft carrier operations was quite incredible.

Initially, however, the aircraft design was constrained by the need to have it operate from World War II–vintage aircraft carriers. This constraint was later discovered to be somewhat artificial, but originally the E-2A was designed to operate aboard the SCB-27C-class carriers (modified *Essex*-class aircraft carriers, a class that included the USS *Shangri-La* [CVA-38] and the USS *Bon Homme Richard* [CVA-31], which were built during World War II and later modified for jet operations). Therefore, height, weight, and length restraints for the E-2A were all mandated by a number of limitations, including the elevators, hangar overhead, wind-over-deck requirements, arresting gear limits, flight deck geometry, deck strength, steam capacity of the catapults, as well as the location of the jet blast deflectors. All of these limitations forced design constraints into the Hawkeye so that it could operate from a class of older aircraft carriers, which after several years seldom if ever occurred.

Although the Hawkeye currently remains the largest aircraft to operate from the deck of a carrier, the requirements mentioned earlier artificially constrained the E-2A. As early test pilots relate, the Hawkeye lacked lateral stability and needed a longer moment arm. This meant that it needed a longer distance from the center of gravity to its rudders in order for these aircraft control surfaces to adequately maneuver the aircraft. This longer moment arm would have allowed the pilot more rudder authority, required in a slow speed configuration. The lack of rudder authority in the Hawkeye is shown by the tendency of the aircraft to display adverse yaw and a lack of directional stability under single-engine control (in an emergency). This situation can be extremely dangerous when the aircraft is on its final approach, particularly to the aircraft carrier. A lack of directional stability occurs as sideslip is induced by rudder deflection, which translates into a yawing motion. In essence, some pilots and engineers believed that the Hawkeye would have benefitted from an extra 5–10 feet in length, which was not available in the initial design, so that the aircraft could fit aboard SCB-27C-class carriers. Perhaps it will never be known if a change in the design would have helped, but this problem still exists.

For all of its original design difficulties, however, the E-2A Hawkeye was an extraordinary accomplishment. As will be shown in succeeding chapters, the service history of the aircraft and the operational capability built into the platform have continued to expand to meet new missions. A revolutionary airplane, the development of the E-2A gave the Navy what it had desired from the beginning: namely, a self-contained platform that could operate from the aircraft carrier and "see" beyond the surface radar horizon and control the battle from its elevated position.

## The Acquisition of the E-2A

The E-2A Hawkeye differed from its AEW predecessors in many ways. It was the first carrier-based aircraft to have a rotating dome with a redesigned radar and the first to have a crew of five aviators. The primary mission of this new aircraft was long-range detection. Therefore, a low frequency and high pulse repetition interval (PRI) was chosen. The high PRI rate equated to a long "listening" period in which the radar wave could travel the full distance out to the target and back. The low frequency enabled the radar to have a large power output, a longer range, and a higher signal-to-noise ratio. The APS-96 B-band radar was designed with all of these considerations and more, including its ability to "see" through weather and sea clutter. All of these features, plus the tremendous advances in detection ranges, often over twice the distance of the E-1B, gave a clear advantage to this system over its predecessors.

The evolutionary process of radar equipment on AEW aircraft becomes plainly evident with the introduction of the APS-96. Switching from the S-band to the B-band (UHF) enabled Grumman to maximize the inherent physical characteristics of this lower frequency. These included longer range, more power out, better detection capabilities, and less susceptibility to the effects of weather. The engineers at Grumman also developed for the first time a self-contained, rotating radar dome for a carrier-based aircraft that sat above the aircraft. Operating from an altitude of 25,000 to 30,000 feet, the E-2A had a radar range in excess of 200 nautical miles and could see all surface ships and aircraft from the surface to over 100,000 feet. Monitors linked to computer-generated automatic course and speed information on all contacts, a first in AEW. No longer was the aircrew forced to tediously track each individual contact, thus freeing them to use their equipment to engage and destroy enemy forces. A tribute to those engineers involved in this project, the E-2A contributed many notable firsts to naval aviation:

- First carrier-based aircraft with a completely pressurized interior cabin
- First carrier-based aircraft to use a nose tow catapult launching system, onboard the USS *Enterprise* (CVAN-65), 8 December 1962
- First carrier-based turbo-propeller aircraft
- First carrier-based aircraft with reversible pitch propellers
- First AEW aircraft to perform a completely automated intercept, 5 February 1963

The engineering team of Grumman and Hazeltine designed an extraordinary platform that served and is still serving in the frontline forces of the U. S. Navy for more than 40 years after its first flight.

## The U.S. Navy Fights to Save the Hawkeye

Yet it was not smooth sailing for the fleet introduction of the Hawkeye. The U.S. Navy was having major developmental problems with the E-2A, and in fact the aircraft was canceled on 15 January 1965 in the midst of production because it could not complete its mission. Avionics reliability was so bad that before special congressional hearings the Navy and Grumman officials could not promise that they could fix the problem. Most of the faults dealt with the inadequate cooling of the avionics components and the hard-wired computer. The computer was an early design, with low reliability, one that literally forced a physical change in the configuration of the computer when to change a part of the program. The E-2A is the only Navy aircraft to serve its entire career while failing its Bureau of Inspection and Survey trials. A poor start indeed.

This whole crisis came from the extraordinary technical difficulty that Grumman was experiencing in developing the new avionics for this radar airplane. Airframe design was relatively straightforward; however, the avionics, in particular the computer and cooling system, experienced severe reliability and maintenance problems throughout the early testing and production phase. Initial results were far from satisfactory, and the E-2A program was canceled after 59 aircraft had been built.

Reliability was so poor that the early Hawkeyes could not be trusted to complete their missions. Corrosion was also a major problem. At one time or another, the entire fleet was grounded, and this problem would continue to plague the community for many years. As one E-2A aircrewman said, "When they worked, they were great. However, when they didn't, which seemed to happen all the time, they were much worse than the E-1Bs."

Incredible as it may seem, almost 10 years after the initial request and five years after the first flight, the E-2A Hawkeye was not performing as advertised. Much of this was because during the long avionics testing phase, four production contracts had been let without any Navy testing of the equipment. To overcome these problems and allow for continued development of the program, Navy officials testified before Congress in 1965 to pressure Grumman Aerospace for greater reliability and more mean time between failures of the avionics equipment. Thereafter, Grumman and the Navy worked together to solve the reliability problem of the E-2A. Instituting new upgrades, Grumman in essence began the development of the E-2B program. Replacing the rotary drum computer with a Litton digital computer and implementing other avionics changes quickly breathed new life into the aircraft. All together, 49 of the original 59 E-2As were upgraded to the E-2B standard.

Was the E-2A a failure? Some would say yes, but those familiar with the incredible difficulties involved in producing an AEW system believe a certain number of developmental problems are to be expected. For all of the troubles the Hawkeye experienced in its introduction to service, the improvements incorporated in the E-2B and E-2C models were to overcome these faults and give the Hawkeye superior performance in the future.

## U.S. Air Force:: The Evolution of the Connie

While the U.S. Navy was developing new AEW aircraft, the U.S. Air Force in the mid-1950s opted to upgrade the handful of more limited RC-121Cs it owned. Nearly all of these models were retrofitted at Lockheed Burbank with the more capable APS-95 radar. Redesignated EC-121Ds, these 30 aircraft of the 551st AEW&CW provided the air defense for the most populated and industrialized region of the United States. By the early 1960s, ADC decided to tie these planes into the budding SAGE network, which linked detection, control, and interception

49

assets electronically. The automation built into the 551st Wing changed their Connies from EC-121Ds to EC-121Hs in 1962, and on the exterior a canoe-shaped fairing forward of the "shark fin" APS-45 antenna was added. These changes also significantly reduced the mission crew required onboard the EC-121 to conduct barrier operations. More importantly, though, these changes in the 551st aircraft also restricted their use to picket duty, so that after the 1962–1963 time frame, all of that wing's special missions were transferred to the 552d Wing, which was still equipped for manual control. What had initially been a significant upgrade to the 551st's planes now sounded their death knell, as defense against a Soviet bomber raid became a lower and lower priority.

**Beyond the Picket: New Missions for the Pregnant Geese and Warning Stars**

While the U.S. Navy was busy introducing new AEW aircraft into its inventory, the U.S. Air Force continued to expand the role and use of its EC-121s. In the late 1950s, the Connies were deployed to the Pacific for command and control of airborne and surface assets during space vehicle recovery and nuclear testing. With the action in its backyard, the 552d qualified several crews in these missions, giving them an occasional respite from the drudgery of the picket operations. Key participants in the pre–Project Mercury suborbital flights, the AEW aircraft not only helped locate the re-entry vehicles, but became command and control ships, helping to monitor the vast amount of air traffic in the area. As many as three 552d planes would be airborne at the same time, patrolling a large swath of ocean, which became progressively smaller with updates on the re-entering spacecraft. When the aircrew had predetermined the atmospheric entry point for the capsule, they would "snap up" the Connie's nose to point the radar at the capsule. The radar return was fantastic, with the ion trail left by the re-entry making a blip over 50 miles long on their display. Later, when American men went into space, 552d EC-121s were on station for the same purpose, beginning with Project Mercury and lasting well into the Apollo missions at the end of the decade.

In addition to its participation in the space program, the 552d provided planes and crews for airborne command and control during atomic testing as early as the end of the 1950s. Designated primarily as a radio relay, the Connies soon proved valuable in command and control and

**E-1B**

Shown here are two *Willie Fudds* in formation. Serving until the last cruise by the USS *Franklin D. Roosevelt* (1976), the E-1Bs were primarily flown as detachments with VAW-111 and VAW-121. The *Willie Fudd* normally carried a crew of four, two pilots and two weapons system operators. Flying at low to medium altitude (5,000–7,000 feet), this "interim" AEW aircraft served the Navy well for its 21-year career. *Department of U.S. Navy*

became the controlling unit for all traffic. Aircrew knew these missions as Operation BLUE STRAW, with operations at Johnston Island and other places, and nearly all of the flights staging out of Hawaii. In addition to the support role for participating aircraft and ships, EC-121s were also tasked with keeping nonparticipant aircraft and ships out of the test area for safety and security reasons. Furthermore, since many of these tests included studying blast effects on American warships and aircraft, the Connies were sometimes tasked with vectoring both air and surface vessels into specific positions prior to the detonations.

## Chapter Three

The U.S. Navy also utilized its WV-2s in missions that were not directly involved in barrier operations. As mentioned earlier, VW-1/2/3/4 were not assigned to conduct barrier flights and were mainly used to support fleet operations or conduct weather reconnaissance (specifically VW-4). An example of the support missions conducted during the late 1950s include surveillance flights in and around Formosa during the Quemoy-Matsu incident from August through December 1958. VW-3 forward-based out of NAS Cubi Point, Phillippines, flew round-the-clock missions, supporting carrier operations around the southern end of Formosa, while VW-1, forward-based at NAF Naha, Okinawa, often flew fleet coverage around the northern end. The operations were extremely hectic for the aircrew as they tried to send accurate reports of air traffic to the aircraft carriers during this tense period. Often flying with a full crew load of 21 to 25 aircrew, the WV-2s averaged 16-hour missions, with some flights lasting as long as 20 hours! During this international crisis, there were, however, some lighter moments as related to me by a former VW-3 aircrew.

It seemed that VW-3 had a pet monkey in the squadron, named "Jocko," that occasionally flew on the WV-2. Jocko usually slept or hung out in his miniature "regulation" bunk that a couple of metalsmiths had made for him, but on one such mission, the aircraft had mechanical problems, and smoke began to fill the aircraft. Cabin pressure was dumped, as was the normal procedure in this type of emergency, and the quick change in air pressure must have awakened Jocko, who was asleep in his bunk at the back of the aircraft. Confused and apparently very agitated, Jocko proceeded to run forward in the aircraft, screaming and defecating throughout the cabin! The aircraft was a mess and it took hours to clean up. Needless to say, it was Jocko's last flight!

For these non-barrier squadrons, weather reconnaissance was also a large tasking. As mentioned earlier, some units, such as VW-4, the Hurricane Hunters, were dedicated to this mission, while others conducted it when tasked or when available. Typhoon and hurricane tracking was very important in this pre-satellite era, and these aircraft were used to warn of impending storms. Both visual and radar cues helped the aircrew follow the hurricanes, and some specially modified WV-2s even flew into the storms to monitor wind speeds and direction. Weather reconnaissance was so important that it would continue to be the primary mission of some VW squadrons well into the 1960s while the rest of the VW units were disestablished.

In the Air Force, there were other new missions for the Connies, too, as knowledge of their ability to provide a timely, "God's eye" view spread throughout the service. For nearly two decades, typical additional tasks included filling in for inoperative land-based radar sites, providing radar coverage in the gaps of land-based radar sites, surveillance of VIP aircraft on overseas deployments, and round-the-clock radar patrols when the president of the United States was away from home. The EC-121s also provided radar surveillance and control of U.S. fighter aircraft on over-water deployments and carried survival kits to drop to any aircrews that were forced to ditch.

Although the 552d was geographically better situated to support most of these new tests and missions, it also received more new tasking, as the 551st was gradually excluded from much of the operational tasking because of its avionics. The 551st also moved one of its squadrons, the 966th AEW&C, from Otis AFB to McCoy AFB in Orlando in 1962. Occasionally supplemented by aircraft from the 552d, these EC-121s provided airborne surveillance and warning for U-2 reconnaissance aircraft flying in the Caribbean. Interviews showed that the USAF aircrew seemed to have enjoyed these missions most of all. Usually, a pair of EC-121s flew these missions, with one at an extremely low altitude, often 50–100 feet above the water, using the ocean to screen out islands and other land masses that severely cluttered the Connies' scopes. Another reason for flying low was so that the EC-121s could bounce the radar beam off the water for high-altitude coverage. Called the "mach effect," this allowed the aircrew to track the high-flying aircraft. The CIC team would have the U-2 flight profile "grease penciled" on their displays, and the 966th crews adapted their routes of flight to provide the best coverage of the U-2s, keeping high-level government sources informed of the mission's progress. As they became more adept at their job, controllers were able to see any hostile fighter aircraft that were trying to reach the U-2s in zoom maneuvers to make firing passes. Knowing the MiGs would shoot at the top of their arc, the controllers were able to predict good times and directions for the U-2s to make defensive turns.

The 966th also flew barrier missions when not involved in these U-2 operations, manning Station 50, 24 hours a day, seven days a week. This station was south of Key West, and the Connies flew at an altitude of 1,500 to 4,000 feet, guarding against a possible attack from Cuba. However, in what was the first public omen of the 551st's ultimate demise, the 552d absorbed the 966th in May 1963. As Cuban defenses became more sophisticated and U-2 flights were reduced, the 966th's mission changed significantly. The 966th still pulled picket duty and did occasional intercept exercises with fighters, but there was a more political mission as well. When President Nixon took office in 1968, he occasionally spent time in the "Florida White House." Perhaps fearing Cuban reprisals, McCoy Connies were airborne 24 hours a day during Nixon's visits to Florida, providing air surveillance. More changes occurred when the 966th became Detachment 2 of the 552d Wing in early 1970. After a move to Miami's Homestead AFB, and with Nixon out of office in 1973, it was deactivated within two years. This had been preceded by the inactivation of the 962d on 31 December 1969, which meant that for all intents and purposes, the 551st had ceased to exist.

All these diverse missions gave the AEW crews the opportunity to showcase the EC-121's and WV-2's capabilities as well as giving the crews a chance to hone their skills and expand the envelope of the Connies' performance. Although the barrier operations fortunately never did warn of the onset of the atomic attack they were built to detect, they did contribute a vital mission in defense of the U. S. coastline. Thankfully, the experience gained from the other, unanticipated operations of the previous decade guaranteed that the Connies would be remembered not for AEW, but as an airborne command and control platform running the air war from three miles up.

# CHAPTER FOUR

# AEW in Vietnam

The use of U.S. Air Force EC-121s in Vietnam began with the loss of two F-105 aircraft to North Vietnamese Air Force (NVAF) MiGS in early 1965. Air Force commanders demanded long-range radar capability, and the Warning Stars were thought to be the answer. Because EC-121s were considered capable of overcoming the limitations of the surface-based radar network, they were sent to Vietnam to augment ground- and ship-based radars to support U. S. military aircraft operating in or near North Vietnam. As U.S. ground and air operations gradually escalated in Southeast Asia, the Seventh Air Force required greater radar coverage of North Vietnam. Since line-of-sight limitations affected the existing ground-based radar network located in South Vietnam (Saigon, Da Nang, Pleiku) and Thailand (Udorn, Nakhon Phanom, Mukdahan, Ubon), EC-121s were used to extend radar coverage well into the high-threat areas.

## The EC-121 and College Eye Task Force

Thus in early April 1965, with only a few hours of warning, the 552d Wing deployed a handful of EC-121s to Tainan, Taiwan, to provide a land-based AEW capability to Southeast Asia. Originally designated Big Eye Task Force on 1 March 1967, this operation was later changed to College Eye Task Force (CETF). Between 4 April 1965 and 15 August 1973, the 552d AEW & CW deployed EC-121s and crews to provide AEW for U. S. aircraft in the Southeast Asian (SEA) theater. Original bases for EC-121s were at Taiwan and Tan Son Nhut Air Base, South Vietnam. In February 1967, operations moved from South Vietnam to Ubon, Thailand.

Operations were shifted twice more in Thailand during 1967, first to Udorn in July and finally to Korat in October. On 30 October 1968, the task force assumed the administrative designation of Detachment 1 (Rotational), 552d AEWAC, and continued to fly from Thailand in College Eye combat missions until August 1973.

Aviation author Rene Francillon summarized the early operations of the U.S. Air Force EC-121 aircraft in this manner: "At the onset of their deployment, the Big Eye aircraft had an important role in providing defensive radar coverage over South Vietnam. Fortunately, as the threat of offensive air operations by Illuyshin IL-28 jet bombers of the (NVAF) never materialized and as ground-based radars were installed to provide adequate coverage over the Republic of Vietnam, the air defense function of the EC-121 was phased out by early 1967."

The Connies also assumed a control responsibility for airborne forces over the Gulf of Tonkin, much like they had done in the Pacific in the preceding years. Unfortunately, outside the ADC community, few other Air Force commanders were aware of what the EC-121s could offer, and the first year of Big Eye was a difficult one, marked by resistance by other aviators. Slowly, however, the 552d's 12 years of experience in the AEW&C business became evident to the other flyers in theater, and there was a growing demand for their services.

The 552d Wing supported Big Eye/College Eye operations with continuous rotations of four to five EC-121s to Southeast Asia. The primary operating area was an elliptical orbit over the Gulf of Tonkin, approximately 50 miles east of Haiphong Harbor. The initial task of EC-121 crews was to provide radar coverage for MiG Combat Air Patrols (MIGCAPs) operating in the Gulf of Tonkin area, with secondary missions including the following:

- Airborne radio relay for passing post-strike reports to the tactical air control center at Da Nang
- Battle management of combat air patrol (CAP), strike, and support missions
- SAR coordination and control of aerial refueling missions

When overflight of Chinese airspace became a politically sensitive issue in 1965 to 1966, EC-121s operated over Laos, near the Plain of Jars, to provide navigational assistance and issue border warnings to

American aircrew. It was during this period, however, that NVAF MiG fighters began making concerted attacks against aircraft strike packages, and the CETF crews were unable to provide reliable warning because of their orbits in Laos. Thus, the EC-121s had to shift their orbits closer to North Vietnam so that by mid-1967, College Eye controllers, using the call sign "Disco," were once again directing airborne intercept control of U. S. military fighter aircraft against NVAF MiGs on a routine basis.

Since the Connies had been originally intended only for over-ocean use, the 552d crews faced many of the same radar difficulties often associated with overland use. Thanks to their earlier experiences, especially near Cuba, the technique of flying the EC-121s low over the water for a clearer picture above the Vietnam land mass proved useful once again. Additionally, because of their earlier employment on picket duty, the EC-121's from the 552d had not been configured for identification responsibility; therefore controlling friendly aircraft without an adequate IFF transponder proved to be both demanding and occasionally unreliable. Compounding these difficulties was the lack of enough radios to talk to the multitude of friendly aircraft under their control. Still, despite these significant shortcomings, 552d crews worked hard to overcome these deficiencies and still provide good coverage and control of Southeast Asian skies. There were significant successes, including the first radar-assisted MiG kill of the war on 10 July 1965, when an EC-121 vectored a patrolling U.S. Air Force F-4 into position against a MiG-21. Additionally, Navy Connies discovered that their radars could trigger the IFFs on some MiGs, which circumvented the EC-121s inability to track the enemy fighters over land. After high-level discussion in the government, the Air Force chose to exploit this capability in Vietnam, enabling some of the early air-to-air victories against MiGs.

The EC-121s also orbited near the Mekong Delta area of South Vietnam, augmenting the tactical air control system of South Vietnam and Thailand. The desired extension of radar coverage into North Vietnam occurred only at medium to high altitudes, because the overland surveillance capability of the APS-20 radar was seriously degraded due to excessive ground clutter. The result was a critical loss of low-level threat detection. Adjusting orbit altitude did little to alleviate the problem; therefore, on occasion, two EC-121s would fly in the same area stacked in low and high orbits. Employing two aircraft to compensate for radar deficiencies was not an economy of force effort, and failed to completely resolve the ground clutter problem. Furthermore, ground clutter prevented accurate radar identification of friendly aircraft, requiring controllers to transmit threat warnings on the UHF Guard frequency rather than a discrete control circuit. Moreover, MiG warnings were broadcast in a general format rather than to specific aircraft or flights, which often did not help a specific fighter section. To compensate for low-altitude detection limitations, EC-121 controllers also monitored NVAF ground-controlled intercept (GCI) frequencies to enhance overall threat awareness.

The Big Eye/College Eye Task Force missions operated in conjunction with Navy platforms to provide surveillance, identification, and fighter control assistance. The U.S. Navy positioned cruisers near the mouth of the Red River and at the 18th parallel to provide radar surveillance of the air space between the North Vietnamese coast and Hanoi. The cruisers, call sign "Red Crown," played an integral role in the Navy's Positive Identification Radar Advisory Zone (PIRAZ) over North Vietnam. "Red Crown" monitored the EC-121 frequencies and augmented threat warnings as required. Despite a redundant network of surface and airborne radars, threat detection within the area of interest was not 100 percent effective. The EC-121 also retained the altitude detection problems characteristic of its predecessors. A transcript of the radio conversation between Capt. Steve Ritchie, "Disco," and "Red Crown" during Ritchie's fifth aerial kill indicates MiG position reports from GCI were accurate, yet neither control agency could provide target altitude information. Captain Ritchie repeatedly requested altitude information on the NVAF MiGs, and had to ultimately rely on his F-4 Weapons System Officer, using onboard systems, to assist with target acquisition.

### Assessment of U.S. Air Force R/EC-121 Operations

The Air Force benefitted from the Navy's experience with the WV-2 by procuring an operationally proven aircraft. Formation of the two AEW&C wings validated the need for, and legitimized the existence of, AEW as a specialized Air Force mission. The demanding environment of the contiguous barrier operations, which required extended sorties flown in extreme climatic conditions, served as a valid proving ground for the EC-121 airframe, its aircrews, and associated AEW components. Optimized for overwater operations, the Connie excelled in air defense missions and integrated well into the SAGE network. However, employment during the Vietnam War revealed several inherent system limitations, precluding utilization of the EC-121 as a fully three-dimensional AEW platform.

Despite system limitations, the Big Eye/College Eye Task Force successfully achieved the objective of providing general threat warning information to aircraft over North Vietnam. Radar control of fighters resulted in over 25 confirmed assists during MiG kills. During the deployed period, EC-121 crews provided control to more than 210,000 aircraft involved in combat operations. Connie crews also issued 3,297 threat and border warnings, and assisted in the recovery of more than 80 downed aircrews. By mid-1967, radar improvements incorporated into the EC-121M enabled weapons controllers to provide greater levels of control, which was especially important in prosecuting the visual identification rules of engagement. Capt. Chuck DeBellevue, an F-4 weapons system officer who assisted in six MiG kills, assessed the effectiveness of the EC-121 thusly: "Many times we would not have been able to intercept an enemy aircraft and affect engagement without the information we received from the EC-121. Its support was invaluable." Airborne weapons controllers also assisted aircraft during refueling operations by providing vectors to fuel-limited fighters and bombers. In addition, the EC-121s also functioned as a radio relay platform in concert with C-135 aircraft, allowing the Seventh Air Force commanders to monitor long-range strike missions from takeoff to landing.

Barrier operations and the Vietnam War validated the efficacy of U.S. Air Force AEW in strategic and tactical environments. Although early problems with the EC-121 system nearly forced the Air Force to relinquish all AEW missions and aircraft to the U.S. Navy, the Connie fleet ultimately proved valuable to theater operations in Vietnam for the U.S. Air Force. Twenty years of AEW experience under ADC enabled Connie crews to demonstrate the worldwide command and control capabilities of the EC-121 platform. Big Eye/College Eye Task Force operations signified the advent of airborne command and control as a means to project power on a global basis. As a result, the 552d Wing received five Air Force Outstanding Unit Awards, two of those for valor for contributing to air operations during the Vietnam conflict.

## VAW/VW Operations in Vietnam

Little has been mentioned previously about the naval AEW participation in the Vietnam War, since it involved such a varied number of aircraft and squadrons. It was in this conflict in Southeast Asia that the Hawkeye received its most crucial operational testing. The Vietnam conflict was the first operation in which the E-2A and E-2B were tested, and unfortunately their results were mixed at best. Overcoming problems with poor reliability, the Hawkeye was constrained by its limited overland detection capability, which negated many of its benefits to the carrier airwing.

What exactly was the role of the carrier-based AEW aircraft during the Vietnam War? Missions performed included strike attack vectoring, fighter control, surface search and control, and more, but not airborne early warning, in the purest sense of the term. The combination of an extremely mountainous terrain, the lack of an airborne moving target indicator (AMTI) radar filter, and the absence of direct threats (whether airborne or surface vessels) tended to mitigate the usefulness of the aircraft in that particular role. However, that is not to say that these AEW aircraft were not important to carrier operations in the Vietnam War. Far from it. In fact, it was during this period that the VAW community continued to refine many of its current tactics and operating procedures.

The two main carrier stations utilized during the Vietnam War were known as "Yankee" and "Dixie," which were generalized operating areas from which several carriers flew strike missions. Dixie station, the southernmost of the two, was used mainly for strikes into South Vietnam and as a training area for the aircraft carriers. Yankee station was to the north, generally around 16–18 degree north latitude, from which strikes throughout North Vietnam were launched. The E-1Bs, E-2As, and E-2Bs flew racetrack patterns 80–100 nautical miles north of the carrier between North Vietnam and Hainan Island. The carrier-based AEW aircraft directed strikes inbound, communicated with the carrier, and detected any unusual surface or air contacts inbound to the carrier. When strike support was desired farther north, a second Tracer or Hawkeye was stationed in racetrack patterns at approximately 20 degrees north latitude. All of these flights were flown without CAP support or onboard defensive weapons.

The APS-82 S-band radar of the E-1B and the APS-96 B-band radar of the E-2A/B were woefully inadequate for the radar environment in which they operated. These radar systems could detect land masses and surface shipping well enough, but attempts by the radar operators to locate airborne contacts over land that were not identified as friendly were abject failures. Therefore, they were often relegated to mundane duties such as checking in aircraft as they went feet dry (over land) or feet wet (over water). They also helped to guide strikes to their coast-in-points (prominent landmarks the pilots used for navigation), join them up to airborne fuel tankers, and conduct surface search and control operations. Other missions included electronic support measures correlation (the matching of radar signals that the E-2B could detect with hostile fire-control systems), such as targeting surface-to-air missile (SAM) sites for attack by other aircraft. The biggest flaw, however, was the inability of the Tracer and Hawkeye to regularly detect aircraft over land. Experiments by different VAW squadrons with lower altitudes reduced the effect of land return and allowed the E-2A a limited overland tracking capability. In fact, VAW-122 coordinated a MiG kill on 10 July 1968 by using these techniques. Still, a better radar system was needed, one that could track aircraft over land on a consistent basis.

Navy land-based AEW aircraft contributing to the Vietnam conflict were primarily "Willie Victors" of VW-1 based in Agana, Guam. This squadron regularly operated detachments of WV-2s throughout Southeast Asia. Primarily used in a supporting role to Seventh Fleet activities, these VW aircrews controlled carrier fighters and attack aircraft, in addition to correlating electronic signals intercept and relaying command instructions. The WV-2 aircraft operations, however, were not without their interesting moments. Capt. Norman S. Bull (ret.) relates an attack that occurred when he and his crew were preparing to launch on the last WV-2 flight from Da Nang, Vietnam, on 1 February 1971. As the crew prepared the aircraft for the mission, shelling by the Vietcong forces wounded three of his crew members. The aircraft, however, was able to launch on time and complete its mission.

Throughout much of the Vietnam War, a mixture of E-1Bs and E-2As operated as the primary AEW aircraft in the region. Yet it was the combination of both the VW and VAW squadrons that enhanced the professionalism of the AEW community. The AEW operators flew their support missions throughout the conflict, growing more experienced with each sortie. They in essence built the professional foundation upon which today's VAW squadrons reside.

# CHAPTER 5

# AEW Reaches
# Its Potential

The mid-1960s were a period of huge changes for the Navy, with land-based naval AEW squadrons closing down their picket operations, while carrier-based AEW squadrons were expanding their capabilities. E-2As replaced the E-1Bs and AD-5Ws in operation throughout the fleet as they became more readily available. By the early 1960s, the VAW squadrons had become huge, often numbering over 1,000 personnel as three plane detachments were provided to all aircraft carriers. Other changes occurred as VAW-12 returned from NAS Quonset Point, Rhode Island, to NAS Norfolk in 1962 after a 14-year absence. This move enhanced the ability of the VAW community to operate with the fighter squadrons based at NAS Oceana, Virginia. Likewise, VAW-11 moved to NAS North Island, where it would stay until 1978.

The biggest change during this time period for the AEW community occurred in 1967. The CNO decided that VAW-11 and VAW-12 were just too large to operate efficiently and instead divided these units into individual squadrons. This was great news to the officers of the community as individual squadrons significantly reduced the chances of having to participate in back-to-back cruises. It also opened up new opportunities for squadron command. Competition was very intense for promotional opportunities when there were more than 100 officers and only one commanding officer. The expansion of the community established more squadrons, which greatly helped to alleviate the VAW community's reputation for "eating its young," a term that indicated a severe lack of potential in the typical career path. An interesting point is that many of the first skippers of VAW squadrons were not necessarily VAW aircrew. Rather, they came from other communities, including Carrier Anti-Submarine (VS), Fleet Air Reconnaissance (VQ), Patrol (VP), and Tactical Electronic (VAQ) squadron backgrounds. Many reasons exist for this situation; however, most point to the lack of senior officers with background and training in AEW aircraft.

## VAW Squadron Reorganization

On 1 April 1967, VAW-12 was disestablished and in its place a new organization on the east coast was born. Carrier Airborne Early Warning Wing Twelve (CAEWW-12) was formed to command the entire AEW efforts for the Atlantic Fleet. The Replacement Air Group squadron RVAW-120 was formed to train aircrew and enlisted personnel in carrier-based AEW aircraft. VAW-121, VAW-122, and VAW-123 were all formed from former VAW-12 detachments that were currently in operation. VAW-121 operated E-1Bs, while the other East Coast squadrons, VAW-122 and VAW-123, flew E-2As. This was because there were still not enough E-2A Hawkeyes to distribute to all of the aircraft carriers in the fleet and because E-2As were rarely operated off from the SCB-27C class aircraft carriers. Thus, the E-1Bs continued to operate in detachments, as had been the practice on the smaller carriers (CVSs). This practice continued well into the 1970s, with the last E-1B returning from deployment with VAW-121 Detachment 42 aboard the USS *Franklin D. Roosevelt* (CVA-42) in July 1975.

The same changes also occurred on the West Coast. VAW-11 was disestablished on 20 April 1967, and in its place CAEWW-11, RVAW-110, VAW-111, VAW-112, VAW-113, VAW-114, VAW-115, and VAW-116 were all formed from former VAW-11 detachments. Like its East Coast counterpart VAW-121, VAW-111 retained the E-1Bs and operated detachments on the smaller carriers. The reason that more squadrons were formed on the West Coast was that the VAW community there was much more heavily involved in the Vietnam War during this period. It is for this same reason that the West Coast squadrons were also the first to receive the E-2As. The East Coast squadrons received Hawkeyes as soon as they did only because the United States was fighting a war in Southeast Asia, and many admirals in the Pentagon still believed that the real battlefield was in the North Atlantic and Mediterranean. They felt that Hawkeyes were needed in the fight for supremacy of the seas against the Soviets, no matter what type of limited insurgency might be going on in other parts of the world.

## The Introduction of the E-2B

Although the hardware problems were not solved by the initial introduction of the E-2B, the development of U.S. Navy carrier-based AEW
continued unabated. The evolution of the VAW community was far from
complete after the reorganization of 1967. Other squadrons, notably on
the East Coast, were later established as more Hawkeyes came off the
production line. VAW-124 was the first to follow on 9 September 1967,
followed by VAW-125 on 1 October 1968, and VAW-126 on 1 April 1969.
Additional squadrons followed including VAW-117 on the West Coast on
1 July 1974 and VAW-127 on the East Coast on 2 September 1983. VAW-
115 had the distinction of being stationed at NAS Atsugi, Japan, as part
of the Navy's forward deployment. First attached to the USS *Midway*
(CVA-41) in 1971, VAW-115 began operating from the USS *Independence*
(CV-62) in 1991, and most recently the USS *Kitty Hawk* (CV-63) in 1997.
The use of a forward stationed carrier enabled the Navy to reduce signif-
icantly its transit and steaming times to crisis regions. It also enabled the
U. S. Navy to have a constant striking source located in the western Pacific.

In addition to the active duty squadrons, the VAW community also
possessed a reserve component. Under the authority of the CNO, reserve
VAW squadrons were formed when the Navy reorganized its forces into
the 2-2-12-3 concept of the Naval Air units. Consisting of 2 new ready
reserve squadrons (one on each coast), in addition to the previous 2
ready reserve squadrons, and 12 active-duty squadrons, there were also
3 selective augmentation units (SAUs). SAUs consisted of qualified
reservists who served with a regular or fleet unit and thereby received
their annual training, as opposed to the ready reserve squadrons who
operate their own equipment.

Normally the ready reserve squadrons performed in a manner similar
to the active-duty fleet squadrons except that they would not deploy on
extended cruises. Qualifying on fleet carriers, participating in weapons
detachments, and most recently operating in the counter-drug (formerly
known as Thunderbolt) missions, their members consisted almost exclusively of former active-duty VAW squadron members who chose to join the
reserves. Active and reserve forces worked together with some interoperability problems, but most of these dealt with differences in equipment
rather than personnel.

Technology was not the only big change that occurred in the AEW
community during the 1960s. With the end of barrier operations in

1965, the VW squadrons were beginning to be phased out and the Navy transferred some of its remaining land-based WV-2s to the U. S. Air Force, except for those in VW-1, VW-4, and a few specialized squadrons. By the end of the 1960s, the Navy was pretty much out of the heavy AEW business and concentrating instead on making the new AEW aircraft, the E-2B, the mainstay of its fleet. In addition, as more Hawkeyes came off the assembly line, they were quickly replacing the E-1B Tracers in fleet operational use. Officers and aircrew from these WV-2 and E-1B squadrons were retained in the community and retrained in the Hawkeye aircraft.

The demise of the WV-2s and the E-1Bs marked an end to the early phase of naval AEW. Much of the pioneering spirit that was associated with the AEW community had been developed in these aircraft. These aircraft were the first to operate consistently as AEW platforms, performing missions all over the world. Many VAW and VW aircrews fondly remember these early AEW aircraft for their accomplishments. Who but the members of VW-2 would name all their aircraft after Norse gods? Or VAW-12 Detachment 62, which named all of their Willie Fudds with "Eye" nicknames? As colorful as they were, however, their mission was now complete, and the time had come to pass the mantle on to the newcomer on the scene, the E-2B Hawkeye.

## Development of the E-2C Hawkeye

Obviously, the Hawkeye, when it operated correctly, was a tremendous improvement over the E-1B Tracer, but it definitely did not live up to its potential in the mid- to late 1960s. Having failed the Bureau of Inspection and Survey trials and with production abruptly terminated in 1965, service life for the Hawkeye appeared to be coming to an end. Under intense pressure from the Navy, Grumman developed quick fixes that enabled the plane to fulfill its mission, if at a somewhat degraded level from earlier expectations. These changes to the E-2A, including improvements to the computer, radar, and cooling equipment, were incorporated into the E-2B, which first deployed with VAW-114 aboard the USS *Kitty Hawk* (CV-63) in November 1970. Of the 59 E-2As built, 49 were converted to E-2Bs, 4 were converted to the TE-2A configuration (pilot trainers), 2 served as C-2A prototypes (cargo versions), 2 served as YE-2C test aircraft (avionics testing aircraft), 1 was used for barricade tests, and the final aircraft was stricken from the inventory and was mounted on a pedestal at the west gate to NAS Miramar, San Diego, California. That aircraft remained there until November 1997, when it was removed and scrapped because the base had changed hands to the U.S. Marine Corps.

While these changes were being completed, the Navy still wanted to develop a follow-on program to ensure the continued production of the aircraft. The E-2B was not the ultimate answer to the problems associated with the Hawkeye program. Therefore, in April 1968 the Navy initiated another reliability improvement program to further upgrade the capabilities of the E-2B and increase the inventory. All told, with only 49 airframes, there were simply not enough aircraft to fill the complements of the fleet. Initially the plan was to assign all E-2Bs to the West Coast squadrons, while the East Coast squadrons would get the new E-2Cs, of which 28 were ordered. The theory was that the next generation of AEW aircraft was to be introduced to the fleet in 1984, and the E-2Bs could continue in service until then. However, this plan was changed in 1976 by the secretary of the Navy's decision to upgrade the entire fleet to E-2Cs.

The preplanned product improvement (P3I) program, which became the beginning of the E-2C program, was a plan to use the original growth capability that was designed into the E-2A from its inception. By utilizing improvements in technology, the engineers at Grumman developed substantial improvements in radar and computer performance without significantly changing the airframe of the aircraft. As the former E-2C (Group 0) pilots would attest, the airframe and cockpit are virtually unchanged from the original E-2A configuration. Some of the instruments and avionics in the cockpit are antiquated. Yet the capabilities of the radar avionics have increased tremendously from the E-2A to the E-2C. The upgrades in the computer and weapons systems alone have given the Hawkeye limited overland and an exceptional electronic support measures (ESM) capability.

The P3I program was approved in 1970, with the first release of funding on 30 September 1971. Production was begun immediately on the E-2C, the Hawkeye that Grumman had envisioned back in 1957. The E-2C was finally able to meet the original capability and reliability thresholds that had been established by the CNO Operational Requirement and the BuAer Specification in 1955, at the outset of the E-2A program. The major change was the introduction of the APS-120 radar, which incorporated a workable AMTI system. Finally the Hawkeye had a limited overland capability, in that it could now detect moving targets over the land mass. In addition, for the first time an ESM package, titled the Passive Detection System (PDS) or ALR-59, was added to the avionics system. If radar is the eyes that can see a target, then the PDS is the ears that can hear it. Able to detect other radar systems at extremely long ranges, the ALR-59 system gives the E-2C operator another tool to use to classify targets.

**E-2C (Group 0)**
When the E-2C was first introduced in 1973, it was the premier AEW aircraft in the world. Shouldering on in fleet squadrons until 2001, the basic E-2C received near continuous upgrades throughout its lifetime. As newer versions of the Hawkeye were created (Group I and Group II), the original E-2C was renamed Group Ø.
*Department of U.S. Navy*

A trend emerged that would continue for the next three decades from 1970 until the present in regards to the E-2C. Changing few external features, the Hawkeye continued to receive upgraded avionics and software to keep up with the anticipated threat from the Soviet Union. These included better radar systems, new processors for the computers, and more software features that saved time for the operator. In fact, the evolution of the E-2C (Group II) is far from complete, with its seventh different radar system, the APS-145, having recently completed its production run, and an entirely new mission with cooperative engagement capability is slated for production in the newest E-2C, renamed the Hawkeye 2000, starting in October 2001.

## Connie's Remarkable Offspring: AWACS

By the early 1960s, the Air Force knew that the Connie would not last forever, and that its vision of the complete airborne command and control platform would never be fully realized on this airframe. Beginning in 1965, several EC-121Ds were modified to Q-models in the BRASS KNOB program, evaluating certain avionics for future use on the next-generation platform, the Airborne Warning and Control System (AWACS). The AWACS solved the seemingly insurmountable "ground clutter" problem of overland detection of aircraft by employing a pulse Doppler radar that could distinguish between flying aircraft and the ground below. A radar that operates on a pulse Doppler principle tracks contacts based on their speed relative to the radar, not their position. Luckily, despite the influence of ADC officers who saw this upcoming system as a new air defense airplane, veterans of the CETF Task Force reminded the Air Force that the EC-121's wide variety of missions had proven its more appropriate application to airborne command and control. Fortunately, the Air Force realized the necessity of upgrading the Connies' avionics to meet their new requirements. The crews' inputs led to the EC-121D+, an upgrade that introduced advanced state-of-the-art "add-ons" enhancing the system in the key areas of hostile detection, friendly beacon tracking, and line-of-sight communications. A secure communication (cross-tell) capability and other classified programs were initiated to greatly enhance onboard threat assessment and lateral information exchange.

These new capabilities made the AEW Connies an even more capable platform, but there was still much to be done to make them the true command, control, and warning platform the Air Force envisioned. System improvements enabled the CETF to adapt to a combat environment and support the needs of tactical aircraft. Although ADC tasking dictated strategic mission prioritization, upgrades to the EC-121 resulted in automated aircraft tracking and improved communications. The introduction of the EC-121T represented a transition from manual to automated system capabilities, and with that came a new designator, Airborne Surveillance and Control System (ASACS). Enhancements represented in the EC-121T included:

- IFF tracking through an onboard computer
- Computer-aided tracking, intercept control programs, and data symbology
- Software programs to support operations in varied geographic areas
- Digital datalink
- Secure, high-power, beyond-line-of-sight voice capability

Upgrades to the U. S. Air Force EC-121 system ultimately enabled weapons controllers to employ for the first time an airborne radar system in a command and control role.

By the late 1960s, the 552d AEW&CW had absorbed all four of the EC-121 squadrons in its effort to coordinate operations in Southeast Asia. However, with the Vietnamization of the war effort beginning during the Nixon administration, the need for EC-121 units was beginning to be reduced. On 31 December 1969, the 551st AEW&CW and 962th AEW&CS were deactivated. Other AEW squadrons were also deactivated as the war in Vietnam drew to a close, including the 965th AEW&CS on 30 June 1971 and the 964th AEW&CS on 30 June 1974.

Lessons learned during the Vietnam conflict dictated that the Air Force resolve ground clutter limitations in airborne radar systems to effectively conduct overland operations. The AMTI concept pursued by the Navy didn't solve the Air Force's requirement for surveillance and detection against a variable terrain background. As early as 1963, the U.S. Air Force Electronic Systems Division (ESD) initiated a far-sighted Overland Radar Technology (ORT) program to determine the viability of long-range pulse Doppler radars with a "look-down" capability to meet military requirements. This program and the associated specific Operational Requirement 206 - Airborne Warning and Control System (AW&CS),

served as guiding documents for the development of specifications for a new radar platform. EC-121s would be used as the test beds for three radar systems under consideration using slotted waveguide antennas and various processing techniques. In early 1966, Westinghouse, Hughes, and Raytheon received research contracts, and by 1967 radar installation feasibility studies began.

To support a new-generation AEW system, Boeing and McDonnell Douglas received funds in 1967 to study the compatibility between an external radar and an existing airframe. Original specifications sought to incorporate an airborne command post with a radar sensor platform, enabling senior military commanders to conduct land, sea, and air operations from a mobile, survivable platform. The Boeing 707 and McDonnell Douglas DC-8 received preferential consideration, although Boeing suggested a 747 airframe to accommodate airborne command post requirements. Even though AWACS had originated from the barrier operations, by the mid-1960s, it had evolved far beyond that mission into an airborne, radar-equipped command center.

After a series of competitive tests, Boeing received the initial AWACS contract on 10 July 1970. The 707-320B became the standard airframe, with a radar mounted above the aft section of the empennage. Interestingly enough, the U.S. Air Force had examined modifying the 707 airframe to increase endurance by fitting the aircraft with eight TF34 engines in twin pods. A number of different pylon arrangements were also looked at before settling on the present configuration. Included in these early proposals were placement of the rotodome on the tail or on a single vertical support in the middle of the aircraft. In the end, though, each radar was housed in a rotating radome, or rotodome, mounted on twin pylons above the aircraft fuselage with a saucer-shaped structure, measuring 30 feet wide and 6 feet thick. IBM and Hazeltine Corporation subcontracted the computer and data display systems. Radar testing of Westinghouse and Hughes radars occurred in Seattle during early 1972. Two 707-320B aircraft (designated EC-137D by the Air Force) flew a battery of airborne tests between April and September 1972. Testing incorporated detection and tracking of F-4, F-106, and B-52 aircraft, in clear and electronic countermeasures (ECM) conditions, against five clutter backgrounds: calm sea, vegetated farmland, rolling woodland, desert, and mountains. In October 1972, ESD declared Westinghouse the radar contractor for the AWACS program. Official production of the AWACS program began on 26 January 1973, and the Boeing E-3A was officially designated as the "Sentry."

The Westinghouse's APY-1 surveillance radar, mounted back to back with Mark XII IFF and TADIL-C datalink antennas, functioned in the following modes:

- Pulse Doppler non-elevation scan (PDNES), to detect targets at very low altitudes without ground clutter
- Pulse Doppler elevation scan, similar to PDNES, except that target elevation is derived from an electronic vertical scan of the beam
- Beyond-the-horizon, using a pulse without Doppler for long-range surveillance
- Passive, in which the transmitter is shut down in selected subsectors, but the receivers continue to detect signals from jammers
- Test and maintenance, used by technicians during repair work
- Standby, to keep the radar ready for immediate use

Unlike earlier radars, the APY-1 did not present "raw" video data for display; instead, incoming signals were digitally processed and fed to a data processing functional group (DPFG). This approach allowed a wide range of versatility in adapting the radar to new requirements, and in manipulation of the data for analysis and display. The radar also utilized many state-of-the-art techniques to counter sophisticated ECM in a hostile environment.

The EC-137D, fitted with additional data-processing equipment and two tracking displays, began a three-month series of airborne tracking demonstrations in the United States, including exercise Brave Shield III at the end of 1972. Full-scale development began on 26 January 1973, and in April of that year, the plane took part in several operational flight tests over Western Europe and the Mediterranean, proving AWACS had the potential to enhance the existing North Atlantic Treaty Organization (NATO) command and control structure. Boeing had by then decided to power the plane with four Pratt & Whitney TF33-P-7/7A (USAF designation TF33-PW-100/100A) engines instead of eight General Electric TF34-2 turbofans.

Full-scale development was divided into two major activities: a system integration demonstration (SID) and a development test and evaluation

(DTE). Both were underway when NATO picked the E-3A for production as a major asset of its C3 components in 1974. During the SID, the same plane was used as in the airborne tracking flights, but modified for the purpose of getting early test and evaluation information. The objective of DTE was "to develop the hardware, software, and technology into an operational configuration and, thus, facilitate the transition between the development and production stages of the E-3A program." DTE was followed in August 1975 by an initial operational test and evaluation (IOT&E) phase. During IOT&E, the E-3A "successfully controlled" close air support, interdiction, search and rescue, airlift, and counter-air missions. It was also "successfully employed as an extension of the North American air defense command and control system in an ECM environment."

The General Accounting Office (GAO) had, in the meantime, published a report in 1974 maintaining the E-3A was being "rushed into production prematurely," that there had been "little or no demonstration of the capability of AWACS to properly manage the tactical situation in a high-density combat environment such as is expected to be encountered in Europe," and that its radar could be jammed and was "subject to performance degradations due to interference from ground-based radars and other electronic systems operated by friendly forces." However, the GAO ended the report on a positive note: "We believe that the AWACS program has the potential for improving the capability of the USAF to manage tactical air operations in a high-density environment. It also appears to us that it could certainly have an important role in limited war, or in contingency situations where no ground facilities exist."

To answer these charges, an E-3A was sent to Ramstein Air Base, West Germany, in April 1975. The plane flew 25 of its 26 scheduled sorties for 100.5 hours, during which it detected small ships and low-flying planes and controlled fighter aircraft in a variety of air defense and anti-ship roles. The Sentry also exercised its "deep-look" capability into Warsaw Pact countries by providing for friendly SAM support and used transponders to identify the status of key installations and the location of maneuvering forces. These tests proved beyond a doubt the ability of the E-3A to interoperate with command and control facilities on the ground, and it also allowed the U.S. Air Force to show off their newest asset to European allies.

**E-3A**

The transition from the EC-121 to AWACS was a major evolution for the U.S. Air Force. With the arrival of the E-3A, the Air Force finally had a true over-the-horizon AEW aircraft that could track aircraft over land in a variety of terrain. Notice the height of the radome above the fuselage in the AWACS. This was done to lessen clutter return from the 707 airframe and to give the operators a clear radar picture. *U.S. Air Force*

## Brave Shield, Vigilant Overview, and TAC-X

E-3A program development continued from January 1973 to December 1975, with the four test aircraft accumulating 1,318 flying hours in 294 flights. North American Aerospace Defense Command (NORAD) integration and naval system compatibility also received evaluation. The first pre-production E-3A (USAF serial number 73-1674) flew in February 1975; the second (73-1675), completely fitted with production avionics for command and control as well as surveillance, left Boeing Field eight months later with representatives from Tactical Air Command, ADC, ESD, and the Air Force Test and Evaluation Center (AFTEC) onboard. AFTEC, an independent test agency located at Kirtland AFB,

73

completed a 16-month operational evaluation in August 1975 during which four E-3As flew 451 sorties for more than 1,800 hours.

Following these initial tests, the E-3As participated in two large-scale operational exercises, Brave Shield XV and Vigilant Overview 77-1, and a specially designed tactical test (TAC-X) conducted at the Nellis AFB range complex from October to December 1976. According to the AWACS report from the 552d Wing history office, the exercise and test scenarios "simulated the required operational missions envisioned for the E-3A in a variety of roles as a command, control, and surveillance system," represented "the most demanding situations the E-3A might be expected to encounter, and closely approximated the associated threats in tactics, number of aircraft, and ECM."

The scenario for Brave Shield, conducted at Eglin AFB, involved the invasion of a friendly nation. Two E-3As relayed data to the Blue control and reporting center, and joint task force headquarters. "The TV downlink presented a continuous, real-time display of the E-3A's total surveillance. It monitored air activity far beyond the exercise airspace and examined isolated air movements within restricted areas of operation." Two E-3As were also on the defending Blue side during Vigilant Overview, which included interceptors from McChord and Fairchild AFB and Comox Royal Canadian AFB. "The Red raids came in three waves, lasted about 4.5 hours, and employed unusually heavy airborne jamming. Despite this, the E-3As directed successful intercepts against most of the enemy penetrators."

TAC-X was designed to assess the E-3A's effectiveness in an environment that "accurately simulated the Warsaw Pact electronic capability and the number of first-line combat aircraft that could be expected to be employed in an actual attack." The two participating E-3As effectively tracked attacking F-4s, F-100s, and F-105s, vectored friendly F-4s and F-15s to intercept them, and resisted all enemy attempts at ECM. "One hundred thirty-four Blue aircraft stood off 274 attackers, eliminating many of them. The E-3As made this possible."

Even as a the Connies were being phased out, the "ADC lobby" pointed to the appearance of a new Soviet intercontinental bomber, the supersonic, 4,300-nautical-mile-range Backfire. With the picket duty Connies gone and American continental radar defenses lapsing in decay, these ADC officers envisioned AWACS answering the same call the EC-121s had heard 20-some years before. The argument was powerful, but the widely varying experiences of the Connies had made their mark. In an article arguing the merits of this expensive new AWACS, two journalists noted: "Although the 42 AWACS aircraft initially ordered would all apparently be assigned to the ADC, the Air Force has said that even if there were no bomber threat, it would still give high priority to the procurement of AWACS as a tactical weapon . . . a flying battlefield command post. Instead of erecting ground-based radars in a disputed territory, the Air Force could station an AWACS plane hundreds of miles from the battle, out of range of enemy weapons, and still control all air operations."

The Air Force originally sought 42 E-3s but subsequently realized a purchase plan for 33 aircraft. Although not part of the USAF fleet, one test bed belongs to Boeing Aerospace, bringing the total number of E-3 aircraft purchased to 34. One AWACS has since been lost with the crash of an E-3B (77-0354) in Alaska on 22 September 1995. All E-3s are currently "owned" by the Air Combat Command, based at Langley AFB, Virginia, while headquarters NORAD exercises operational control of CONUS E-3s. The 552 Air Control Wing at Tinker AFB actually operates most of the USAF fleet and currently reports to Twelfth Air Force at Davis-Monthan AFB. Operational squadrons at Tinker AFB are the 960th, 963rd, 964th, and 965th Airborne Air Control Squadrons (AACS), the 966th Airborne Air Control Training Squadron, and the 552d Training Squadron. Pacific Command (PACOM) operates four Sentries through the Fifth and Eleventh Air Force, with two E-3 squadrons, the 961st AACS at Kadena AFB and the 962d AACS at Elmendorf AFB, each currently having two aircraft assigned.

Of the 32 surviving E-3A aircraft, 22 airframes were upgraded to the E-3B configuration during the 1980s. This upgrade included enhanced computer functions, additional radios (including the Have Quick jam-resistant system), an austere maritime surveillance capability, and five additional situation display consoles (increasing the number from 9 to 14). The Air Force subsequently ordered the conversion of 10 Standard E-3A aircraft to E-3C models from 1984 to 1988. At the time this book was published, the U.S. Air Force operated a fleet of AWACS that was a mix of 23 E-3Bs and 9 E-3C models, with Boeing continuing to operate the remaining E-3C as a test bed aircraft.

The authorization for the 34 AWACS the USAF purchased originally envisioned that one-third of the planes would be based overseas for theater early warning and control, with the remaining two-thirds stationed in the

United States for continental air defense. But in the end, because of the AWACS' versatility, plus the fact that this new Soviet bomber threat, as with the first one, never really matured, the AWACS found its home in Tactical Air Command as perhaps the most important air asset in contemporary air combat.

## The EC-121: Denouement and Aftermath

With the delivery of the first E-3 AWACS only a few years away, the 552d was notified in late 1974 that it would be deactivated within two years. The 552d detachment in Thailand, which had returned to Korat in 1973 after a two-year hiatus to Kwangju, South Korea, was inactivated first, followed by the Iceland detachment. Some 552d Connies were transferred to the Air Force Reserve at Homestead AFB, fulfilling an ongoing rotational commitment in Iceland (since 1968) to watch those strategic waters just as Navy barrier EC-121s had done beginning in the early 1960s. The 552d Wing then became the 552 Airborne Early Warning and Control Group (AEWACG), with one active squadron (963rd AEWACS) and nine operational aircraft. On 30 April 1976, the 552d AEWACG deactivated. Then on 1 July 1976, the 552d AWAC Wing (AWACW) was formed at Tinker AFB, Oklahoma. The Air Force Reserve absorbed the EC-121 fleet, and the 552d AWACW accepted the first production E-3A on 23 March 1977. By reforming the 552d AWACW, the U.S. Air Force paid perhaps the ultimate compliment to the men of the 552d AEW&CW, who proved the airborne command and control concept for over two decades of EC-121 employment.

Today, there are a few EC-121s in museums around the country. The Connie that assisted in the first MiG kill of 1965 is at the Air Force Museum in Dayton, Ohio. Another Connie sits in the McClellan Aviation Museum and another at Tinker AFB, Oklahoma City, but these Connies are ironies in themselves. Despite their Air Force paint scheme, both of these aircraft were flown by the Navy and used on the barrier patrols. Most visitors would not pay much attention to these planes, for they sit adjacent to famous fighters and bombers which are more likely to attract attention. Few of those smaller, sleeker aircraft, however, flew for over 20 years, nor saw as much of the world as the EC-121. It was truly a remarkable aircraft, and a worthy parent of today's AEW platforms.

# CHAPTER 6

# AEW
# Operational Use

Air operations in World War II and Korea reinforced the need for centralized air control. Likewise, in Southeast Asia an AEW system was needed to extend the coverage of ground-based radars and provide surveillance, warning, and control, occasionally in an autonomous mode. The lessons learned provided much needed data to enhance the development of the E-2 and E-3, especially in the area of low-level detection. In the late 1970s, as the various services responded to the drawdown in force structure, many officers realized that AEW aircraft were even more important in giving commanders the information that they needed in these high-threat environments.

Training and operational experience combined to reinforce the combat capabilities of crews beginning in the early 1980s. AEW aircraft involvement in composite force training exercises exposed crew members to the dynamics of tactical employment. In the Air Force, key exercise scenarios utilized the airborne battle management functions of AWACS, resulting in widespread exposure and increased awareness throughout the tactical Air Force. Likewise, with the introduction of more capable AEW aircraft, VAW squadrons gained increased recognition throughout the carrier battle group (CVBG).

Specialized career and joint interoperability training provided additional benefits to AEW crew members. Attendance at the Carrier Airborne Early Warning Weapons School, Fighter Weapons Instructor Course, Counter Air Tactics Awareness Training Course, Weapons and Tactics

Instructor Course, Army Air Defense Artillery, and various electronic warfare courses increased the E-2 and E-3 community's knowledge of service-unique and joint tactical employment. Navy exchange tours, whereby U.S. Air Force E-3 qualified crew members fill billets in VAW squadrons and on AEGIS cruisers, broadened the joint experience and knowledge levels of the AWACS communities. A liaison office at Tinker AFB, staffed by AWACS-qualified Navy personnel, also enhances the joint capabilities of the system. AWACS and VAW exchange billets are staffed with the U.S. Marine Corps and Joint Staffs. Furthermore, naval fleet staffs, such as a Commander Third Fleet, maintain a billet for AWACS-experienced personnel to address interoperability issues. The traditional joint orientation of both AEW communities facilitated joint operations before it became popular to do so. And in doing so, the crews of these platforms proved over and over again how incredibly versatile these AEW aircraft really are.

**E-3 Operations**

U.S. Air Force E-3s support a myriad of worldwide tasking in conjunction with joint and combined forces. The E-3 Sentry provides highly mobile, flexible, and survivable wide-area surveillance and C3 functions, while overcoming the inherent limitations of ground-based radar systems. When deploying with combat forces, E-3s execute various C3 functions while en route to, or upon arrival at their destinations. AWACS operates in conjunction with other C3 systems to integrate airborne elements of command, air surveillance, air support coordination, airspace management, and control. Further enhancing the operational stature of the E-3 is its ability to conduct all-weather surveillance above various types of terrain. Since the arrival of the first aircraft at Tinker AFB, the robust C3 capabilities of AWACS have kept the E-3 in demand around the world.

Like its EC-121 predecessor, the Sentry played an important role in strategic air defense operations during the late 1970s and 1980s. NORAD assumed operational control of E-3s in January of 1979, maintaining aircraft on alert at Tinker AFB and supporting numerous air defense operations and exercises. Sentry deployments to Europe, Asia, and Alaska tested AWACS interoperability capabilities, and in a unique exchange program, the Canadian Air Force supported air defense operations by posting operationally qualified personnel at Tinker AFB. These Canadian aircrew have flown in AWACS since 1979 as a part of the Royal Canadian Air Force (RCAF) commitment to NORAD. The United States and Canada had envisioned a number of AWACS aircraft dedicated to NORAD use for picket duty, but as the role of the E-3 evolved, so did the mission of the RCAF aircrew. Originally composed of 14 aircrew, this complement was expanded to 54 (three crews) in 1987. The majority of these personnel are stationed at Tinker AFB (43), while 11 aircrew are stationed at Elmendorf AFB in Alaska with the 962d AACS.

The 552d AWACW also provided aircrews and aircraft to support air defense operations in the Icelandic region. From October 1978 to mid-1989, the 960th AWACS at Keflavik, Iceland, provided long-range surveillance and airborne intercept control against Soviet bombers. An interesting side-note is that when the AWACS were deployed to the United States to cover striking air traffic controllers from December 1980 to April 1981, VAW aircrews covered the Icelandic patrols with U.S. Navy E-2Cs. In addition, AWACS were deployed to Saudi Arabia from 1981 to 1989 on a near continuous basis as a part of the European Liaison Force (ELF) One Detachment One. During this detachment, the E-3s flew more than 6,000 sorties for 87,000 hours to monitor the Iran-Iraq War.

From the 1980s to the present, AWACS crews consistently have received valuable interoperability and large-force employment training during Red Flag, Green Flag, Maple Flag, Copper Flag, Cope Thunder, Team Spirit, Gallant Eagle, Cobra Gold, Bright Star, and numerous other joint and multi-national exercises. AWACS crews also gained operational experience during politically sensitive Joint Chiefs–directed contingencies from the early 1980s to the present. Aside from strategic defense operations, E-3s exist as an integral part of multi-service ground radar elements. One of the key tactical responsibilities of the E-3 is to function as an airborne element of the theater air control system (AETACS). The E-3 can be used to extend the surveillance area of a ground radar system, provide additional radar control capability, and/or perform both functions in areas where the ground radar systems are not operational. Doctrinally, AWACS provides interim C3 until the U.S. Air Force Theater Air Control System (TACS) elements arrive on location. The E-3 as an AETACS platform performs all functions of a fully integrated TACS from mobile, rapidly deployable platforms. From a battle management perspective, AWACS provides real-time situation information, affording increased response times for air and ground commanders.

The AWACS fleet maintains a commitment to providing worldwide "airborne diplomacy" as a peaceful show of the American flag. A large portion of the E-3's history involves overseas deployments to areas of political and military tension. The long-range AWAC system provides a non-threatening presence while projecting airpower abroad. Operational deployments to Europe, Saudi Arabia, Egypt, Korea, and Sudan have characterized the E-3's ability to provide rapid response during times of crisis. AWACS supported combat missions in Operation Just Cause in Panama in December 1989 and Operation Desert Storm in 1991, often flying missions in excess of 22 hours. Although the E-3 has performed numerous peacetime missions, the Joint Chiefs have consistently directed AWACS employment during contingency operations and hostilities.

## Daily Operations

To get a better sense of the day-to-day operations of the E-3, let's examine the organization of the AWACS community. Primarily based at Tinker AFB, Oklahoma City, there are also two squadrons, the 961st and 962d AACS, that operate two plane detachments in Elmendorf and Kadena AFB. The four operational squadrons stationed at Tinker (960th, 963rd, 964th and 965th AACS) operate and support NORAD, Joint Chiefs, and U.S. Air Force AWACS missions. The fifth flying squadron also located at Tinker, the 966th AACS, is primarily tasked to provide Initial Qualification Training (IQT). These five flying squadrons as well as the 552d Training Squadron make up the core of the E-3 community and are home to many aircrew.

The officers that fly the AWACS are generally divided into the flight deck personnel (pilots and navigators) and the mission crew (13B). The pilots undergo their initial flight training in Undergraduate Pilot Training and then receive their assignments to E-3s where they receive academic and simulator training at the 552d Training Squadron and E-3 flights at the 966th AACS. Likewise, 13B E-3 aircrew undergo basic, air intercept, and battle management training at Tyndall AFB and then, after receiving their assignments to E-3, undergo academic and simulator training at the 552d Training Squadron. The controllers receive seven flights in the 966th AACS and a final evaluation check flight. This IQT is primarily a safety check to ensure the pilots and operators know how to operate their E-3 equipment safely.

Once in an operational squadron, E-3 aircrew will serve for up to five years, progressing through the upgrades of Weapons Director (WD), Instructor Weapons Director (IWD), Senior Director (SD), and Instructor

Senior Director (ISD). It normally takes about two years for a WD to upgrade to an SD. This progression on the weapons side is paralleled by the WDs who upgrade to become Air Surveillance Officers (ASOs). The addition of the Electronic Combat Officer (ECO) adds new options with a possible career progression including ECOs fleeting up directly to ASOs. This normal upgrade progression is aided by the IWDs and ISDs, who facilitate this training within the operational squadrons. The 966th AACS then conducts a Mission Qualification Training (MQT) to ensure that these E-3 aircrew are tactically ready to conduct missions all over the world.

## Typical Missions

With all of these different and varied operations, it is difficult to describe a "typical" mission for an E-3, but the following paragraphs attempt to show how the AWACS aircrew accomplish their tasking. Unlike other aircraft with smaller crews who often will mission-plan the day of their sortie, mission planning for the E-3 crew is a full-day process usually taking place on the duty day prior to the flight. Mission planning consists of a series of meetings, some involving the entire crew and some involving only key players from the flight deck and mission crews. The initial meeting is run by the Aircraft Commander and the Mission Crew Commander (MCC), who together will outline the big picture for the flight. Objectives and timing are discussed, as are scheduled weapons and surveillance missions and any training events for the flight deck, such as aerial refueling, touch-and-gos, check rides, or chemical warfare training. Individual sections then split up for specialized mission planning. Around midmorning, the mission crew leadership meets for a coordination meeting to iron out the communications plan, determine training priorities, plan daily emergency procedures drill, and identify any maintenance problems with the aircraft that could impact the mission. By early afternoon the whole crew is ready to meet for a summary briefing to explain details of the mission and discuss any changes. The day wraps up with the weapons and surveillance sections having specialized briefings to discuss the details of their training plans for the flight.

Early on the morning of the sortie (2 hours 15 minutes prior to takeoff), the crew shows up at the squadron for a final "step brief." Emergency procedures are reviewed, and any passengers and last-minute changes to the mission or aircraft are briefed. The crew then boards a bus to ride out to the aircraft. Upon arriving at the aircraft, the crew begins its preflight

**E-3B**
The E-3B serves throughout the world as a sign of American foreign policy. Many analysts say the arrival of the AWACS signals a shift in national strategy. The deployment of the E-3 is a clear sign that the United States is interested in maintaining air superiority in a region, and thus should be viewed as a deterrent measure. *U.S. Air Force*

inspections, which for the flight engineer and technicians are often quite extensive checks of the aircraft and mission systems. For the rest of the mission crew, a quick check of their seat and oxygen equipment is usually followed by a trip to the flight kitchen for breakfast, while the flight deck will stay at base operations to check the weather, do last-minute flight planning, and file the flight plan. During the breakfast stop, crew members pick up in-flight box lunches for the rest of the crew and the technicians who had to stay on the aircraft to finish their preflight.

For takeoff and the first 10–15 minutes of the flight, the mission crew members are passengers. Once the aircraft has reached sufficient altitude and the temperature of the outside air is low enough to cool the mission systems, the technicians begin their power-up sequences. The communications technician and radio operator turn on and configure all of the mission radios, while the computer and radar technicians bring up their systems. The computer system must initialize, which on most jets takes 15 minutes or so, and the radar and IFF transmitters must time-out, which takes 20–30 minutes as well. During the power-up process, the technicians keep the MCC aware of any problems they encounter, especially if they will impact later parts of the mission. The MCC will notify the flight deck of any problems and vice versa. Once the sensors, computer, and radios are all functioning properly, the rest of the mission crew (the weapons and surveillance teams) will begin work. The surveillance section will contact the closest NORAD Sector Operation Command Center (SOCC), in accordance with a plan briefed the day before, and establish datalinks and begin tracking and identifying aircraft in a briefed area of responsibility. The surveillance section will normally train with the SOCCs and practice datalink procedures. Often, on missions to the southern portion of the United States, the E-3 assumes a customs support role, looking for drug smugglers trying to fly under ground-based radar coverage.

Meanwhile, the senior director will contact the FAA center they will be coordinating with, to ensure that the E-3's radar picture matches the FAA's by doing a correlation check, and requesting that the center release whatever airspace the E-3 is controlling to the AWACS crew. If the weapons directors were able to brief with their fighter pilots on the previous day, those briefings and objectives are reviewed. If not, attempts are made to contact the pilots either over the squadron operations frequencies or another discrete frequency. The weapons and surveillance sections work together during the time that the weapons directors are controlling aircraft, which varies greatly from mission to mission. There may be several fighter missions in the same area, resulting in the E-3 staying in one place all day, or there may be one mission followed by a gap of several hours, in which the Sentry moves to a different airspace and controls fighters from a different unit at a different base. During lulls in fighter activity, the crew may practice emergency procedures, run tests on the mission equipment, conduct simulator training, or even break for lunch. When the weapons section is not controlling fighters, they will debrief their missions internally and prepare debriefs to send to the fighter pilots.

The flight crew is obviously more busy while the E-3 is moving from one orbit area to another, but while on a particular station, the autopilot normally keeps the plane flying so the flight deck personnel can take turns stretching their legs and watching the mission crew at work. Often missions change while in flight. Fighters may cancel or change their timing, requiring the weapons team to change their plans. Or the weather may change in the patrol area or at Tinker AFB, requiring an alteration of the flight plan. All of these events require close coordination between the flight and mission crews to ensure that the maximum training is accomplished while maintaining a high level of safety. At some point in the mission the E-3 may meet a tanker aircraft for refueling, at which point the mission crew largely becomes passengers again, as the sensors must be placed in standby and only some radios can be used during the refueling operation.

Once all desired training is accomplished (or the jet reaches bingo fuel), the E-3 will return to Tinker AFB or its temporary base. During the flight home, the technicians will power down and run diagnostic checks on their equipment, noting any problems to debrief with maintenance. Upon arrival at Tinker, the flight crew will usually shoot a few practice approaches before landing for the day. The crew then secures the aircraft, debriefs with maintenance, then debriefs among themselves to evaluate how well they accomplished their training objectives. Areas for improvement or lessons learned are noted, and following the completion of all required paperwork, the crew is dismissed. From landing to debrief conclusion, postflight activities usually take 1.0–1.5 hours. A typical "out and back" training sortie usually consists of an 8–10-hour flight, which adds up to about a 12–14-hour workday.

While these paragraphs might describe a typical mission, a nightmare for any crew is the possibility of a blue-on-blue incident. This is exactly what happened in one of the more recent contingency exercises, Operation Provide Comfort. This exercise was begun in April 1991 in the immediate aftermath of the Gulf War in an effort to establish a security zone in northern Iraq to protect Kurdish rebels and bar Iraqi forces from this area. A no-fly zone was established in Iraq above the 36th parallel. AWACS based out of Incirlik, Turkey, were flying routine surveillance missions to not only observe possible flight violations of the zone but also to track friendly aircraft. On 14 April 1994, a pair of U.S. Army UH-60 Blackhawk helicopters conducting aerial resupply and transport in northern Iraq were shot down by two U.S. Air Force F-15 Eagle fighters, killing all U.S. personnel onboard the helicopters. Although the Blackhawks had established communications with the AWACS, radar tracking was intermittent due to the mountainous terrain and the fact that the helicopters were landing at different sites. Therefore, there was confusion on the AWACS as to where the helicopters really were.

**E-3 (Interior View)**
The interior of the AWACS is quite large, and is filled with numerous consoles. Each of these consoles is identical, with the operator configuring his or her respective display for the mission. Most of the rows of consoles are three across, and the area where the air controllers work is often called "The Pit." *U.S. Air Force*

**E-3 (Interior View)**
Shown here is a typical workstation aboard an AWACS. Each of the different consoles can be tailored for different missions depending on the operator's or aircrew's needs. The E-3 operator receives synthetic tracks with all the amplifying data available to them. *U.S. Air Force*

The F-15s had checked on station with the AWACS and the lead fighter pilot had picked up an unknown contact on his radar. Not knowing that Army helicopters were operating in the vicinity caused confusion between the F-15s and the AWACS controller regarding the identity of the contact. The fighter pilots were not advised of the previous radar and IFF correlation, but they also made an inaccurate visual identification. The lead F-15 declared the contact a Hind (a Soviet-built helicopter) and both F-15s shot missiles, destroying the Blackhawks. This blue-on-blue incident resulted from many factors that included a faulty command structure, and the mistakes by both the AWACS crew and the F-15 pilots. In the end, 26 personnel were dead and the AWACS community received a black eye from which many people feel it has only recently recovered.

This tragedy does not overshadow the many outstanding contributions of AWACS aircrew throughout the world. Day in, day out, these men and women fly missions in support of Joint Chiefs– and U.S. Air Force–directed tasking, all over the world. There is no typical mission for the E-3; these aircraft and aircrew have proven themselves useful over the years, and capable of adapting to any number of operational situations. The AWACS community celebrated two decades of service in 1997, and since then the versatility of this AEW aircraft has continued to prove itself over and over.

## E-2C Use Around the World

The introduction of the E-2C to the U.S. Navy in the early 1970s was a godsend. Finally delivering reliable performance at extended ranges for maximum endurance, it was for a few years the premier AEW aircraft in the world, until the introduction of the E-3A AWACS. Commencing Bureau of Inspection and Survey trials in April 1973, the first E-2C aircraft were delivered to a fleet squadron in May 1973. Performing work-ups on the USS *Saratoga* (CVA-60), the Screwtops of VAW-123 made the first operational deployment with the E-2C in September 1974. Recognition for the aircraft and community did not come easily. Flying in a support role, E-2C aircrews ensured their reputation only by performing mission after mission to near perfection. With consistent superior performance, the VAW aircrews became trusted and valued members of the air wing. This fight for recognition from the air wing and carrier battle group was very important, because it proved once and for all just how advanced this new AEW aircraft really was. From the late 1970s through the mid-1980s, the VAW squadrons tested and evaluated the E-2C in a variety of operational and training environments. On every carrier after the last cruise of the USS *Franklin D. Roosevelt* (CVA-42) in 1976, they have participated in virtually all important naval operations for the past 25 years.

Introduction of other new carrier aircraft greatly enhanced the capabilities of the E-2C by interfacing their respective avionics systems. This was especially true of the E-2C/F-14A team. Considered the finest Anti-Air Warfare (AAW) team in the history of naval aviation, the F-14A (Tomcat) was designed to operate with the Hawkeye from its onset. Using its datalink (Link-4), the E-2C designated contacts and targets to the Tomcat without using voice communications. In turn, the F-14A replied to these directions without radio calls, including relaying vital information such as fuel and weapons capacity back to the E-2C. The Tomcat was not the only aircraft that benefitted from the introduction of the E-2C. The modern air wing is composed of a host of aircraft, including the F/A-18C, F-14B/D, the S-3B, and the EA-6B, all of which operate with the Hawkeye on a daily basis. The integration of these different aircraft creates a synergistic effect that enables the carrier air wing to act as an agent of national policy. A true force multiplier, it is the E-2C Hawkeye that allows this to happen.

**Daily Operations**

VAW squadrons are located at NAS Norfolk, VA, Atlanta, GA, Atsugi, Japan and Naval Air Weapons Station (NAWS) Pt. Mugu, CA. In July 1998, the four West Coast squadrons and AEW wing (CAEWWP) moved from Marine Corps Air Station (MCAS) Miramar to NAWS Pt. Mugu, as a result of the downsizing in the U. S. military. These bases act as the home to the E-2C communities and provide the daily training operating areas for these squadrons. The main VAW bases of NAS Norfolk and NAWS Pt. Mugu also host the two VAW wings (CAEWWL and CAEWWP), while the sole training squadron, VAW-120, is located at NAS Norfolk. VAW-120 operates as the central clearinghouse of E-2C training for the entire fleet. New pilots and NFOs arriving from flight school undergo an extensive, year-long syllabus, while more senior aircrew returning for their department-head and commanding-officer tours undergo an abbreviated training program. Until the downsizing efforts of the mid-1990s, VAW-110 existed at NAS Miramar, but it was disestablished beginning in September 1994, and its aircrew, personnel, and aircraft were merged with VAW-120.

There is no such thing as a "standard" mission for an E-2C aircraft, but there are functions and taskings that Hawkeye aircrew do every single flight that comprise a "typical" mission. Like their Air Force counterparts, the VAW aircrew do detailed flight planning, although they do not always have the luxury of setting aside a whole day for this effort. On the aircraft carrier, aircrew will typically fly every other day. Back at their home stations, tactical missions are usually flown every couple of days. The Combat Information Center Officer (CICO) is normally the mission commander for the crew, and as such he or she will normally be responsible for coordinating mission planning. This doesn't mean that the CICOs have to do all the planning by themselves, and normally they won't. Typically, the CICO will task the Air Control Officer (ACO) and the Radar Operator (RO) along with the pilots to divide up the work load. Although E-2C mission planning is less formal than the Air Force counterpart, there is no less attention to detail.

As part of the flight planning on the aircraft carrier, typically the RO and ACO will go to the respective ready rooms of the aircrew that they are going to control, and discuss specifics. For AAW missions, this could include CAP setup, commit criteria, communications and Link-4A/16 usage, as well as a dedicated study of the flight's timeline for intercepts. For a strike mission, the NFOs will typically talk to the strike lead as well as the flight's escort to determine what kind of information they want to hear over the radio. The E-2C aircrew likes to try to build the situational awareness of the strike package without overwhelming the fighter pilots. Detailed discussion will occur, with the E-2C NFOs telling the strike aircrew what the Hawkeye can and cannot do for them. While the ACO and RO have been getting their specific portions of the flight briefed and planned, the CICO normally does a quick tour of combat spaces in order to get a good overview of current operations. Typically the CICO will talk to the intelligence officers, the Tactical Action Officer (TAO), the Link-11/16 supervisor, the surface watch officer, and a host of other ships' company and air wing personnel to get the latest information on what is going on before he briefs the rest of the crew. Thus, when the carrier air-wing is at sea, there is a great opportunity for VAW aircrew to interact with a number of operational personnel, which is a unique opportunity usually not available to their AWACS brethren.

Usually, two hours prior to takeoff, the crew will brief with the CICO, outlining the mission and then conveying the tactical situation. Following this, the pilot will brief the takeoff, en route, and launching criteria along with any emergencies. Normally this process takes about 45 minutes, at which time any remaining questions are checked out by the various aircrew. This could mean that the ACO walks down to the FA-18 ready room to get a detailed CAP brief, or the CICO goes to ship's combat for the latest update. Either way, about 50 minutes to an hour before launch, the crew will go to maintenance control and read the maintenance book on the assigned aircraft. Normally, in a squadron with four E-2Cs, one aircraft will be undergoing maintenance evaluation and three aircraft will be available for flight operations. Once the pilot is satisfied with the condition of the Hawkeye, he will sign for the E-2C and the crew will walk out to the aircraft to begin their preflight. Each aircrew has a preassigned section of the Hawkeye to check, and once they are complete, the crew will man-up and begin preparation to start the aircraft.

Normally the pilot will start the starboard engine first, as this allows the back-end crew to immediately start their time outs for cooling, computer, and radar systems. The port engine can then be started, and the pilots will monitor engine performance and begin to communicate with the tower. However, with the introduction of Group II aircraft and the ability to crossbleed air from one engine to another, the order of engine start has lessened in importance. Meanwhile, the CICO will task the ACO and RO to load the computer and input various commands to initialize the system. If the CICO has time, he will set up his Link-11/16 settings in order to receive the picture from other platforms while still on the deck. The crew can also begin to receive a passdown from other E-2Cs as they may be getting ready to land. However, all turnover will slow down and then stop once the pilots begin to taxi, as the aircrew will need to turn their seats forward and get the system ready for takeoff. Because the aircrew can time-out their avionics system on the deck using an internal cooling system, the Hawkeye is ready to start operating as soon as it launches. The NFOs will wait to complete their turnover and system evaluation until after the takeoff, whether from a land base or the catapult, and as soon as the airplane is safely airborne, the NFOs will turn their seats back sideways, close up the windows, and begin their mission.

The E-2C normally flies a double-cycle mission off the aircraft carrier. Airborne for 4.5 to 5.0 hours, the aircraft is limited to this time period because of the lack of airborne refueling capability and because, without the ability to rotate mission crew members, the NFOs tend to lose their effectiveness after several hours. Thus, a "typical" mission will involve SSC and fighter control. In a standard setup for many Hawkeye missions, the RO will coordinate the SSC aircraft, vectoring them to look for potentially hostile shipping. The RO is normally the junior aircrew in the aircraft and thus can use the slower pace of SSC missions to feel more comfortable in the aircraft. Also, since the Hawkeye is minimally manned, if there are equipment problems, the RO will normally move forward into the forward equipment compartment (FEC) to troubleshoot the system. Likewise, the ACO will typically control the fighter missions, working two to four sections of aircraft at a time. The ACO will normally be in NFO training to become the mission commander who sits in the center seat. So why, you ask, does the CICO sit in the center seat? Because from there they can hit both of the other aircrew on the helmet with a flashlight when they say something stupid over the radio. All kidding aside, the main reason that the CICOs sit in the center seat is so that they can touch and control most of the radar and radio controls as well as the Link-11/16 settings. If the crew is flying a double-cycle mission off the boat, then there may be a short period of 10 to 15 minutes between the cycles to relax. Unlike the AWACS with its galley and racks, the E-2C crew generally is limited to soda or bottled water and maybe a bag lunch. They will normally take these breaks in their seats, still hooked up to their parachutes and communications cords.

With only three NFOs onboard, it is only natural that the pilots are much more actively involved in the mission than the flight deck of an E-3. In fact, the pilots of the Hawkeye do a varied amount of operational task-ing, including monitoring radios and checking aircraft in and out. Proposals for future versions of the Hawkeye include a scope on the copi-lot's side console to enable him or her to monitor the tactical situation. Overtasking, as you can imagine, can be a problem in the E-2C. With a myriad of capabilities, often the crew is asked to perform a number of simultaneous operations. The task saturation and limited on-station time are often cited as the biggest constraints of the Hawkeye. However, as you have read in preceding chapters, the flexibility and availability of the Hawkeye often overshadow these limitations.

As the flight draws to a close, the NFOs will begin to transfer control back to other ships or ground stations and relay passdown information to their relief E-2C. Normally the back-end crew will try to have all items turned over before the pilots begin their descent to land, but that is not always the case as it is always a good practice for the NFOs to back up the cockpit crew on the approach and landing phase of the mission. After landing, the crew will debrief with any fighter or attack aircrew and check out with combat watches to update their intelligence plots.

An interesting variation to the normal aircraft carrier landing is the Hawkeye-Controlled Approach (HCA), which is of course an update of the tactic used by Guppies three decades earlier. Normally the Carrier Air Traffic Control Center (CATCC) on a aircraft carrier (CV) will conduct the nighttime control of aircraft lineup and approach, but if they have a casualty, whether radar or communications, the aircrew of the E-2C can coordinate the aircraft stack in their absence. Practiced by Hawkeye crews, the HCA is an all-hands effort, with the back-end and front-end aircrews working together to ensure that the aircraft in the stack are spaced correctly and that each aircraft pushes on time for its approach. This is a great test of the E-2C and its system and, when done correctly, can demonstrate to the air wing how truly versatile the Hawkeye is.

Of course flying in the Hawkeye is not all work. The author would like to relate one flight that he participated in that highlights a unique capability of the E-2C. Not many people realize that one of the collateral missions of the Hawkeye is to act as the "heavy" bomber for the carrier air wing. Ever since the demise of the A-3 and A-5 series of attack aircraft, the Navy has lacked this heavy bomber capability; thus, the E-2C has been dedicated to fill that role. Although the Hawkeye has no weapons systems, no targeting systems, no self-protection systems or weapons delivery capability, this aircraft regularly flies attack profiles during the annual air wing bombing derby. The aircrew will hand-carry Mk.76 practice bombs onboard, and as the pilots begin their final weapons delivery profile (less than 150 knots, less than 500 feet), the NFOs will pop open the ditching hatch and position their intrepid bombardier in the airstream. Targeting is done using the copilot's Mk.1 Mod 0 eyeball and his thumb. Careful coordination between the cockpit and the bombardier can often result in a direct hit on the "target." Although not practical for any purpose other than crew morale, these flights are always a fun evolution.

Flying the Hawkeye is the primary duty of E-2C aircrew assigned to VAW squadrons, and as such, the NFOs and pilots receive upgrade training throughout their tours. Typically, junior pilots graduating from VAW-120 will undergo an 18 to 24-month period of evaluation in which they can receive increasingly higher levels of qualification until they become Carrier

Aircraft Plane Captains (CAPCs). Likewise, NFOs will upgrade to become CICO within a two-year period. CAPC and CICO qualifications are considered the highest qualification for E-2C aircrew, and all officers who wish to continue flying and stay in the Hawkeye community must maintain this status. This continuing effort to train and upgrade squadron personnel is what ensures that when the need arises, the men and women of the VAW community are ready for combat.

### The Hawkeye in Combat

During the early 1980s, confrontations between the U.S. Navy and the Libyan Air Force (LAAF) were frequent as the Navy conducted Freedom of Navigation (FON) operations in the Gulf of Sidra. The United States and other democratic nations are always interested in maintaining this area as international waters because it is one of the few open-ocean areas in the Mediterranean where large-scale exercises can be conducted. So, whenever a CVBG operated in this area, CAPs consisting of F-14As were established and controlled by E-2C aircraft. Since the E-2C had such a superior surveillance system, the CAPs were never in much danger of being put into an unfavorable position. This cat-and-mouse game continued until 19 August 1981, when two F-14As from VF-41 were engaged by LAAF Su-22s. This time the naval chain of command supported the decision made by the naval commanders on the scene as well as the National Command Authorities (NCA) to shoot them down. Receiving permission to engage, aircrew from VAW-124 (Bear Aces) ordered the Tomcats to retaliate, and the Fitters were soon destroyed. A similar scene would occur on 15 January 1989, when four F-14As from VF-14 and VF-32, controlled by aircrew from VAW-126 (Seahawks), shot down two MiG-23s. Final score: U.S. Navy – 4, LAAF – 0. These actions, punctuated by the Operations in the Vicinity of Libya (OVL) during 1986, are prime examples of how effective the E-2C Hawkeye can be when working with the F-14A Tomcat. A synergistic effect is gained by this team, which has been a winning combination for the Navy during the past 30 years.

Other Hawkeye squadrons were also involved in combat missions with the E-2C. VAW-122 and VAW-126 operated off the coast of Lebanon during the fall of 1982, following the bombing of the U. S. Marine Corps battalion landing team barracks in Beirut on 23 October. Retaliation was slow as the political leadership in Washington deliberated, until finally on the morning of 4 December 1982, the Battle Group Commanders for both the

*Independence* and *John F. Kennedy* were ordered to launch an immediate strike at Lebanese anti-aircraft positions. Because there was little notice of this strike, aircrews were rushed trying to get airborne, and the Hawkeyes from the Steel Jaws and Sea Hawks hurriedly tried to coordinate these two separate strike groups as they launched off of the carriers.

The strikes did not go well. Aircraft orbited the carriers for 30 minutes as sections were joined up and the pilots were getting updated intelligence from the carrier. Because the carriers were close to shore, all of this activity was monitored and tracked by Syrian early warning radars, and when the strikes pressed inbound, they met with heavy retaliatory attacks of anti-aircraft fire and SAMs. Two aircraft (one A-7E and one A-6E) were shot down, and there was much debate over the effectiveness of this raid. In fact, the lessons learned from this raid became the basis for the formulation of the U.S. Navy's Strike University in 1984.

### Achille Lauro

There was one incident that best summarizes the flexibility and capabilities of the E-2C Hawkeye and the carrier battle group. It involved VAW-125 on the USS *Saratoga* (CV-60) during a Mediterranean deployment in the fall of 1985. The Tigertails, as they were commonly called, were attending a funeral service onboard the carrier on 10 October 1985 for one of their officers who had been killed in an automobile accident while serving as a naval liaison officer ashore. With the carrier en route to a port call the next morning, nobody expected an alert launch that evening, but that is exactly what was called over the ship's intercom. Racing to launch the aircraft, it took only 27 minutes from the initial announcement until the Hawkeye was airborne.

The reason for the emergency launch was that terrorists had taken over the cruise ship *Achille Lauro* on 7 October. Led by Abdul Nidar, these terrorists had killed an American tourist, Leon Klinghoffer, and sailed the ship to Alexandria, Egypt. While many people in the United States were outraged at this act of piracy, Lt. Col. Oliver North of the National Security Council had discovered a method of bringing these men to justice. He learned that the terrorists were flying in an airliner from Egypt to Tunisia and proposed to President Ronald Reagan that the U. S. Navy intercept the terrorists.

The speed at which the operation came together left many mission specifics very vague. The Hawkeye was launched to intercept an unknown airliner flying across the Mediterranean from Egypt to Tunisia. The take-off time, airline, and aircraft type were only discovered later and had to be relayed to the crew airborne. A second E-2C was launched when a very high frequency (VHF) radio tested faulty on the first Hawkeye. The E-2C at that time was the only aircraft on the aircraft carrier that could communicate via VHF radio to the airliner. All other Navy aircraft on the CV possessed UHF-only radios. This would become very important later, during the actual intercept phase of this operation.

The second E-2C (with the squadron skipper, Comdr. Ralph K. Zia, onboard) successfully located Egyptian Air Flight 2843, a Boeing 737 en route to Tunisia. This was accomplished by vectoring two F-14A Tomcats, with navigation marker lights off to mask their approach, to a position on either side of the airliner. To ensure it was the correct airliner, Commander Zia directed that the fighter pilots shine their flashlights on the vertical stabilizer to identify the tail number.

Reaching a point southwest of Crete, the airliner was denied landing rights by the Tunisian authorities and told to return to Egypt. Commander Zia used his VHF radio to trick the Egyptian airliner pilot into believing he (Commander Zia) was in the F-14A that was escorting him. He told the 737 pilot to fly west and land at Sigonella, Sicily. The Egyptian Air 737 pilot initially disagreed, until he was "persuaded" by the sight of the two now-lit F-14As on either wing. At this point, the airline pilot dutifully turned west and headed to Sicily. Unfortunately, the Italian air traffic authorities were not prepared to handle this situation and initially denied landing rights. They wanted the airliner to land at a nearby civilian field instead of the military one at Sigonella. Commander Zia, communicating via another radio to the Italian air traffic control authorities, insisted that the airliner land at Sigonella. The F-14As were able to persuade the airliner to land by flying very close to the airliner and frightening its pilot. The Egyptian Air pilot declared emergency fuel and received permission from the Italian air traffic controller to land. Upon touchdown the airliner was immediately surrounded by members of the armed forces.

A minor operation, the capture of the terrorists by the U. S. Navy illustrates just how incredibly flexible a CVBG can be. Using the tremendous capabilities of the E-2C Hawkeye, these aviators were able to accomplish a daring and potentially dangerous mission with no briefings or in-depth analysis. A tribute to the men that accomplished this deed, this may well be the ultimate in successful AEW operations. The interception of

Egyptian Air 2843 exemplifies the qualities that AEW aircraft possess that make them so useful to the Navy and in particular to the battle group commander. The E-2C Hawkeye is the only aircraft in the world that could have controlled this operation on such a short notice to a successful conclusion. This incident also underscores the fundamental utility, flexibility, and value of sea-based aviation. Because basing or landing rights were not in question, this mission could be carried out with the utmost speed and urgency. The success of VAW-125 in this mission demonstrates the ability of AEW aircraft to perform missions and tasks that were dreamed about for over 40 years, specifically to detect, track, classify, and engage contacts beyond the range of surface-based radars.

**Operations in the Vicinity of Libya (OVL)**

The *Achille Lauro* incident was not the only major activity taken by the United States in the Mediterranean during the Reagan administration. The U.S. Navy had been denied the opportunity to operate in the Gulf of Sidra since 1981, from the first LAAF shootdown, but this was changed in late 1985. By January 1986, naval forces had been assembled once again to conduct FON operations. Called "Attain Document," three exercises were conducted, with the last one, Attain Document III, being held in March of 1986. Three CVBGs were present, with the USS *Coral Sea* (CV-43), the USS *Saratoga* (CV-60), and the USS *America* (CV-66) representing a major striking force if needed. Combat air patrol flights were flown and controlled by the three AEW squadrons, VAW-123, VAW-125, and VAW-127. The Hawkeyes constantly monitored LAAF activity and ensured that no Libyan fighters were able to maneuver into advantageous firing positions.

The exercise concluded on 27 March and the fleet sailed north, with the *Saratoga* CVBG returned to the United States, thereby completing its deployment. However, on 5 April 1986, a terrorist exploded a bomb in a popular West Berlin disco frequented by U. S. servicemen. Traced to Libya, President Reagan ordered immediate retaliation, and the two remaining battle groups sailed south and took up attack positions on the morning of 15 April. Launching for a 0200 local time on target, aircraft from the *Coral Sea* and *America* CVBGs attacked five targets within Libya using a combination of precision-guided munitions and iron-bombs. The VAW squadrons controlled these strikes and coordinated the flow of 18 U.S. Air Force F-111s and EF-111s from Lakenheath AFB, England.

Overall, as compared to earlier evolutions, the Libyan strikes went well and validated many of the lessons learned from earlier operations.

## Counter-Narcotics Operations

Not all combat missions involved foreign nations. AEW aircraft are natural platforms to be used in the "war on drugs," and the Sentry and Hawkeye are no exceptions. The look-down capability as well as the ability to detect the "low-slow flyer" are significant factors that make AEW aircraft attractive to conduct counter-drug operations. So, from its inception in the mid-1970s, the AWACS has been looked upon with an eye toward its use in detecting smugglers flying light aircraft. However, there were significant legal obstacles to overcome in order to use the E-3 in a drug surveillance role. Specifically this involved the Posse Comitatus Act, which was enacted after the Civil War to prohibit direct active participation of U.S. military personnel in civilian law enforcement activities. Thus, throughout 1977 the U.S. Air Force and specifically the 552d AWAC Wing at Tinker AFB examined the requirements of cooperating with the U. S. Customs Service (USCS) to support counter-drug missions. Guidelines were developed by the U.S. Air Force Tactical Air Command (TAC) in July 1977 which stated the following restrictions:

- Support will be limited to scheduled training missions
- Support will not degrade crew training
- Surveillance data, voice told to SAGE, may be used by the USCS
- E-3A aircrews will not attempt to identify border violations
- E-3A weapons directors will not control intercepts for USCS
- USCS personnel will not regularly fly on the E-3A

This policy was followed in November 1977 by the approval of the "over the shoulder" program, where USCS agents could fly in the AWACS and use the surveillance data gathered on these missions on a not-to-interfere basis. Success came early as the USCS agents flying in the E-3A were able to quickly radio information back to chase planes. However, the very success of the Sentry in other missions was to eventually spell the end of the USCS program. Because the AWACS had to fly in military operational areas to support training sorties, and since it was decided in early 1980 to deploy the E-3A worldwide, the number of missions available for counter-drug surveillance dropped dramatically. During the first 13 months of this operation, from August 1978 to September 1979, USCS agents flew 97 flights. This dropped to 32 missions from January to July 1980, and the situation degraded even further after that to the point where on 11 January 1981, the "over the shoulder" program was officially canceled. Because AWACS could not be dedicated for specific counter-drug missions, ultimately the USCS needed to operate its own AEW aircraft to obtain the type and quantity of support that they desired. So the end of USCS direct involvement with the E-3 Sentry flights brought a period of testing as the USCS evaluated a number of different methods of utilizing AEW aircraft to support its operations.

The first of these tests was called Operation Thunderbolt. In this exercise lasting from 1 October to 16 December 1981, the USCS, in conjunction with the U.S. Navy East Coast VAW squadrons and the Department of the Treasury, flew numerous missions off the southeast coast of Florida. Results were mixed. While the E-2Cs intercepted 31 aircraft and participated in the seizure of more than $300 million worth of cocaine, it also cost the USCS $816,000 to "rent" the Hawkeyes for this period. In addition, the operation "cost" the U.S. Navy and in particular, VAW squadrons, much needed training opportunities for both pilots and NFOs. While obviously these aircrews did participate in these exercises, the missions themselves did not afford the kind of training required or needed by the Hawkeye squadrons for their air wing turnaround training cycle. However, Operation Thunderbolt did evaluate the ability of the APS-125 radar to detect the "low-slow flyer" for USCS requirements, which led to the USCS decision to purchase E-2C Hawkeyes for their own use.

Concurrent with Operation Thunderbolt were changes in the laws concerning military cooperation with civilian law enforcement officials. President Ronald Reagan signed Public Law 97-86 into effect on 1 December 1981 that permitted not only the sharing of military information, but also the use of military facilities, equipment, and personnel to assist in various operations. Members of the armed forces were restricted from actively participating in the interdiction, search, seizure, arrest, or any similar "police-type" activity, but the requirement of having a USCS agent on board the surveillance platform to transfer information was specifically eliminated.

The partial success of Operation Thunderbolt spurred serious interest by many governmental agencies in the use of AEW aircraft in counter-drug operations. Congressional hearings in February 1982 and June 1983 supported changes in legislation that would allow dedicated drug interdiction missions by E-2 and E-3 aircraft. On 13 January 1984, the U.S. Air Force updated their regulations that dealt with official support to civil law enforcement officials (AFR 55-35). However, the biggest change in legislation came on 8 April 1986, when President Ronald Reagan signed a new National Security Decision Directive. This policy specifically linked drug trafficking to terrorist groups, labeled as illegal the international drug trade, and made this threat a national security concern. This directive increased the ability of the DOD to conduct operations in support of counter-drug missions.

One of the major problems associated with the use of the E-2C has always been its "short legs." With typical flight windows of 4.5 to 6.0 hours, the Hawkeye often cannot cover a large area for the duration required for certain missions. As early as the late 1960s, Lockheed had proposed designs for a new, land-based "heavy" AEW platform using the E-2A APS-96 radar and the P-3A Orion in their CL-520 design. After this initial concept, Lockheed conducted numerous experiments using the different E-2C radar systems (APS-125/138/145) on land-based aircraft with longer legs such as the C-130 or P-3C. U. S. governmental agencies—primarily the USCS and the U. S. Coast Guard (USCG)—have also led the research effort into adapting different platforms, although both the U.S. Air Force and U.S. Marine Corps have expressed interest as well.

The USCS modified a C-130 as well as four P-3 Orions to perform AEW missions. Acquired in 1989, these four Orions replaced the E-2Cs that the customs service had used from 1986 to 1990 as an interim fix for their detection assets. Since the customs agents are primarily interested in the low-slow flyer in an overwater scenario, older versions of the Hawkeye radar (APS-125 and APS-138) were used in this initial modification. A successful adaptation of two proven systems, the P-3 AEW aircraft has proven itself repeatedly in the past 10 years as a major counter-drug platform.

In addition to the customs service, the USCG has also played a major role in the interdiction of contraband into the United States. Tasked with stemming the tide of illegal drugs, the USCG acquired two E-2C aircraft and stood up an AEW squadron (CGAW-1) on 22 January 1987. Operating from borrowed facilities and closely tied to the U.S. Navy Carrier Airborne Early Warning Wing Twelve (CAEWW-12 since renamed CAEWW-Atlantic [CAEWWL]) at NAS Norfolk, these USCG aircraft flew counter-drug missions for more than two years until they were transferred to a new Coast

Guard Air Station (CGAS) at St Augustine, Florida. Acquiring another two aircraft in August 1989, CGAW-1 grew in size and eventually reached a force of 140 personnel. Operating detachments all over the Caribbean, the USCG Hawkeyes proved a very valuable tool in helping to counter the flow of drugs into the United States.

A number of events, however, conspired to quickly end the Coast Guard use of the E-2C. On 24 August 1990, a USCG Hawkeye (CG3501) crashed on short final to NAS Roosevelt Roads, Puerto Rico. All four crew members died. The aircrew had reported a fire in the aircraft during the mission and had attempted to land but were overcome with smoke and fumes. The loss of this Hawkeye, along with declining budgets and the realization that the E-2C was an extremely expensive aircraft to operate, eventually led to the cancellation of the program. The last Hawkeye with USCG markings flew on 14 October 1991 and all aircraft were returned to the U.S. Navy.

The loss of the E-2C was not, however, the end of the USCG involvement with AEW aircraft. During 1990 to 1991, a C-130 was converted to an AEW platform by adding an E-2C radar system (APS-125) to the airframe. Combining proven experience in both avionics and aircraft usage, the EC-130V (CG1721) allowed the USCG to remain on-station for up to 10 hours, and it was also compatible with the C-130 fleet for maintenance issues. Accepted by the USCG in July 1991, the EC-130V was based at CGAS Clearwater, Florida, until August 1993, when it was transferred to the U.S. Air Force and redesignated NC-130V. Although this aircraft was an incredibly capable platform, the USCG could simply not afford a one-of-a-kind aircraft of this type during this period of intense budgetary cutbacks, and was forced to give up its last remaining AEW capability. To prove how close these service AEW communities truly are, this same EC-130V platform is now being used by the U.S. Navy and Northrup-Grumman to test advanced features for the Hawkeye 2000 (HE2000).

With the demise of USCG fixed-wing AEW aircraft, the USCS is now the only non-military, governmental agency that still flies AEW aircraft in counter-drug missions. To date, seven former U.S. Navy P-3 aircraft have been converted to the AEW configuration for use as an AEW platform. However, the VAW community has been increasingly tasked throughout the late 1980s and to the present time with flying numerous dedicated counter-drug missions in conjunction with the USCS. E-2C squadrons have flown detachments from a number of locations in the Caribbean,

**C-130 AEW Aircraft**
The U.S. Coast Guard modified a C-130 aircraft by adding an APS-125 radar and dome to the fuselage. The platform was eventually scrapped due to budgetary pressures and has since been transferred to the U.S. Air Force, which used it as a testing model. Recently, the U.S. Navy acquired this aircraft to conduct tests for its HE2000 systems. *U.S. Coast Guard*

including Key West, Pensacola, Puerto Rico, Guantanamo Bay, and Howard AFB (Panama). The drastic downsizing of the 1990s has not slowed down these flights, and in fact, VAW-122 was allowed to remain established for two years after the rest of its air wing had disappeared, solely to act as a counter-drug unit. Most recently, on 1 October 1995, VAW-77, a new reserve squadron, was stood up at NAS Atlanta. Possessing only civilian maintenance personnel, the squadron cannot deploy to sea, and its primary reason for establishment is to fly counter-drug missions! However, VAW-77 cannot cover all counter-drug tasking, so for the foreseeable future, VAW squadrons from both coasts as well as VAW-77 will continue to fly in these operations.

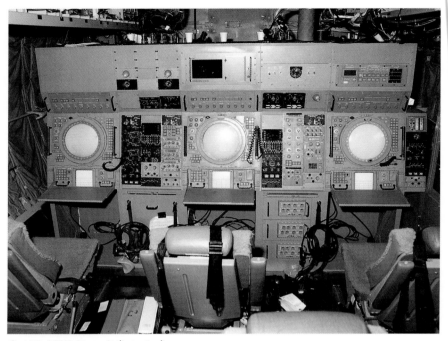

**C-130 AEW Aircraft (Interior)**
This is a mock-up of the interior of the C-130 aircraft as an AEW platform. Notice that the scopes and seats are in the same configuration as the E-2C Hawkeye, but the consoles are aligned athwartships in the fuselage vice fore and aft. This setup is almost exactly what the Group Ø consoles look like in the E-2C. *U.S. Coast Guard*

## Aircraft Losses

AEW aircraft like any other airframes are subject to many dangers inherent in flying. People tend to forget this and begin to think that these are command and control assets that are somehow immune to the laws of physics. Therefore, the next several pages are dedicated to the men and women who have lost their lives flying in AEW aircraft in support of their country. This section will cover some of the more recent crashes of both the E-2 and E-3 to allow you to better understand the risks involved for these aircrew every time they man up an aircraft. We will start with the U.S. Navy and the E-2, since they have experienced more accidents over a longer period of time. While this section will not cover every Class "A" accident (more than $1 million or loss of life), it will explain the seven most recent incidents.

The first accident involved the loss of a VAW-78 E-2B on 14 January 1978. The reserve aircrew were flying a local training mission from NAS Norfolk when the elevator pushrod became disengaged. What this meant was that the pilots no longer had control of the elevators, and the plane began to do a series of ever increasing sine-wave maneuvers as the pilots tried to wrestle with the aircraft. At some point a decision was made to bail out, and the pilots popped the main entrance hatch (MEH). Unfortunately, mechanical and human error combined to trap all five aircrew in the aircraft. At that time, the MEH had an extra safety device installed to keep the door from dropping on unsuspecting maintenance personnel. Apparently a combination of operator error and a cable kink jammed the MEH in a partially opened configuration. As the wild oscillation continued, the aircrew were not able to try alternate escape routes and all five bodies were found near the MEH in the wreckage. Subsequent accident investigation into this crash led to changes in both the elevator pushrod assembly and the MEH.

A second accident involving VAW-78 occurred on 13 November 1979 during a carrier qualification (CQ) period off the East Coast. On their return from the boat, the two pilots (there were no NFOs onboard for this pilot training hop) were faced with low cloud cover over much of the mid-Atlantic area. Trying to land at their primary and alternate airfields without success, the pilots flew their Hawkeye north toward what was supposed to be better weather. However, over southern Pennsylvania, the E-2B ran out of fuel and the aircrew attempted to bail out. Only one pilot was successful, and until 1991, this was the first and only successful bailout from the Hawkeye.

The next fatal crash of a Hawkeye involved another E-2B, this time from VAW-115 operating onboard the USS *Midway* (CVA-41). Recovering after a night sortie on 17 August 1985, the pilot failed to use the power lever lock on the landing and accidentally retarded the throttles to the flight idle detent. Receiving a waveoff, the pilot was unable to move the throttles forward and the aircraft settled into the water off the angle deck. Three aircrew survived the crash: the copilot, the CICO, and the RO. After-action reports and debriefs indicated that there were less than 5 seconds from impact until the aircraft was totally submerged under water. The copilot reported that the overhead ditching hatch was much farther aft than he expected, and he believed that the pilot got tangled with the steering column. The death of the ACO is a little bit of a mystery. Because the location of the aft ditching hatch is directly over the ACO's seat, the normal ditching procedure is for the ACO to exit first. However, in this case, for some reason the ACO left his seat and went aft into the aft equipment compartment (AEC). Both the CICO and RO reported that they saw the ACO in the aircraft as they quickly departed the sinking airframe. Further investigation reveals that the ACO was a poor swimmer, which may explain his reluctance to exit the aircraft. To answer the perennial question, "What happens to the dome when a Hawkeye crashes?"; well, in this case it floated. Somehow the rotodome separated from the rest of the aircraft and was still floating the next day. The dome was subsequently shot and sunk by Marine gunners from the *Midway*, as it was considered a hazard to safe navigation.

The next fatal accident of a Hawkeye, an E-2C, occurred with a USCG aircraft on 20 August 1990. The aircraft was conducting a counter-drug mission from NAS Roosevelt Roads in Puerto Rico when the crew reported smoke and fumes and began to divert their aircraft back to the base. Monday morning quarterbacks have suggested that the crew should have landed as soon as possible rather than as soon as practical. However, in their defense, up to that time, the E-2C had not had a serious fire for over a decade and was considered a very safe aircraft. That was soon to change. The USCG crash was the first in a series of four accidents that were to plague East Coast squadrons and claim the lives of 14 aviators over a 31-month period.

The next incident involving an E-2C fortunately did not result in the loss of any aircrew. VAW-122 was operating in the Mediterranean Sea on a routine mission onboard the USS *Forrestal* (CV-59). Immediately after takeoff on 8 July 1991, this particular Hawkeye developed a serious fire in the starboard engine that could not be extinguished with the internal fire extinguisher. Quick decisions and actions by the crew allowed all aircrew to bail out while the aircraft was still controllable and in straight and level flight. The plane was so stable that an FA-18 was vectored to shoot it down so that the E-2C would not continue to fly and crash into land. The Hornet lined up for a Sidewinder missile (AIM-7) shot, slightly behind and below the abandoned Hawkeye, pulled the trigger, and missed! For a number of reasons, the missile did not hit the E-2C, so the now chastened pilot brought the FA-18 around again and this time shot down the ailing aircraft with his machine guns!

Much if not all of the credit for the successful bailout of this crew lies with the quick decision by the CICO, then–Lt. Comdr. John Yurchak. A seasoned aviator, "Yurch" knew that the fire on the starboard engine was out of control and that it was only a matter of time before the fire consumed the rest of the aircraft. Therefore, he directed the pilot, Lt. Vince Bowhers, to blow the MEH early enough to affect a successful bailout of the entire crew. Not everything ended on a good note for these aircrew. The ACO, Lt. Bob Forwalder, was subsequently killed in another crash of a Hawkeye a mere 18 months later. However, the mere fact that all five aircrew successfully bailed out of a burning E-2C was a first in the history of naval aviation.

Tragedy struck the VAW community less than a year later on 31 July 1992, when an E-2C from VAW-126 operating from the USS *John F. Kennedy* (CV-67) crashed in the Caribbean. Once again, smoke and fumes inside the aircraft were the problem and the aircrew did not have a chance to ditch or bail out before they were overcome by the fire. Apparently the problems started as the aircraft was on the downwind leg of the landing pattern, immediately after the carrier break. Investigation of the wreckage revealed that a chafed hydraulic line sprayed a mist into the FEC that was somehow ignited to produce a blowtorch across the passageway of the FEC. The smoke and fumes were so intense that the aircrew had trouble flying the aircraft while trying to don oxygen masks. Communications with the ship were sporadic, and in less than two minutes after the initial report, the aircraft crashed into the sea, six miles astern of the carrier. Because the E-2C was at pattern altitude (800 feet), it was too low to affect a bailout, plus the ferocity of the conflagration probably prevented any aircrew from trying to escape via the MEH. Thus, the only option was ditching, which could have been accomplished if the crew had recognized the danger immediately and descended. However, since they could not or would not, all five aircrew were killed when the aircraft plummeted to earth. The total time for the crew to react was less than two minutes, not much time if you really think about it.

The final major accident involving the Hawkeye afflicted another East Coast squadron, the Bear Aces of VAW-124. Operating onboard the USS *Theodore Roosevelt* (CVN-72) on 26 March 1993, the squadron was literally flying their first full day in the Mediterranean after a quick trans-Atlantic steaming period. The E-2C that crashed was the last scheduled recovery of the night, and by all accounts, it was a very dark night. Several pilots later reported vertigo, and the lack of sensory cues was attributed as a direct cause of this accident. Also, the aircrew were very tired. They had been strike planning the day before and were "pumped up" because their mission was the first in a series of flights in support of operations over Bosnia. The final recovery developed problems when an S-3B Viking ASW aircraft popped a springback upon landing. Springbacks are metal spacers that keep the arresting wires 6–8 inches above the flight deck. Refitting a springback is not a ship casualty, but it does require a few minutes to re-rig, this of course requiring the Hawkeye to waveoff. As the aircrew transitioned in the climb for a turn downwind, the pilots flew the aircraft into the water approximately 3–4 miles in front of the aircraft carrier.

No one survived the crash. Wreckage recovered the next day found a bloody gauze bandage which was construed by many to mean that someone in the crew had a minor medical problem, perhaps a cut, that diverted his attention during the critical landing phase of the mission. The actual cause of the accident, however, was labeled as pilot error. The accident board theorized that the pilots experienced vertigo during their long descent to the boat. When the waveoff signal was received, the pilots then should have begun a gentle climb, but instead the aircraft momentarily rose to a height of 400 to 500 feet before it started an imperceptible descent that ended a few minutes later.

Since there were no survivors nor any radio communications of problems, the cause of the accident might never be known, but it is believed that the pilots suffered from a vertigo effect known as the Coriolus Factor, or Vestibular Illusion. This is where the semi-circular canals in your ears have movement in two or more axes at once. Without a visual reference, the pilots are forced to rely on their instruments because their senses are confused. Thus, when the E-2C began a climb after the waveoff, the pilots "felt" that they were climbing too steeply and put the nose over. Now the pilots believed that they were in level flight, whereas they were actually in a very gradual descent that only ended when they crashed into the water. Maybe the crew was distracted with an internal injury of an aircrew (hence the bloody gauze), maybe the long planning and flight day took its toll, maybe we will never know, but for whatever reason, the aircrew did not notice the descent as the aircraft crashed into the night sea.

The VAW community has not been alone in its share of accidents. AWACS aircraft have also experienced tragedy, namely with the loss of Yukla 27, an E-3B (77-0354) that crashed after takeoff at Elmendorf AFB (Alaska) on 22 September 1995. This aircraft was part of the 962d AACS attached to the Third Air Force Wing, and it used "Yukla" or the local Tanaina Indian name for "Eagle" as its call sign. Assigned a 6.2-hour reconnaissance mission with the flight concentrating on southwestern Alaska, this was a code M mission that included a full mission crew of 24 aircrew including two

Canadians. Destined to become the worst accident in Third Wing history, the crash of Yukla 27 is also the only fatal accident of an E-3 Sentry.

The aircraft began its takeoff roll on Runway 05 at 0746 (AST), but was only airborne for 42 seconds. Apparently, the Sentry flew into a flock of Canadian geese, which fodded both port engines. The aircraft flew in a slight left turn until the crew could no longer maintain control. Unable to fly with two of four engines inoperable, the aircraft only reached a height of 270 feet before crashing 3,500 yards from the runway at 0747:12. Carrying 125,000 pounds of JP-8 onboard, the resultant fireball killed all aircrew and could be seen for 30 miles. There was no chance for the crew to escape.

A more recent accident involving an E-3 was the ground abort by a NATO Sentry on 14 July 1996. Starting their takeoff role from Forward Operations Base (FOB) Prevezia, Greece, at 1520 GMT, the aircraft was launching to conduct a mission in support of Operation Decisive Endeavor over Bosnia. During the takeoff roll, the pilots experienced what they believed to be a multiple bird strike. Since there were no secondary mechanical problems, and it was prior to rotate speed, the pilots elected to continue. At rotation speed, the aircraft took more bird hits and the number 2 engine failed. With the nose gear lifting off the runway, the pilots decided to abort. Departing the runway at 50 knots, the aircraft was traveling at a very high speed and subsequently failed to stop on the runway. Sliding off the end of the runway, the aircraft stopped on a rock seawall, with portions of the aircraft in the water.

There was significant damage to the aircraft, and for all intents and purposes, the E-3 was a loss. The airframe was cracked in half, with the floor buckled and several feet of seawater inside the lower lobes. Radar, computer, and communications equipment all detached from their racks, and the lights fell off of the overhead. Aircrew had to crawl over their consoles to escape, and everyone survived with only the flight engineer experiencing a back injury. And to answer the perennial question, yes the rotodome did stay attached to the airframe. There was no official comment from NATO, but operations are now centered on 17 vice 18 aircraft, and all parts that could be stripped and recovered were taken from the disabled aircraft. While some have questioned the decision to abort at takeoff, the pilot did save the whole crew, and coming so soon after the Elmendorf crash, it is no wonder that some aircrew may have been a little gun-shy. However, all aircrew in this case are still on flying status and, most importantly, still alive.

# CHAPTER SEVEN

# AEW Forces in the Western Hemisphere and United States:

## Organization and Development from the 1990s to Present

This book is a history of all AEW systems, not just those of the United States, so this chapter will cover the development and procurement of these aircraft by other countries. Since AEW platforms are so expensive and technologically complex, there are simply not that many variations in AEW radar systems in the world. Many nations have purchased E-2 or E-3 aircraft, since these platforms have proven themselves in combat over the past two decades. However, some countries, such as Sweden and Israel, have also developed their own aircraft. So it is interesting to look at the different approaches taken by a number of countries around the world in developing an organic AEW capability. In addition, the sales of these platforms, especially in Taiwan, Saudi Arabia, and Israel are demonstrations of U. S. support to these nations. A component of national strategy, the procurement of AEW aircraft can strengthen a bilateral relationship.

Until recently, all AEW aircraft in the Western Hemisphere, were owned by the United States. But that is no longer the case. Chile, Peru, Brazil, and Mexico have all either recently acquired AEW systems or are in the process of doing so. These other nations have recognized the inherent value of these platforms and are attempting to purchase this capability for their own sovereign use. In general, though, most of the AEW aircraft flown within the Western Hemisphere and the United States are operated by the U.S. Navy and U.S. Air Force. These services have the longest history of operating these aircraft and have invested the most time and money in their development. In the next few sections, I will explain in general how the services are organized and equipped with AEW aircraft.

## U.S. Navy Hawkeye Organization

VAW squadrons are located at Naval Air Stations Norfolk, Atlanta, Atsugi, and Pt. Mugu. In July 1998, the four West Coast squadrons and Commander CAEWWP moved from MCAS Miramar to NAS Pt. Mugu, as a result of the downsizing in the U. S. military. These bases act as the home to the E-2C communities and provide the daily training and operating areas for these squadrons.

The main VAW bases of NAS Norfolk and NAS Pt. Mugu also host the two VAW wings, while the sole training squadron, VAW-120, is located at NAS Norfolk. VAW-120 operates as the central clearinghouse of E-2C training for the entire fleet. New pilots and NFOs arriving from flight school undergo an extensive year-long syllabus, while more senior aircrew returning for their department head and commanding officer tours undergo an abbreviated training program. Until the downsizing efforts of the mid-1990s, VAW-110 existed at NAS Miramar, but it was disestablished in September 1994 and its aircrew, personnel, and aircraft were merged with VAW-120. One reserve Hawkeye squadron is located at NAS Norfolk (VAW-78), and another is at NAS Atlanta (VAW-77). The latter conducts purely counter-narcotics operations and utilizes contract maintenance. (In addition, VAW-115 is homeported at NAS Atsugi in Japan to support Western Pacific operations as part of CVW-5.) Together, these 13 active and reserve squadrons make up the total U.S. Navy AEW assets.

## United States Air Force AWACS Organization

The AWACS community is primarily based at Tinker AFB, Oklahoma City, Oklahoma, with two squadrons, the 961st and 962d AACS, operating two-plane squadrons in Elmendorf and Kadena AFB. The four operational squadrons (960th, 963rd, 964th, and 965th AACS) operate and support NORAD, Joint Chiefs, and U.S. Air Force AWACS missions. The fifth flying squadron, the 966th AACS, is primarily tasked to provide Initial Qualification Training. These four squadrons as a well as the 552d

**E-2C Group I**
The basic E-2C was first introduced to the fleet in 1973. This Hawkeye has been
gradually updated with a number of software and radar upgrades, including an
APS-96 radar and an ALR-59 PDS system, although the model remained the same.
By 1988, the nominal fleet E-2C carried an APS-138 radar with an ALR-73 PDS
system and a TRAC-A dome. However, more changes were in store with the
introduction of the Group I system in 1989. *Leigh Armistead collection*

Training Squadron make up the 552d Air Combat Wing and form the core of
the E-3 community.

The recent reorganization of the U.S. Air Force into Air Expeditionary
Forces (AEFs) was a direct result of hard lessons learned from the AWACS
community. Due to the extraordinarily high tasking of certain key airframes and units by the Air Force in Operation Southern Watch, a move
was made to develop 10 units or AEFs that can deploy to crisis areas in
the world. In this manner, the U.S. Air Force could spread out the pain of
deployment and perhaps increase morale among their aircrew and maintenance personnel, by giving them long-range schedules that they could

count on. For the AWACS community, this meant the recommissioning of the 960th to give Tinker four full operations squadrons, so they can fit two detachments from each squadron (eight total) plus the 961st and 962d AACS to fill out the 10 AWACS slots needed for the AEF concept. Implemented in Fiscal Year 2001, it will be interesting to watch the U.S. Air Force maximize its forces with this new plan.

## Hawkeye Development

The E-2C aircraft that was introduced in 1973 had an APS-120 radar with an ALR-59 passive detection system (PDS). These components were upgraded to the APS-125, then the APS-138, as well as the ALR-73 respectively, but throughout these changes were still called the E-2C. Additional adaptions to the dome in the form of a TRAC-A antenna also improved the radar's performance, but once again no changes were made to the nomenclature of the airframe. This was done for a number of reasons: First, it costs money to redesignate an aircraft. Second, it involves congressional scrutiny. These two factors and others have led the Navy to limit the changes in aircraft designators. Today, 27 years later, the Hawkeye is still called the E-2C, but it only resembles the original model on the outside. Virtually every part of the aircraft has been changed or upgraded over this period.

As mentioned previously, the basic E-2C Group 0 composition consisted of an APS-125 radar, ALR-73 PDS system with the Allison T56-A-425 engine and a TRAC-A rotodome. Operated in the various VAW squadrons beginning in 1983, it wasn't until the year 2000 that the last active duty unit, VAW-126, began this transition to an upgraded platform. The turnover, however, had actually begun over a decade earlier. In 1989, testing began on the E-2C Group I, which was an interim upgrade developed by the U.S. Navy. Consisting of new aircraft engines (T56-A-427) and a new radar (APS-139), the Group I aircraft were only flown by the West Coast VAW squadrons during this short five-year testing cycle.

The Group I was never meant to be "the" permanent replacement for the original E-2C model. Only 19 of these models were built, and instead another upgrade entitled the E-2C Group II was introduced to the fleet with testing beginning in 1993. But the future of the Hawkeye was not assured with the introduction of the Group II. In 1992 the production line was stopped for U.S. Navy E-2Cs, and it was only the sale of aircraft to foreign nations and an innovative multi-year package that has kept the skilled workforce in place. In a later section, the current production of the E-2C Group II emphasis for the U.S. Navy will be discussed. The E-2C Group II model is also receiving a lot of interest from foreign nations interested in buying a medium-sized AEW aircraft. Egypt, Taiwan, France, and other nations have all contracted for this latest update to the Hawkeye. It is, for the moment, probably the best deal for a proven air battle management system that is moderately priced. Nonetheless, the U.S. Navy is not finished improving on this venerable aircraft.

As you can guess, the U. S. Navy continues to place a high value on AEW. Thus, the evolution of the E-2C will continue for the foreseeable future. The Hawkeye 2000 is the next upgrade of this aircraft, and as of 2001, it is finishing its testing phase and beginning production. Specific upgrades include:

- Changes in the navigation system (NU)
- Changes in the flight controls
- A new mission computer (MCU)
- New CIC displays (ACIS)
- Upgraded vapor cycle (VC)
- SATCOM
- Cooperative Engagement Capability (CEC)

The final upgrade, CEC, is a system that allows a number of platforms to share track data that is accurate enough to develop a fire-control solution. CEC will help the surface fleet engage targets beyond their sensor range as well as target the ballistic theater missile threat. A major advance for the Hawkeye, it is funded by the surface Navy community who are looking to the E-2C to pass a coherent data picture to their units.

### AWACS Development

The U.S. Air Force has been busy upgrading its fleet of E-3 Sentries, with improvements that will confirm their viability beyond the year 2020. The new Radar Sensitivity Improvement Program (RSIP) enables detection of targets one-tenth the minimum radar cross section of the current system. The block 30/35 ESM upgrade will provide a long-overdue passive detection capability, reinforcing the E-3's role as a force multiplier during autonomous operations. Upgrades to the communications system will facilitate two-way secure voice and data capability with fighters, ships,

**AWACS (Interior)**
This photo shows a portion of the AWACS aircraft, and highlights an operator testing radar equipment. Notice the difference in the room available to the AWACS and the different equipment worn by the operators. A typical E-3 aircrew will fly only in their flight suit and wear a headset. *Boeing*

and other platforms. A computer modification will increase the computing power of the computer by a factor of four, and feature bubble chips with disc access, thereby improving processing and adding room for expanded memory. The addition of the Global Positioning System (GPS) also provides an improved navigation capability. With current and future upgrades, AWACS will support power projection and forward presence with state-of-the-art technology, and possess the capability to counter evolving threats until at least the year 2035.

While the 30/35 program did a lot to improve the communications connectivity and add an electronic warfare suite to the E-3B/C models, the new RSIP will vastly improve the overall radar performance. Its overall goal is to:

- Improve detection of low radar cross section targets
- Improve electronic protect capabilities
- Improve overall reliability and maintainability of the radar system

The RSIP upgrade will also bring the U.S. Air Force AWACS back to some parity with the NATO systems. Currently the NATO E-3A AWACS have almost completed the mid-term upgrade, which has a computer and radar system that is superior to the 30/35 upgrade. When the U.S. Air

**AWACS with 30/35 Upgrades**
The U.S. Air Force improved the venerable E-3 with an upgrade program called the 30/35 program. Distinguishable by the ESM "bulges" on the sides of the fuselage aft of the cockpit, this upgraded aircraft is designed to keep the U.S. Air Force current with other AWACS that are being sold around the world. *Boeing*

**AWACS E-767**
Because the Boeing 707 pipeline is shut down, the U.S. Air Force has been interested, for a number of years, in switching their AWACS radar system to a different airframe. Shown here is the Boeing 767 modified to an AEW platform. Notice how much larger the aircraft is than a 707, and that it only has two engines compared to the four of a typical AWACS. *Boeing*

Force aircraft receive their new RSIP upgrades, their radar systems will be superior to the NATO fleets', but their computers and display system will not. That will have to wait for the proposed 40/45 upgrade in fiscal year 2008! The RSIP upgrades have been underway since 1999 and will continue through January 2006.

Since the Boeing 707 airframe is no longer being built, if Boeing wants to export their AWACS technology to foreign nations, they must use other airframes. The most successful upgrading of platforms has been the development of the Boeing E-767. Sold to the Japanese Self Defense Force, (JSDF) the 767 AWACS has 50 percent more floor space than the 707 airframe and twice the internal volume. Therefore, the E-767 has room to grow, a benefit not currently available in the older AWACS airframes. The aircraft itself is a technological upgrade from the 707-700 platform as well. Using fuel-efficient CF6-80C2 turbofan engines, the operational altitude is 40,000 feet, which gives the E-767 a 390-knot ground speed and an unrefueled 13-hour mission profile. That equates to a 4,500-nautical-mile range and can be extended up to 22 hours with inflight refueling. Because the combination of the 767 airframe and the AWACS radar antenna was a new pairing, the aircraft underwent certification by the FAA beginning in 1996 before it was approved for export. Specifically, it completed a supplemental type certification under Part 25 of the FAA rules. This was done to help Boeing in any future foreign military as well as prospective U.S. Air Force sales.

## JSTARS Development

Every aircraft that has been discussed so far has been an airborne early warning and control platform. The Joint Surveillance Targeting and Attack Radar System (JSTARS) is a relatively new aircraft whose mission is to conduct airborne, theater-wide battle management using a side-looking, phased-array radar for ground surveillance. This aircraft is still in production, with a total of 16 systems scheduled for delivery to the U.S. Air Force by May 2004. However, the U.S. Air Force still has an operational requirement for 19 JSTARS aircraft.

JSTARS originated from a 1973 DOD study of ways to locate and track armored vehicles beyond enemy lines. In 1982, the U.S. Air Force and U.S. Army merged their programs. Originally, the two services wanted to use three different aircraft—the OV-1, TR-1, and a modified 707—but in June 1984 a decision was made to only use one platform, a 707-700 series aircraft renamed the E-8C. In September 1985, the U.S. Air Force awarded Grumman a contract to build an airborne system. For JSTARS is not just aircraft, but it also has special ground sites that are operated by U.S. Army personnel who collect data and transfer it to the ground commanders as needed. These Army Common Ground Stations (CGSs) are typically mounted on tracked vehicles for easy mobility, and they receive the JSTARS data over a secure, jam-resistant surveillance and control datalink. Unfortunately, this datalink is not compatible with the other AEW aircraft. Therefore, to date there is no common database of tracks within these different systems. At the present time, the JSTARS is not a standalone platform; therefore, until its datalink is integrated with other common systems, disconnects will occur.

JSTARS
The E-8 is an AEW aircraft, but it tracks ground-based moving targets, vice aircraft, or ships. The JSTARS conducts their mission through the use of the MTI radar located in the ventral canoe on the aircraft. *Ted Carlson photo*

The ground station started out in 1984 as a link to the OV-1 Mohawk. As the program grew, the module became more sophisticated, with upgrades purchased in 1986, 1992, 1994, and finally 1997. The latest iteration of the common ground station cost $4.1 million. This station can support a multitude of airborne components, including not only JSTARS, but also Unmanned Aerial Vehicles (UAVs), U-2s, and Comanches. There currently are 17 HMMV-mounted systems operated by the U.S. Army in support of the JSTARS program. The eventual goal is to purchase 100 of these CGSs and distribute 25 per theater. In addition, the U.S. Marine Corps and NATO have also contracted for two systems each to evaluate as prototypes.

All of the 707s used for the JSTARS program were originally built in the 1966 through 1973 time frame, with at least 25,000 hours already flown, mostly as commercial air carriers. The U.S. Air Force has been refurbishing the aircraft while they are being modified to carry the radar in the 40-foot-long canoe under the forward fuselage. The main operating modes for the JSTARS radar system are the wide area surveillance moving target indicator and the sector search moving target indicator from the synthetic aperture radar. These modes can be interleaved or changed to accomplish the mission objective. Capable of detecting ground targets in a 120-degree cone on either side of the flight path in an area 50–250 kilometers from the aircraft, the JSTARS aircraft is at this time the supreme example of an airborne system for ground battle management. There are efforts by the United States to try to export these aircraft to various nations and entities such as NATO, but at $225 to $270 million apiece, most Air Forces cannot afford JSTARS.

By 1990, there were two developmental aircraft undergoing testing by Northrup-Grumman. Pressed into service early to help coalition forces during the Persian Gulf War, these platforms flew their first operational sortie on 14 January 1991 and completed 49 combat missions, accumulating over 500 hours in support of Operation Desert Storm. Key success stories from this campaign include:

- 22 January – JSTARS located a 60-vehicle armored convoy moving toward Kuwait. An air strike was called in and 58 of these tanks were subsequently destroyed.
- 24 February – On the first day of ground operations, JSTARS directly interdicted enemy forces attempting to block operations of coalition troops.
- 26 February – JSTARS was the key surveillance asset that first identified the mass exodus of Iraqi units from Kuwait City. Attacks on these convoys resulted in the "Highway of Death."

These same two developmental aircraft were again pressed into service in December 1995 to monitor events in Bosnia. Flying 95 operational sorties for more than 1,000 combat hours, once again the JSTARS, using preproduction aircraft, proved its worth to coalition forces. Yet the use of test aircraft was to change, for on 11 June 1996, the 93rd Air Control Wing accepted their first production aircraft. Declaring Initial Operational Capability on 18 December 1997, the 93rd currently has received 10 of their 16 production airframes as of 02 June 2001. Of the 16 aircraft under order by the U.S. Air Force, 15 have been fully funded with long-lead funding for the 16th system. The Pentagon still maintains a requirement and has approved full production for the 19 aircraft that were part of the original requirement from the U.S. Air Force. The original planned buy (19) will equip three squadrons with five operational aircraft each, while still allowing two aircraft to undergo long-term maintenance and dedicating the other two airframes to training.

In addition, different mission tasking for JSTARS is undergoing evaluation. Tests conducted at Green Flag in 1998 using the E-8C to track mobile ballistic and air defense missiles were very successful. The coordination between the Air Operations Center and the different air battle management platforms with the strike platforms noticeably improved during the exercise; however, reporting and integration procedures needed more practice. The operational use of the JSTARS aircraft continues. Heavily utilized in both Operation Joint Endeavor and Noble Anvil, the E-8C has been crucial to the information superiority shared by the United States and coalition forces throughout this period. A true force multiplier, the success of JSTARS has sped up acquisition efforts by other nations as well as NATO for this type of capability.

The JSTARS aircraft are also undergoing upgrades to keep its systems modern. The major replacement will be with the computer system. As part of a $141 million contract, the U.S. Air Force plans on replacing five computers on each aircraft with two more powerful models that give the system 100 times more battle management processing power, 25 times more storage, and 10 times more radar processing power. These new computers will go onto the rest of the production aircraft and be retrofitted onto existing JSTARS during depot level maintenance over the next five years. The extra computer power is needed to accommodate the planned upgrade for the Radar Technology Insertion Plan (RTIP).

This radar upgrade is not only for the JSTARS aircraft but also will be an upgrade for the Hawkeye 2000 as well, since they are both Northrup-Grumman products. The RTIP upgrade turns the radar into an electronically steered array vice a mechanical antenna that greatly enhances the overall detection capability. Specific upgrades through FY06 are shown below:

- Block 10 (fiscal year 1999) – Baseline aircraft improved with TADIL-J, digital autopilot and Y2K compliance
- Block 20 (fiscal year 2000) – Adding networked communications, including Army-improved data modem and Singars radios
- Block 30 (fiscal year 2002) – Adds UHF satellite

> communications, broadcast intelligence, TADIL-J upgrades,
> and Global Air Traffic Management
> - Block 40 (fiscal year 2004) – Adding enhanced and inverse
>   SAR, improved moving target indicator (MTI), and extremely
>   high-frequency & super-high-frequency (EHF/SHF) satellite
>   communications
> - Block 50 (fiscal year 2006) – Upgrading aircraft with RTIP,
>   electronic intelligence (ELINT) capability, combat identification,
>   helicopter detection and tracking, automatic target
>   recognition, maritime detection, and an automatic tracker

There have also been unsolicited proposals by CFM International to upgrade the E-8C aircraft CFM56-3 engines to enhance the JSTARS performance and on-station time. The changes would be similar to what the U. S. Air Force is doing to its 23 RC-135s in the facility. However, no official proposal has been accepted by the U.S. Air Force to date.

The U.S. Air Force has the two best airborne radar platforms in existence today with the AWACS and JSTARS aircraft, but they do not normally communicate directly with each other. One is designed to detect airborne and surface targets, while the latter can track ground-based moving contacts. What if these two platforms could be combined? That is the goal behind the Multi-Mission Aircraft (MMA) concept. The first problem, however, deals with physics. Radar systems are designed to do certain tasks, and their characteristics are often constrained by these parameters. For example, long-range detection capabilities may necessitate a lower frequency and thus a larger antenna. Or in another case, an AEW radar is not necessarily suited for detecting ground-based moving targets, although it can with advanced technology be adjusted to have a limited role.

At $240 to $300 million a copy, no nation, not even the United States, can afford many of these expensive aircraft, so planners are investigating methods of combining the capabilities of these two systems into one aircraft. In addition, by using newer computers and the RTIP technology, there is the possibility of fitting the system into a much smaller aircraft like a business jet. In essence, the airplane may look very much like the Erieye AEW aircraft. It also may look very much like a Hawkeye. The U.S. Navy has been evolving their AEW aircraft as well, and proposals to upgrade the E-2C to conduct both missions are spelled out later in this book. Many companies are lining up proposals for this new system.

## Aerostat

This is a picture of an aerostat that houses a two-dimensional radar. These platforms are playing a major role in the future of AEW systems as they grow in capability. Notice the tremendous look-down capability this platform can have. These aerostats are unmanned and all data is fed back down through the tether to the control center, unlike earlier ZPG-3Ws, which flew with operators. *Courtesy of TCOM*

Boeing, General Dynamics, Bombardier, Northrup-Grumman, and Raytheon have all presented proposals for this platform. They realize that whoever wins this competition could corner a huge market worldwide, if they won the bid for the NATO Air-Ground Surveillance (AGS) Program.

However, the current funding for RTIP by the U.S. Air Force is in doubt, with reductions from $60 million to $20 million reported in fiscal year 2002 and more cuts to follow in fiscal year 2003 and fiscal year 2004. In the meantime, the U.S. Air Force is spending $250,000 to study alternatives to RTIP. One idea is to develop modular systems that may possibly ride on smaller aircraft, UAVs, and even satellites. As of the summer of 2001, there were still no definitive answers from the U.S. Air Force.

**Southern Border Aerostat**
This map shows the locations of the different aerostat stations that the U.S. Air Force utilizes as part of Operation Sowrball. These aerostats are tied into a counter-narcotics network, and are an important part of the United States' southern defense system. Stretching from Yuma, Arizona, to Puerto Rico, these aerostats give a virtually unbroken radar picture of all southern approaches to the United States.
*Courtesy of TCOM*

## Other U. S. AEW Development

As mentioned earlier, the U.S. Air Force operates a fleet of 12 aerostats along the southern border of the United States to counter the low, slow flyer attempting to smuggle drugs into these areas. These tethered radar systems use static balloons that carry radar sets aloft to an altitude of 10,000 to 15,000 feet. Using the Lockheed Martin L-88-A radar, this tethered aerostat radar system (TARS) provides coverage of the United States' southern border to include the Gulf of Mexico and the Caribbean. Linked to NORAD, U.S. Southern Command, U.S. Customs Service, and the Joint Interagency Task Force East, these aerostats give good, long-term surveillance coverage for the counter-narcotic mission.

Designed and built by Tactical Defense Systems (TDS), a subsidiary of Lockheed Martin, these aerostats come in different sizes ranging in cubic volume from 56,000 to 596,000 cubic feet, with the largest being over 70 meters in length. The radar is housed in a synthetic fabric blister beneath the main envelope, with a maximum payload weight of 3,400 pounds.

In addition, TCOM of Columbia, Maryland, has also developed a large line of aerostats for use in surveillance operations. Together, these two companies have sold AEW platforms to four countries (South Korea, Kuwait, Saudi Arabia, and the United Arab Emirates (UAE) ) and four U. S. government agencies (U.S. Coast Guard, U.S. Army, U.S. Customs Service, and U.S. Air Force). Tied into the Customs counter-drug surveillance program called Project Sowrball, the aerostats give virtually an unbroken surveillance coverage from California to the Bahamas.

Unmanned aerial vehicles are defined as remotely controlled, autonomous airframes that can carry a payload. They have been used in combat as recently as Operation Enduring Freedom and as earlier as Operation Peace for Galilee. Although typically UAVs are limited to reconnaissance missions, new technology has broadened their scope to include surveillance and AEW-type missions. In a recent NATO conference (April 2000), 19 nations were listed as possessing a UAV program, and there were 98 different programs in a development or production phase in these countries. This incredible amount of activity and financial expenditures have pushed the rapid development of UAV research. In addition, at less than $10 million a copy, the UAVs are a huge bargain compared to manned AEW aircraft. If these platforms can develop an organic radar capability, they may in the future become a viable candidate to replace the current AEW systems.

In the United States, the UAV that is receiving the most attention from an AEW perspective is the R-4A Global Hawk. A High-Altitude Endurance (HAE) program that hosts an Electro-Optical/Infrared (EO/IR) imagery system to provide long-range, long-loiter capability, the Global Hawk is also being experimented with to act as a relay station for AEW data. Specifically, the U.S. Air Force is testing the Global Hawk with the E-3C AWACS to relay track data back to ground command and control sites.

A final AEW platform was originally developed by Lockheed Hercules in 1987, as they delivered four AEW-modified P-3 Orion aircraft to the Customs Service. These maritime aircraft were fitted with an APS-138 radar, similar to the Group Ø system on the Hawkeye. In addition to the normal AEW components, the Customs Service also added a Hughes APG-63 multi-mode radar very similar to that carried in the F-15 Eagle. This combination gives the operator a detection system that could not only conduct long-range over-the-horizon searches, but also track-while-scan intercepts. Named the UP-3A, these P-3 AEW aircraft have served almost exclusively in the counter-narcotics role for the U. S. Customs Service.

**Brazil/Chile**

The United States is not the only nation in the Western Hemisphere that is engaged in procuring AEW aircraft. Brazil has ordered eight Embraer 145 aircraft, of which five are to be fitted with the Erieye system. The Brazilians will use the aircraft mostly for surveillance over the Amazon River basin and will integrate it with their SIVAM air traffic and air defense system. This program is designed to survey the entire Amazon basin, which is a greater area than the whole of Western Europe. Brazil envisions the EMB-145 AEW aircraft for border surveillance as well as general air defense missions. The Chilean Air Force has been testing Phalcon radar systems on Boeing 707s since 1995. Also called the Condor, this platform is a combination of Boeing, Israeli Aircraft Industries (IAI), and ELTA efforts to export the Phalcon technology. Although the phased array radar can be installed in up to four locations, including the bulbous nose extension, cheek extensions, fuselage panels, and the tail, the Chilean model only uses the nose and cheek fairings. Designed to operate in the extreme environments of the Andes and rugged coastlines of Chile, the performance may not have been up to the desires of the Chilean Air Force, as no production aircraft have been ordered.

# AEW Development in the Soviet Union/Russia and Europe

W hile the British and the French inherited some AEW capability from the United States, the second country to indigenously
produce such aircraft was the Union of Soviet Socialist
Republics (USSR). As in all matters concerning the Soviet Union, secrecy
makes it difficult to separate fact from rumor, and there are inevitable
gaps in the story. However, with the breakup of the USSR, the increasing
openness of Russia has made enough information available to trace the
highlights of its development of an AEW system.

Probably impressed by the capabilities of the EC-121 and E-2, the
Soviets appeared to have initiated an AEW program sometime prior to
1967. The first indication of a Soviet AEW program was the 1968 release
of a documentary film showing a transport-type aircraft which appeared
to be carrying a saucer-shaped radome.

Possibly influenced by Israeli E-2C performance in the Bekaa Valley
during Operation Peace for Galilee, the *Aviatsiya Voyenno-Morskoyo Flota*
began development of a naval tactically oriented AEW system as early as
1982. The development of an organic AEW system is neither easy, cheap,
nor fast, as the Soviets would quickly learn. Conceived by shortening the
fuselage of an AN-72 and placing a rotodome on the top of a forward-swept
tail fin, only two versions of the resulting AN-74 (code-named MADCAP by
NATO) were created before disappointing test results ended the program.
Another variant, the AN-71K, was designed for use on the aircraft carrier

*Admiral Kuznetsov*. This large aircraft would have used rocket boosters for carrier launch, but it lost the design competition to the smaller YAK-44.

The YAK-44 was an original AEW design probably intended for carrier operation. First demonstrated in full mockup in 1993, the model used twin-engine counter-rotating turboprops, a high wing and twin fins. Smaller than the AN-71 and using turbofans for better low-speed thrust, the YAK's appearance would undoubtedly have earned it the nickname "Hawkeyeski" if Russian carrier construction had not been curtailed. Development of the YAK-44 also stopped, although the system has been offered for export.

Thus, with no fixed-wing AEW assets, the Russian Navy has been forced to rely on helicopters for their AEW platform. The KA-31 is a derivative of the proven KA-29 "Helix B" transport helicopter. Fitted with an E-801 Oko radar system, a 5.5 x 1.0–meter antenna has been mounted below the fuselage. The antenna is stowed for landing and in cruising flight, while in the AEW configuration it is deployed below the fuselage and the landing gear is retracted. The expected endurance is 2.5 hours at 3,500 meters, and the crew consists of a pilot and systems operator. The KA-31 was accepted for naval service in 1992, and at least three KA-31s exist and have been tested aboard the *Kuznetsov*. Little information is available about the performance characteristics of the radar system except that the antenna can rotate 360 degrees and this aircraft was expected to operate with the fleet. Although the helicopters debuted in 1995, the lack of funding by the Russian Navy has effectively suspended any further development within that country until recently. In 2001, India ordered a total of nine of these platforms to serve as part of their naval forces.

The *Voyska Protivo-Vozdushnoy Oborony* (Troops of Air Defense) have had greater success in the development of organic AEW aircraft than their naval brethren. Some of that is because they can use larger platforms that are not constrained by having to operate off of naval vessels. Yet the aircraft produced by the Soviet Union have generally not been comparable to Western designs. As you will read in the section on Soviet AEW systems, their overall operational service has been limited, and no export sales have been recorded. This is not to say that certain technologies or concepts from Soviet aircraft have not been utilized by other nations, but in general, the TU-126 and A-50 are generally not regarded as AEW success stories.

The aircraft code-named MOSS by NATO later was determined to be a modified TU-126. Estimates are that 8–12 of these aircraft were produced by 1972. Operated by the National Air Defense (PVO-Strany), the Tu-126 was intended to vector advanced interceptors against attacking aircraft in areas of poor radar coverage. It was assessed to have a secondary role of providing assistance to friendly aircraft operating on offensive missions. A military version of the Tupolev TU-114 airliner, the MOSS was a four-engine turboprop with a wingspan of 51 meters and a maximum weight of 170,000 kilograms. Operating with a crew of 12, the aircraft had a reported endurance of 10 hours (without air refueling). The Liana radar (NATO code-named FLAT JACK) was assessed to be a two-dimensional L-band radar, probably having some moving target indicator capability. Many analysts, however, believe that the large counter-rotating metal propellers used by the *Kuznetsov* NK-12M turboprop engines represented a huge radar return that compromised the performance of the system. Consequently, only a few versions of the MOSS were developed, and many consider it a failure as far as its AEW capability.

There appears to be little documentation available on MOSS operations, but a squadron was reportedly stationed at Siaulai Airfield, Lithuania. This is consistent with assessments of poor overland and look-down performance, although the aircraft could have provided coverage over the Baltic. Fortunately, MOSS was never put to the test for which it was built, namely, a full-scale nuclear or conventional war with NATO. However, several sources have contended that the Soviets provided a MOSS to assist the Indians in their 1971 war with Pakistan. Reportedly operated by Soviet Air Force personnel, the MOSS flew at 20,000 feet well within Indian territory and parallel to the Pakistani border. Operating as a strike coordination center, the MOSS directed Indian SU-7s and Canberras that were conducting low-level night attacks over 100 miles inside Pakistan. While this would seem to contradict assessments of the TU-126's overland performance, it should be noted that strike coordination using IFF vice radar symbology, particularly in the absence of enemy air opposition, is a far easier mission than MOSS' primary one of air defense.

The deficiencies of the Liana radar system led to development of a follow-on system called Shmel. When the TU-126 proved unsuitable for such an upgrade, other aircraft were tried. Finally, an AEW platform based on the new IL-76 transport was developed. Designated A-50, it was officially named MAINSTAY by NATO, but unofficially it was promptly dubbed the Soviet Union's AWACS. A prototype airframe was tested in

December 1978 and the aircraft entered service with Troops of the Air Defense in 1984. The A-50 resembles the IL-76 transport except for the addition of an in-flight refueling probe, the deletion of glazing in the lower nose, and of course, the rotodome above the aft fuselage. Although capable of air refueling, the A-50 typically flew on-station a four-hour mission, typically loitering in a figure-eight pattern at 32,500 feet. Intended to operate with the advanced interceptors such as the MiG-31 and SU-27, the A-50 was supposed to be able to handle up to 50 targets at maximum ranges of 150 miles. These aircraft have an extensive but very heavy avionics suite including voice radio, datalink, IFF, and navigation equipment and an ECM system. Initially operating from bases in the Baltic region, in 1990 the A-50s were shifted north to their current operating base at Perchora. A-50s have participated in exercises in the Far East operation areas, reportedly guiding MiG-31s to intercept cruise missiles while simultaneously controlling intercepts against bombers and supplying submarines with tactical information. During the Gulf War, two A-50s staging out of southern operating locations monitored events from orbits over the Black Sea.

## AEW Development in Europe

The Air Forces of the European nations have had a long history of AEW aircraft development and use. Both the Royal and French navies procured U.S. Navy carrier-based AEW aircraft (the AD-4W and TBM-3W, respectively) and used these platforms throughout the 1950s. What is very interesting now within Europe is the fact that while all 19 nations of NATO enjoy AEW coverage via the NATO AWACS fleet, a great number of these countries are endeavoring to procure their own organic AEW aircraft as well. In fact, there is a huge market for future radar platform sales within the NATO nations using the small business jet and the Erieye system.

To truly analyze the European AEW market, though, one must first study where the different nations have been and how they came to acquire the current systems that they have. We will begin with the United Kingdom, because it has the dubious honor of having the longest procurement history of any nation in developing an organic AEW aircraft.

## United Kingdom

In 1960, the RN-received the long awaited replacement to the aging AEW Mk.1 (AD-4W). The AEW Mk.3 Fairey (later Westland) Gannet was a step in the right direction for a Navy that was quickly reaching its heyday in terms of carrier capability. Much like the AD-4W Skyraider, the AEW version of the Gannet was a spinoff from a previously developed and deployed series of aircraft.

Deployed first on HMS *Hermes* in July of 1960, the Gannet proved to be a sturdy and reliable, if unorthodox, aircraft. The basic Gannet anti-submarine aircraft which was adapted to the AEW role was powered by a unique engine system known as the Armstrong Siddeley Double Mamba, which produced 3,875 ehp. This system consisted basically of two turbo-prop engines placed side by side, each powering one of two co-axial, counter-rotating propellers. In order to increase range and loiter time, one of the two engines could be shut down and its associated propeller feathered. Both engines were used on takeoffs and landings and in combat situations. In the AEW version, the rear cockpits were removed and accommodations provided within the fuselage for the two radar systems operators, much like the Skyraider.

Further in line with its heritage, the aircraft continued to use the APS-20 radar with the familiar lines of the radome appearing on the underside of the aircraft just aft of the engine. Thirty Gannets were modified to the AEW Mk.3 version by 1962, and all received a radar upgrade in 1972–1973. The AEW Mk.3 would serve with the Royal Navy until the decommissioning of Britain's last big conventional takeoff and landing carrier, the HMS *Ark Royal*, in 1978.

Yet the Gannet AEW Mk.3 was obviously not the answer to the pressing need for an AEW aircraft for both the Royal Navy and Royal Air Force. Therefore, in the early 1960s, a series of studies was begun to develop a capability similar to that being introduced with the new E-2A. Promising results from tests conducted with a fore and aft scanner system (FASS) convinced many in the United Kingdom that this arrangement was superior to the rotodome mounting used in the Hawkeye. Thus, for the next 25 years, one can notice a large emphasis in British designs on the use of the FASS antennas for both carrier- and land-based aircraft proposals.

The first project that drew a lot of attention was the Blackburn P.139, which—because of its portly dimensions—was dubbed "The Flying Pig." Designed to operate as both an AEW aircraft or in a carrier onboard delivery role, this airframe was never built because of the drastic reductions in the Royal Navy that took place in the mid-1960s. However, the FASS arrangement did not die. Because the United Kingdom still desired a suitable AEW aircraft, further studies continued, with the RAF eventually proposing an AEW version of the Comet airliner. Known as the Nimrod, the initial design was developed in 1966. Unfortunately, the avionics designed for this aircraft never did work as advertised, and in 1986, after 20 years of research and development, the Nimrod AEW aircraft was officially canceled.

Design studies and proposals aside, the decision to eliminate the conventional aircraft carriers from the RN had a drastic effect on its AEW aircraft. Because the Gannet AEW Mk.3 could not operate from the vertical takeoff and landing (VTOL) aircraft carriers, these aircraft were retired in 1978 and their APS-20 radars were transferred to the RAF to use as backups for their aging AEW Shackleton aircraft. Thus, the RN was forced to rely on the RAF–modified Shackleton patrol aircraft that had been developed in 1970 to 1972 as a stopgap measure of AEW capability.

So now there was a modified World War II patrol aircraft, using a modified World War II radar, as the *only* AEW aircraft in the UK inventory from 1978 to 1982! Sometimes called "30,000 rivets flying in formation," the Shackletons were unable to fly in support of the RN during their Falkland campaign. Thus, the RN was ill-prepared to fight a war 8,000 miles from home in the south Atlantic Ocean. Although the loss in aircraft throughout the conflict was limited to ground fire, this was not the case for the surface fleet. In all, a total of 17 ships were sunk or damaged by the direct or indirect actions of Argentine attack aircraft. The most significant loss was, of course, the HMS *Sheffield* (D-80).

While many believed that the Shackletons were at best a temporary measure, in fact they served with the RAF from 1972 to 1991. Originally consisting of one squadron of 12 aircraft based at Kinloss, these ancient aircraft were slowly reduced in numbers (six in 1981) and moved to Lossiemouth as they reached the end of their engineering lifetime. Clearly inadequate for the high-threat environments of the 1980s, the Shackleton AEW Mk.2 was unfortunately forced to shoulder on when the Nimrod debacle caused delays in procurement of its eventual replacement.

Named after the characters in "The Magic Roundabout" television series, the aircraft normally carried a crew of nine, including four systems operators. Using three scopes, the fourth operator flew onboard to allow for crew rest, especially on those long, 12-hour missions. The radar in the Shackleton was upgraded to the APS-20F version, which gave the operators a ground-stabilized display. However, even with these upgrades, the Shackleton was antiquated and the threats would not wait. On a spring day in 1982, the British government would pay for its indecision.

From 1978 to 1982 the RN would do without an AEW platform, but the effects of the Falkland Islands War on the British fleet saw the emergency acquisition of modified Westland Sea King helicopters to fill the vacant role. Necessitated by the lack of a carrier that could accept a conventional AEW aircraft like the American E-2C Hawkeye, the Sea King helicopter option was the only viable solution available in the near term and at a price which was acceptable to the British government.

So once again the AEW role would be filled by an asset modified in order to accept the necessary equipment. The basic Sea King was a copy of the Sikorsky SH-3D, with a watertight hull and retractable main gear. Powered by two 1,660-shaft horsepower Rolls-Royce Gnome engines, the helicopter has the ability to lift close to 10,000 pounds, cruise at a speed of 130 miles per hour, and fly as high as 10,000 feet. Combat radius for the AEW version of the helicopter averages 150 miles with a loiter time of up to two hours, depending on altitude. Under Project LAST (Low-Altitude Surveillance Task), initial modifications were carried out on two Sea King Mk.2 helicopters. Each aircraft had approximately 4,000 hours on the airframe prior to the modification, which took a period of 11 weeks. Although this period was relatively short in terms of development and fielding a project, it proved too long, as the aircraft were unable to reach the south Atlantic before hostilities ceased.

The heart of the AEW system aboard the helicopter would be the newly acquired Thorn EMI Searchwater radar. Previously installed in Nimrod maritime patrol aircraft, only slight modifications were required to install the system and apply it in the AEW role. Proclaimed by the manufacturer as the most advanced maritime search radar in the Western world, the system has several unique features. An I-band frequency-agile radar with maximum power output of 65 kilowatts, the system uses pulse compression techniques and a pitch and roll stabilized antenna with controllable tilt and automatic sector scan. IFF systems are incorporated for the interrogation of both aircraft and surface vessels. A signal processing system is used to enhance the detection of small surface targets including antennas and periscopes.

The system can also be coordinated to provide over-the-horizon targeting for anti-ship weapons. All equipment is stored in the cargo compartment of the craft with the exception of the air-pressurized "Kettledrum" antenna, which is stowed on the starboard side of the helicopter and hydraulically deployed. Number 849 Squadron was recommissioned in 1984 to serve as a home for the AEW helicopters and their crews. Interestingly enough, several former Gannet AEW Mk.3 crew members and pilots have made the transition to helicopters from their fixed-wing upbringing. In all, 10 systems were modified for the Royal Navy, and a further six Sikorsky SH-3Ds were modified for Spain after the system proved itself. The Royal Navy operates their Sea Kings in the 849 Squadron at Culdrose, which is divided into three aircraft detachments that operate from the *Invincible* class of aircraft carriers.

While the SH-3 AEW Mk.2 is a definite advance in technology over the Gannett and Shackleton, it is still basically a point defense weapons system. With only two operators and limited in altitude, the Sikorsky can become overwhelmed in a multi-axis, multi-threat environment. Likewise, the Mk.2 also suffers from a common problem with many search radars in regard to sea return. This deficiency is especially acute when using this system to detect surface targets. For example, at an altitude of 5,000 feet, the radar has a physical limit of about 75 miles. Combine that with its sea return "hole" and you end up having a "donut" that the operator must tailor to keep the track in view. This "donut" will get smaller or larger depending on how high the helicopter flies, but it will never substantially gain in width. This discussion is not meant to denigrate the SH-3 AEW Mk.2 platform or its aircrew, but to show that the technology of AEW aircraft is quite expensive and there are no shortcuts. Improvements to the SH-3 AEW are desperately needed. Without a datalink, the Mk.2 can often have great difficulty incorporating into a coalition air defense environment. Because the operators have to pass their tracks verbally, this is very aircrew intensive and difficult to correlate with real-time targets. In some cases, the old Mk.2s were simply told to go away because it was too hard to integrate them into the coalition datalink architecture.

The United Kingdom has, however, attempted to solve this problem. The Royal Navy is currently upgrading its own organic AEW aircraft and bids were submitted in mid-1995 to convert its 10 Sea King AEW Mk.2s to Mk.7 standards with an option to upgrade six more. The Royal Navy wanted to take advantage of advances in radar technology, particularly in terms of

## SH-3 AEW

After lessons learned in the Falklands, the Royal Navy developed a crash program to build an aircraft with AEW capability. Shown here is a picture of the SH-3 AEW helicopter. Because their platform had to operate from a VTOL carrier, the Hawkeye was not an option. At that point, AWACS was still too expensive, so the Royal Navy opted for a point-defense AEW system, housed in the Sea King platform. *Crown Copyright*

look-down capability and clutter rejection, and they also wanted to enhance the automation of the aircraft. The Searchwater 2000 AEW radar is a relatively new system that uses three different beams operating at the high, low, and maritime levels. It's a high-power pulse Doppler surveillance system that can search and track simultaneously, thereby decreasing operator workload. Taken together, these SH-3 AEW Mk.7 upgrades include:

- Upgrades to the radar system (Searchwater)
- Integrating the IFF Mode 4 interrogator/transponder
- Adding a ring laser gyro

**SH-3 AEW (Interior)**
This is the interior of the SH-3 AEW helicopter. Notice that the aircrew members sit side by side, and that they wear flight helmets while airborne. As you can see from the one scope, concentric circles mark the different range rings that the operator uses to track contacts and identify potentially hostile targets. *Crown Copyright*

- Adding Joint Tactical Information Distribution System (JTIDS) Link-16 components
- Upgrades to the man-machine interface

The previous sections illuminated how the RAF got into the messy situation of flying antiquated AEW aircraft during the 1980s, and what the RN did to acquire an AEW platform. The next section illustrates the trials and tribulations of the RAF. The British military and the Parliament were vainly trying to use an organic English aircraft, namely the Nimrod, which was originally an anti-submarine warfare platform (Mk.1), to develop to an AEW platform. The Nimrod AEW aircraft began as a study for fleet protection in the 1960s after the RAF was forced to pick up this role.

Originally desired for its overwater detection capability, it was the over-land detection capability that quickly became more important. The first test aircraft was flown in 1977, and tests continued throughout 1979 for airframe performance and handling qualities, airframe systems opera-tions, and testing of the high-capacity cooling system for the avionics suite. The modifications made to the Nimrod included a new aft fuselage section, 3-foot extensions of the horizontal stabilizer and the vertical fin, and, most distinctively, the large nose- and tail-mounted radomes added to house the Marconi Avionics radar. A second aircraft was put into test-ing in late 1979 with a complete radar and avionics suite. It was a test bed for subsystems operation and systems compatibility. The first opera-tional Nimrod was to be supplied to the RAF by early 1982. However, the testing of these aircraft marked the beginning of a period of frustration for the British military.

The original deadline of 1982 came and went, with no Nimrod in oper-ation for the RAF. Likewise, 1983 was also Nimrod-less, with the first plane now promised by the end of 1984. With all of the airframes ordered now flying or in the factory being modified, it soon became obvious that the avionics were the source of the delay. Now labeled as the Nimrod Mk.3, these aircraft were to provide the RAF with four basic capabilities:

• Low-level radar coverage
• Early warning radar coverage
• Command and control of air defense fighter aircraft
• Surveillance of surface traffic, on land and sea

In addition, the Mk.3 aircraft was to serve as:

• A radio communications relay link
• Command and control center for ground attack aircraft
• Limited air traffic control facility
• Search and rescue coordination center
• Standby/emergency control and reporting center

The British had also planned the Nimrod Mk.3 to be their contribu-tion to NATO's AEW force. In order for the Nimrod to carry out these mis-sions, it required the latest in technology. The Mk.3 contained both pas-sive and active sensors, along with a sophisticated data handling system.

135

Long-range, downward-looking radar utilized two antennas: one in the nose and one in the tail. These antennas alternately transmitted during half of their sweep to provide 360 radar coverage. Using a twisted Cassegrain antenna with an aperture eight feet wide and six feet high, the radar system itself was a coherent pulse Doppler designed for low side-lobe and narrow main beam transmission. The system was stabilized in relation to the aircraft's motion and used a medium and low PRF to help distinguish aircraft from ground clutter. In addition to azimuth determination, the radar also determined altitude. The passive system used two wingtip-mounted pods containing two early warning support measures antennas. These four antennas were angled to provide overlapping 360-degree coverage, and they fed into a single receiver. Integrating these sensors systems was the data handling system, capable of automatically initiating and maintaining the track of aircraft and automatically classifying targets by IFF and passive sensor inputs. By comparing a signal against an onboard library, the system could classify a target as friendly, hostile, or unknown. Another significant feature was the datalink capability to other AEW platforms, ground stations, and other datalink capable aircraft. Tying this all together were the six console operator stations. With operator-controlled constraints available, the operators could limit the amount of data presented to them by the system. The ability to control minimum or maximum altitudes, speeds, or sectors also enabled a more efficient use of resources.

While the advanced electronics enabled a highly capable system, they were not without drawbacks. The Mk.3 generated a staggering 124-kilowatt heat load, 79 kilowatts more than the projected 45 kilowatts. This in turn generated the need for an additional cooling system, which was solved by splitting the cooling system and using the wing fuel tanks as a heat sink. Other problems which had occurred up to 1983 were high-voltage sparking in the radar transmitter, and a high rate of false alarms in the transmitter resulting in automatic shutdowns. In February of 1985 more bad news came to the Nimrod production. With no operational aircraft yet in service, the cost of the AEW project was re-estimated from $500 million to more than $1.3 billion. In addition to that revelation came the statement that the earliest the Nimrod could be available was now 1987. Disgruntlement with the British Aerospace Corporation was now settling in full force. Five years later than the proposed delivery date and $800 million over budget was cause to take a step back and rethink the Nimrod project. The pressing need for AEW support was still foremost in Britain's mind, and a problem-plagued, overdue product was not what it needed. At this point serious talks between the Ministry of Defense and British Aerospace/GEC Avionics began in earnest. By January 1986, the problems slowing the completion of the Nimrod production were significant enough to warrant talks by the British Defense Ministry about canceling the project and purchasing an AEW aircraft from the United States in its place. The Nimrod was at this point four years late and over budget by $2 billion.

In addition to these major problems, the Avro Shackleton aircraft that the Nimrod was intended to replace were now over 35 years old, and it was doubtful if they would last till 1988. By March of 1986, Britain had decided to hold a competition for its new AEW aircraft. This meant that the Nimrod was no longer a guaranteed buy by the British Government. Thus, GEC lost their cost-plus contract, but were still the primary contractor, and would have to furnish 50 percent of the cost of the next six months' spending on the Nimrod. At the end of the six months, the Defense Ministry would have finished its evaluation of alternate AEW aircraft, and GEC Avionics would make its proposal for the continuation of the Nimrod program. Britain's new proposal was hard-nosed and to the point: "Demonstrate that you can produce an AEW aircraft to our specifications, and we will purchase it!" The least expensive option facing the British at this point was buying into the NATO AWACS program. This was the same program they had left in 1977 to start the Nimrod program. However, the drawback to this option was the fact that during any operations out of the NATO area, the British would not have AEW capability! This prospect was unacceptable to the government, as the recent Falklands War had demonstrated.

By May 1986, three U.S. companies, Grumman International, Boeing, and Lockheed-California, submitted bids to replace the Nimrod. Boeing and Lockheed both submitted new aircraft proposals: the E-3A and the P-3 AEW respectively, while Grumman proposed utilizing the Nimrod airframe and some of its less "vital" components, and attaching the E-2C's radar and central computers. Meanwhile, GEC Avionics was laboring intensively to bring the Nimrod up to standards and keep the cost within budget. Grumman's proposal intrigued Britain, and the six-month deadline was extended another 10 months in order for Grumman to complete its proposal. This did not give GEC Avionics more breathing room, as it was still required to meet the six-month deadline to demonstrate its capability to meet the RAF specifications. GEC had more riding on the Nimrod program then just another contract, as they had their reputation as a leading aviation manufacturer on the line. In order to win the contract, GEC started making changes to the Nimrod in the form of new radar antennas, a new computer system, and improvements in the computer software to upgrade the tracking capabilities of the system. These advancements were enough to warrant granting GEC a 30-day extension, with the possibility of another 30-day extension to further work its problems out.

Ultimately, however, these changes were not ready in time to make a difference. Because of serious developmental problems including system integration, the Nimrod was not chosen, and in September 1986, Great Britain narrowed the field down to two finalists: the Grumman-modified P-3 and the E-3A AWACS. England had also teamed up with France for the final evaluation process. This meant that France was a strong possibility for a new AEW market, and the winner could get the bonus of supplying additional AEW platforms to France. Both aircraft had to meet the cardinal points spelled out in the competition rules, namely:

- An on-station time of nine hours
- 700 miles from base
- A 360-degree capability to track surface and airborne targets, including fighter-sized aircraft, at ranges in excess of 150 Nautical Miles
- The ability to track 400 targets simultaneously

Boeing, in an obvious attempt to influence the decision, made the British a 130 percent offset offer in conjunction with the AEW contract, of which only 10 percent would be related to the E-3A buy. Therefore, it is not surprising that in the second week of December 1986, the British government decided to purchase the E-3 aircraft. This was a huge step for the British defense industry—choosing an American-made aircraft over a domestically produced one. For $1.238 billion, Britain purchased six E-3s, with the option of purchasing two more within six months. This ensured that Britain would have an AEW platform operating by 1991, a long nine years from the projected delivery date of the initial Nimrod aircraft. Therefore, after 14 long years, the Royal Air Force finally had a new and updated AEW fleet. No longer dependent on outside sources for its early warning capability, the service once more had sufficient resources to conduct a war in today's technologically advanced arena. In September of 1990, the first British E-3D flew at the Farnborough Air Show from RAF Waddington in Lincolnshire, the home base for the UK's AEW fleet. By 1993, Britain had developed datalink capability between its Tornado F-3 aircraft and its U.K. Boeing Sentry Mk.1 (E-3D). With this advancement in tactical aviation, Britain reestablished itself as a formidable air power. Today the United Kingdom operates a fleet of seven E-3Ds.

When the U.S. Air Force first proposed the AWACS as a system, AEW and surveillance were seen as its primary role. Likewise, the United Kingdom procured the E-3D under Air Staff Requirement 400, which emphasized the platform for AEW vice air battle management. The focus on air defense deficits centered on the fact that the aircraft had only two consoles, which meant it could accommodate only two controllers. In intense operations, these aircrews can quickly become overwhelmed. These problems are evidenced by the evolution of the use of the E-3D over the past nine years. In 1992 to 1993, during Operations Sky Monitor over the Balkans, and also during Operations Deny Flight from 1993 to 1995, the primary mission was surveillance, so there was little tasking for the weapons controllers, and a false sense of security arose. Things began to change during Operation Deliberate Force against Bosnian Serbs in 1995, when the control requirements grew rapidly, often stretching the controllers beyond their capabilities. Even after augmenting the crews with an additional controller, the 10-hour missions often saturated the platform.

Operation Allied Force in 1999, a campaign of air strikes designed to drive the Yugoslavian forces of President Milosevich out of Kosovo, was a huge challenge for the E-3D. It flew alongside the NATO E-3As, U.S. Air Force E-3B/Cs, and French E-3Fs, and its aircrew were expected to pick up control from these assets at any time. Still using only three controllers, these aircrew were tasked with 30 to 40 aircraft at any one time, thus forcing them to leave important control frequencies unmonitored. Fatigue and sustainability were huge issues, as controllers often spent long periods (9-plus hours) on the console, leading to more mistakes and greater risks of midairs.

To lessen these dangers, the Royal Air Force has requested the following remedial actions, based on lessons learned from these recent combat operations:

- Augment weapons teams
- Additional radios
- Enhanced Mission Data Exchange System

In addition, the Royal Air Force has also identified that nine consoles were inadequate, of which only three were for weapons controllers, and that five additional work stations were needed to bring the E-3Ds up to standards with the U.S. Air Force and NATO. This deficiency was a result of cost-cutting measures in the procurement of the AWACS by the RAF as well as its initial acquisition requirement for primarily a surveillance asset. Notwithstanding these deficiencies, the E-3D is still a superlative platform, and when called upon, performed admirably in the Kosovo campaign.

The Erieye is not the only unique AEW radar system to come out of Europe. Pilatus Britten-Norman in conjunction with Westinghouse (now a division of Northrup-Grumman has modified the APG-66 F-16 radar to enhance its surveillance capabilities and has installed the system on its Britten-Norman Islander aircraft to market the airframe as an AEW platform. Two different models exist, named the Defender 4000 and Multi-Sensor Surveillance Aircraft, that offer alternatives to those customers looking at the low- to medium-size AEW market. The system is currently used by the U.S. Navy to monitor its Chesapeake Test Range and by Pakistan's Maritime Safety Agency for coastal patrol work, and several interested customers have announced options to purchase this system.

Pilatus Britten-Norman modified the Defender 4000 maritime surveillance aircraft by using a pod similar to the Searchwater radar system employed by the SH-3 AEW helicopter. Proposals for an AEW configuration include two consoles, which might be very useful for nations looking to acquire a small or limited capability. A more advanced version called the Multi-Sensor Surveillance Aircraft has also been developed that adds a Westinghouse APG-66SR radar to the nose. Similar to the F-16, this version has a larger planar array antenna, which gives it a ground surveillance capability. The APG-66SR can also track maritime and air targets with a range of 80 nautical miles. In this model, the console is located at the rear of the aircraft and uses a common Microsoft Windows format. The potential for the AEW Defender 4000 is high, especially as a border patrol aircraft. The U.S. Army employs OV-1 Mohawks for this mission, and the Pilatus platform could be a good replacement. Able to detect moving ground targets or low-flying aircraft, the AEW Defender can be a huge force multiplier in a crisis or wartime scenario.

The British have contracted a requirement for a new surveillance system called the Airborne Stand-Off Radar (ASTOR). This platform is being developed for U. K. military requirements and may be a prime competitor for the JOSTAR competition at NATO. Originally developed as the CASTOR program in 1995, the requirement for an AGS system by the RAF has gone through a very lengthy evolution process. The ASTOR is a surveillance system, not a battle management platform, designed to conduct 24-hour, all-weather surveillance of moving and static targets. Originally the United States fought hard to sell the JSTARS system to the RAF, but the E-8C was viewed by many as only first-generation technology. The U. K. requirement was for not only a (MTI) radar but for a (SAR) capability as well. Although plans were presented to update the JSTARS platform, in the end, the RAF selected a different aircraft. The main competition boiled down to Raytheon/E-Systems, which based their bid on a Bombardier Global Express regional jet using radar technology similar to the Hughes ASARS 2 (U-2), and the Lockheed Martin proposal, which was hosted in a Gulfstream V aircraft with a new radar system developed by a RACAL/Texas Instrument coalition. In development since 1993, the contract was awarded in December 1999 to Raytheon Systems Limited for £850 million ($1.4 billion). The first production system is expected to be delivered in November 2003. The in-service date is projected for November 2005, with an eventual total of five aircraft planned for delivery.

Thus, ASTOR will use a combination of MTI/SAR components in the projected airframe of the Global Express business jet. Linked to a tactical ground station in a similar manner to the JSTARS, ASTOR is proposed as a major component of Britain's overall intelligence collection capabilities. As this system is compatible with the E-3D through Link-16/JTIDS, the tentative plan is to base the support facilities at RAF Waddington with the AWACS crews. The primary information will be passed over a dual wide-band and narrow-band datalink to either the Operational Level Ground Stations or the Tactical Ground Stations that are collocated with Army units. However, as the U. K. Ministry of Defense has indicated, the ASTOR is fundamentally different from existing airborne surveillance systems and will present command, control, and communications challenges that must be overcome. Yet the real significance of the RAF decision may lie in the upcoming JOSTAR program at NATO. Now that Raytheon has won the bid for the United Kingdom, that corporation is quickly becoming the odds-on favorite to win the NATO competition as well.

Chapter Eight

## France/Sweden

As mentioned earlier, France has a long history of using AEW aircraft, operating TBM-3Ws from their straight-deck carriers in the 1950s. However, they also have a history of independent military forces and thus have endeavored to build a world-class force capable of conducting operations around their region and the world. In that vein, they have purchased their own AEW platforms in recent years to build a highly respected naval and Air Force fleet.

With the construction of the large-deck aircraft carrier *Charles de Gaulle*, the French Navy desired an organic AEW aircraft. While they could have gone the route of the British or Spanish Navy and purchased a number of SH-3 AEW helicopters, instead the *Aeronautique Navale* desired a higher-end system, one that could operate to protect their fleet and not simply a point-defense system. Therefore, after a series of negotiations, the French Navy signed a contract with Grumman to deliver four E-2Cs to fly from their aircraft carrier. The first two Hawkeyes were built to the Group II standard and were delivered in December 1998 and April 1999 respectively. The third aircraft will be a Hawkeye 2000 model and is scheduled for delivery in 2003. Plans are in work to upgrade the first two aircraft to the Hawkeye 2000 standard, and a fourth aircraft is under contract as well. In addition, French naval officers have received training at VAW-120 in Norfolk and are acting as liaisons with the U.S. Navy. The carrier's deck had to be extended 15 feet to accomodate the Hawkeye.

The *Armee de L'Air* acquired an impressive AEW capability in the form of E-3F Sentries in the late 1980s. Signing a contract with Boeing for three AWACS aircraft in February 1987, the French Air Force added a fourth aircraft to the contract in 1989. Somewhat different from a standard E-3, these aircraft are powered by French-built CFM-56 engines. The first aircraft was delivered in October 1990, with all four aircraft based with the 36th *Escadre de Detection Aeroportee* in Avord. As mentioned earlier, these AWACS flew missions in support of Operation Allied Force in 1999, and there has been discussion to upgrade these platforms. Recently the DOD requested to install RSIP modification kits on their AWACS at a cost of $190 million. In addition, the French Air Force is also upgrading the flight suites of the aircraft with GPS navigation units.

The sea and air services are not the only military units within France that desire an over-the-horizon surveillance capability. The French Army has been developing an organic SAR platform for at least the last decade.

142

Originally called the Orchidee (*Observatoire Radar Coherent Heliporte d'Investigation des Elements Ennemis*), this system consisted of a 3.5-meter antenna mounted below a Super-Puma helicopter. The current AEW system utilized by the French Army also is helicopter based and consists of an MTI radar connected via a datalink to a ground station. Mounted underneath an Aerospatiale Super-Puma Mark 2A, this steerable antenna can be folded out of the way for takeoffs and landings. The Horizon program, a follow-on to the older Orchideeprogram, does not have an SAR capability; therefore, it uses digital maps. The data can be processed at either the ground station or onboard the helicopter. Tested during the Gulf War, the first operational system was fielded in 1996, with two complete systems purchased by 1998. These helicopters saw action in Operation Noble Anvil with a detachment in Skopje.

The Swedish aircraft industry has always designed unique and interesting aircraft, and it shows in the production of their AEW platforms. Ericsson-Radar Electronics has developed the first airborne phased-array radar that is small and light enough to fit on a commercial airliner and has tested the radar on the Fairchild Metro III and a Saab 340 airframe. This system is unique in that not only does the radar data integrate with Sweden's command and control system (StriC-90) and NATO's datalink, but the mission control area can actually be unmanned, with the controllers and technicians operating the system from a ground station.

The Swedish Air Force intends to use these platforms as surveillance assets for their borders as well as an integrated part of their air defense command and control structure. In that manner, the Erieye system is deliberately designed to operate in a low-manning or unmanned status for operators to minimize the costs involved for training airborne radar aircrew. The radar called the Erieye is far different from the technology used by the Hawkeye or Sentry. The Erieye antenna is a long, narrow, non-rotating, fixed design that uses 200 solid-state transmit/receive modules on each side that can scan two 120-degree sectors on either side of the aircraft. Although this configuration leaves two 60-degree sectors centered on the nose and tail uncovered, this limitation is not as big a problem as one might think, because most surveillance missions tend to have a threat axis and do not require a full 360-degree coverage. Reported ranges include 200 miles for a fighter-size target and the instrumented range is 270 miles. The S-band frequency agile pulse Doppler radar is also highly resistant to ECM interference.

Ericsson Erieye is the world's first high-performance AEW mission system that can be mounted on a number of small commuter-type aircraft like the Saab 340. This feature provides low overall system costs, and enormous flexibility. *Courtesy of AEWA*

Originally tested on a Fairchild Metro III airframe in 1990, this early model can only seat two operators if an airborne manned capability is desired. The larger Saab 340 aircraft was modified and first flew with the Erieye radar system in January 1994. Five aircraft were built for R&D testing, with Ericsson receiving $200 million for this contract. This aircraft has room for up to four consoles, with an on-station time of eight hours within 180 kilometers of home base. Ericsson has also proposed fitting the Erieye system on even larger aircraft such as the Fokker 50 or C-130.

In 1997, the Royal Swedish Air Force accepted the delivery of its first Saab S100B Argus AEW aircraft with the Erieye radar system. A total of six are expected to be delivered, and all of these aircraft have built on the success of the long R&D testing cycle undergone on the previous airframes. The latest platform to accommodate the Erieye radar is the

Embraer ERJ-145, a regional jetliner aircraft that is used by the Brazilian military. The airframe was structurally reinforced and new navigation and communications suites were installed in addition to adding an enhanced auxiliary power unit, increased fuel capacity, and a revised interior layout. All of these changes have ensured the capability of the EMB-145 to support the Erieye system. This surveillance aircraft will also have SAR, FLIR, TV, ELINT processing and an onboard processing system, with Ericsson delivering the first EMB-145 in 2001.

While the EMB-145 is the latest aircraft to fly with the Erieye radar, a large number of countries are interested in buying the Erieye system to mount on their indigenous aircraft. These include Pakistan, India, Indonesia, Malaysia, Thailand, and South Korea. The total number of this radar and its related aircraft platforms is expected to grow steadily through the next decade as more and more third world nations line up to buy these less-expensive AEW platforms. Thus, it is the Erieye and the modified business jet that have the most potential for the future of AEW. If a manufacturer were to sell a jet modified to perform both JSTARS and AEW missions, then the market could easily exceed 50 aircraft worldwide. Proposed airframes for this conversion include the Jetstream 41 and 61, Donier 328, Hawker Siddeley HS-748, de Havilland Dash 8, and the Bell-Texitron V-22 Osprey. There are also proposals to fit the Erieye radar on helicopters as a possible replacement for the SH-3 AEW system; this would be useful to nations such as Spain, Italy, and the United Kingdom.

## NATO

Besides individual European nations, the largest user of AEW aircraft in Europe is the political and military union of the North Atlantic Treaty Organization (NATO). Defending Western Europe against a potential Warsaw Pact attack presented NATO with a seemingly endless series of strategic challenges during the early Cold War years. Many of these were based on geography. The nature of the terrain in Europe, with its mountain ranges, narrow valleys, rugged coastlines, and wet climate, complicates efforts to rapidly deploy offensive forces to the front in time of war, but it also gives troops in strong defensive positions a distinct tactical advantage, provided they are forewarned.

With that in mind, the North Atlantic Council in September 1960 approved the formation of an integrated air defense system including a string of 40 NATO air defense ground environment (NADGE) radar sites between Norway and Turkey. While NADGE potentially gave NATO an extra few minutes' notice of a hostile air strike, enough to scramble most of the alert fighters, it had a weakness shared by all ground-based radars, namely that of extremely limited range against low-flying targets. Ground-based radars cannot detect aircraft flying at or below 1,000 feet at ranges much beyond 30 to 35 nautical miles because of the earth's curvature.

Although the Soviet Union and its Communist allies in Eastern Europe did not possess all-weather combat planes that could fly at such low altitudes around the clock during the 1950s and 1960s, by the early 1970s this was not the case. Three major NATO commanders, the Supreme Allied Commander Europe (SACEUR), the Supreme Allied Commander Atlantic (SACLANT), and the Commander in Chief Channel (CINCHAN), decided NATO needed an AEW system following publication in 1972 of a series of Supreme Headquarters Allied Powers Europe (SHAPE) Technical Center studies on the state of NATO's air defenses. These studies showed the Warsaw Pact had high-speed fighters that could fly low enough to escape long-range radar detection, and the electronic countermeasures to support an effective first-strike. An early warning radar looking down from 30,000 feet would give NATO an additional 30 minutes' notice of an attack and, thereby, move the location of the war's first air battles 200 to 300 nautical miles further to the east.

SHAPE planners saw AEW aircraft playing a wide variety of roles in the event of a major European war involving the superpowers. SACEUR, for example, might use the radar planes to detect a low-level strike package before it crossed the front lines and vector friendly fighters to intercept it. SACLANT could have the AEW aircraft direct their sensors at enemy aircraft and warships threatening NATO convoys in the Atlantic. Finally, CINCHAN would need AEW planes to reduce the chances of friendly ships being surprised and sunk in the English Channel, and to follow the movements of Soviet surface vessels in the Baltic.

But what AEW aircraft did NATO have in mind? Certainly not the piston-powered EC-121, which could not climb much above 19,000 feet and whose radar could not separate low-flying targets from ground clutter. And the Shackleton AEW Mk.2s which entered service with the RAF in September 1971 were similarly limited. Therefore, NATO had no choice but to look elsewhere. NATO evaluated three AEW systems beginning in 1973: Boeing's E-3A, Grumman's E-2C, and Hawker Siddeley's Nimrod AEW. The NATO Conference of National Arms Directors in 1974 selected the E-3A because it could detect and track fixed-wing aircraft at low altitude over all types of terrain, operate in hostile electronic environments, and serve as a backup to command and control centers on the ground.

While the carrier-based E-2C could perform many of the E-3A's surveillance functions, from a practical standpoint it took four E-2Cs to perform the same mission as the E-3A over distant land masses. The E-2C also had shorter endurance (5.6 hours vs. 11.5 hours), flew considerably slower (270 knots vs. 420 knots at cruise), had room for fewer mission crew members (3 vs. 13), operated at a lower altitude (20,000 to 25,000 feet vs. 29,000 to 38,000 feet), and used older radar technology (1968 vs. mid-1970s) than the E-3A. The E-3A's longer endurance meant it could remain on-station for extended periods, about 6 hours when operating 1,000 nautical miles from its base. Also, the E-3A's greater speed resulted in less time spent in transit, and flying at a higher altitude provided the aircraft with a revolutionary ability to look far beyond the Iron Curtain.

The bulb-nosed Nimrod AEW, a spinoff from the civilian Comet 4C, was a proposed variant of the Nimrod MR.1 maritime reconnaissance planes operated by RAF Strike Command. It flew about 40 knots faster and had a higher service ceiling than the E-3A, and some judged its Marconi-Elliott mission system avionics superior to those of the E-3A in overwater operations. With its sensors mounted in the nose and tail, less aerodynamic drag was induced and theoretically the FASS arrangement caused fewer radar blind spots than the E-3A's dorsal radome arrangement. But in 1974, Boeing had experience in the high-tech Minuteman Missile Program and Lunar Orbiter programs to draw upon, and was much further along than Hawker Siddeley in AEW aircraft and radar development, facts which no doubt played a major part in NATO's decision. NATO support of the E-3A at this point was fortunate, for the British government would cancel its Nimrod AEW Mk.3 program in December 1986 in favor of the Sentry AEW.1 (NATO designation E-3D) after spending $1.4 billion over a nine-year period on the failed Nimrod program.

The E-3A being developed for the U.S. Air Force up to that point was in the basic "core" configuration. But NATO, following a series of contract definition studies conducted between 1975 and 1977, wanted a modified version with a computer fast enough to track high-volume air traffic, a third high-frequency radio, a radio teletypewriter, a radar with full maritime surveillance capability, and an electronic countermeasure–resistant communications system. During this period, Boeing studied seven versions of the

E-3A for NATO and made nine proposals. But neither the U.S. Air Force nor NATO could afford to finance two standalone programs, so a compromise was made to develop a "standard" configuration combining major elements of both. NATO defense ministers in December 1977 authorized initial funding of $1.9 million for three months of predevelopment engineering work, set to begin in April 1978. The British had by then already withdrawn from the NATO program and invested fully in the Nimrod AEW, a decision the NATO Military Committee later endorsed by setting a "mixed force" requirement of 18 NATO and 11 Nimrod AEW aircraft.

The NATO Defense Planning Committee, meeting at the ministerial level in May 1978, reviewed the program and issued a statement of understanding authorizing $5 million to continue AEW predevelopment funding through the end of September, and to obtain by then the consent of all the participating nations. That same month, the E-3A was officially given a new name: Sentry. The United States had two reasons for wanting to downplay the plane's command and control capabilities. One was that over the years, the "C" in AWACS, the control element, had somewhat disappeared, as more and more of that function has been handed over to a ground-based authority through the developments of technology, especially with regards to the EC-121H and the SAGE system. Also, the philosophy of datalinks and the air defense ground environment concept emphasized deterrence, especially considering that these Western European countries had invested heavily in the NADGE radar network and felt uncomfortable with a command center outside national boundaries and control. Proponents thus structured the ground control segment of the program to link the E-3A as an additional data source for NADGE, stressing that the system could counter the low-flying threat.

NATO defense ministers (except those from France and Greece) voted on 5 December 1978 to support a NATO E-3A Cooperative Program estimated at $1.83 billion. Two days later, they signed a multilateral memorandum of understanding calling for 18 standard-model E-3As to be delivered by mid-1985. This included the airborne early warning ground integration segment (AEGIS) upgrade to NADGE that allowed ground radar controllers to monitor targets detected and tracked by AEW aircraft. In addition, facilities consisting of a NATO AEW Force Command headquarters at SHAPE, a main operating base (MOB) in Geilenkirchen, West Germany, and forward airfields in Greece, Italy, Norway, and Turkey, were all approved.

On 8 December 1978, alliance foreign ministers approved the charter for a NATO Airborne Early Warning and Control Program Management Organization composed of a board of directors with members from each participating nation, and the NATO Airborne Early Warning and Control Program Management Agency. The general manager's mandate was an extremely difficult one because he was tasked to manage the largest commonly funded acquisition program ever undertaken by the alliance. He was given "total responsibility" for the entire procurement process and "full contractual authority." Cost-sharing by the 12 participating NATO countries was based on a complex formula that considered such things as gross domestic product (GDP), national economic conditions, prior AWACS research and development investment, and industrial participation. The United States paid about 42 percent ($769 million), West Germany 28 percent ($512 million), Canada 9.5 percent ($174 million), and Italy 7 percent ($128 million). Belgium, Denmark, Greece, Luxembourg, the Netherlands, Norway, Portugal, and Turkey all split most of the remaining 13.5 percent ($247 million). The cost of the 11 Nimrods to be provided by the United Kingdom as a NATO AEW was considered a "contribution in kind" and was estimated at more than $500 million. The aircraft component, including development, training, logistics, and maintenance support, accounted for five-sixths ($1.52 billion) of the program budget, with one E-3A costing about $80 million with spares, and $70 million without. AEGIS was budgeted for $182 million, facilities for $70 million (in addition to $60 million provided by the West German government) and administration another $50 million.

Boeing in February 1979 awarded a $107 million subcontract for NATO E-3A systems integration to Dornier, a West German aerospace company. Dornier set up special laboratories and check-out systems at its Oberpfaffenhofen plant, procured ground service and other equipment, installed and tested avionics manufactured in the United States, Canada, and West Germany as part of an industrial collaboration program, and inspected the aircraft before delivery to MOB Geilenkirchen. In June 1979, Boeing began flight-testing the new APY-2 radar off the Washington State coast in cooperation with the U. S Coast Guard. What made the APY-2 different from the older APY-1 was a maritime mode, which used a very short, compressed pulse to decrease sea clutter for detection of ships and other surface vessels. The radar system also had a digital processor that could compensate for variations in sea clutter and blank out extraneous land returns. Before each flight, the Coast Guard would provide the E-3A crew with the location of all known ships in the test area. By comparing these known target locations with in-flight radar returns, the crew was able to determine how accurate the APY-2s maritime mode was. The modified radar can spot ships and patrol craft under very rough sea conditions, ships that are motionless or moving very slowly, and vessels that are snuggled up close to land masses.

APY-2 radar components and software were installed by Westinghouse in July 1980, and the U.S. Air Force made a preliminary operational effectiveness assessment of the equipment between 15 July and 30 August. The purpose of the assessment was to determine if the E-3A radar modified for maritime use met operational specifications. The study found that it was likely that these aircraft could satisfactorily conduct combined air-maritime operations.

AEW contracts valued at more than $2 billion over five years were signed by Boeing, the U.S. Air Force, and NATO in September 1980. The U.S. Air Force portion of the contract was valued at $255.7 million for production of three AWACS aircraft in fiscal year 1980, long-lead funds and production options for two systems in 1981, and production options for two aircraft each in fiscal years 1982 and 1983. The definitive contract for the NATO systems was valued at $1.4 billion. All major assemblies for the first standard-mode NATO E-3A (serial number 79-0442) were completed and joined at Boeing's Renton facilities in November 1980.

The aircraft was flown to Seattle on 18 December and subsequently fitted with a rotodome and a small amount of associated equipment, such as the bearing, radar, IFF antenna, and antenna drive. Bearing the letters "NATO OTAN" centered on a four-pointed star (OTAN is the acronym for *Organisation du Traité de l'Atlantique Nord*, or NATO in French), the plane was rolled out of its Boeing Field hangar on 27 January 1981 before 200 dignitaries and industrial subcontractor representatives, and about 1,600 Boeing employees. The aircraft, also known as N-1, underwent a series of flight checks at Boeing Field before it was ferried virtually empty to Oberpfaffenhofen on 31 March 1981. Less than 10 months later, the aircraft was formally turned over to NATO on 22 January 1982, "on schedule and within budget." Although N-1 had NATO markings on the fuselage and wings and the number 90442 painted on the tail, it could not be flown to its permanent home before it was registered. But to whom? According to NATO AEW Force Commander Maj. Gen. Leighton R.

Palmerton, "There were those of us who wanted to register the airplanes with NATO, but NATO insisted on national registration."

Since NATO is not a national entity and, therefore, could not legally operate the aircraft with its own insignia, the alliance ironically turned to a country without an Air Force to register its aircraft, the Grand Duchy of Luxembourg. After securing a written guarantee from NATO absolving it "of any financial or legal liability in case of international incidents," Luxembourg on 23 February 1982 agreed to register N-1 and eventually the rest of the NATO AEW fleet. With the registration issue resolved, N-1 (or rather LX-N 90442) was cleared for delivery to Geilenkirchen, where it touched down on 24 February 1982 at precisely 1633 local time.

N-1's arrival in Geilenkirchen represented the achievement of the NATO E-3A Cooperative Program's second major milestone. The first was the activation in January 1980 of NATO AEW Force Command, and its attainment on 17 October 1980 of full NATO headquarters status. West Germany formally handed over the Geilenkirchen air base to NATO on 31 March 1982, which was followed on 28 June 1982 by the official activation of the NATO E-3A Component. NATO then opened a FOB at Konya, Turkey, on October 1983 and a forward operating location in Oerland, Norway, the following month. The eighteenth, and last, NATO E-3A was delivered on 3 May 1985, and two more foreign operating bases, Trapani (Italy) and Preveza (now Aktion, Greece), were activated in January 1986 and April 1987, respectively.

The UK's contribution to NATO AEW is the E-3D, based at RAF Waddington in No. 8th Squadron. Possessing seven aircraft, this unit reached initial operational capability on 1 July 1992 and was declared fully operational on 31 December 1994. At that time NATO's AEW "mixed force" was finally complete. It took more than 16 years to complete the task, but by the end of 1994, NATO had developed a major command, control, and communications capability with its AWACS component. NATO took a calculated risk back in December 1978 when it decided to invest $1.83 billion in a cutting-edge weapons program. It paid off in the long run, despite the fact that NATO and the United Kingdom went their separate ways at first. NATO's decision to procure E-3As instead of Nimrods for its AEW fleet was a wise one, because it saved untold millions of dollars and time. The E-3A was already an outstanding aircraft when Boeing first introduced it more than 20 years ago, and thanks to NATO's investment in modernization programs, it will continue to operate well into the next century. The NATO AWACs were sent to patrol the

skies above the United States as part of the Chapter V contribution following the attacks on the World Trade Center on September 11, 2001.

## Upgrades to NATO AWACS

In late 1986 the major NATO Commanders initiated a study to
upgrade the AWACS aircraft. Published in December 1987, this requirements document became known as the NATO AEW System Improvement
Plan. It divided upgrades to the AWACS aircraft into near-, mid-, and
long-term objectives, with the first portion approved in December 1990.
Budgeted for $1.4 billion, this first modernization program lasted from
1992 to 1999 as all aircraft were retrofitted in block upgrades. This
upgrade, as mentioned earlier, makes the NATO E-3As the most advanced
AWACS aircraft in the world as of the summer of 2001.

What is very interesting about the NATO AEW Force (NAEWF) and their
upgrade program is how the foreign military sale system works. The United
States and Boeing fought hard to export AWACS in the mid-1970s, and the
platform sold to NATO was a bare-bones version of the U.S. Air Force model.
Yet with their upgrades and substantial dollar increases, 20 years after their
original purchase, NATO finally has the aircraft that they originally requested.
The NATO AWACS near-term upgrades consisted of:

- Computer Memory Upgrade
- Anti-Jam UHF Communications
- Link-16
- Color Display Consoles
- Electronic Support Measures
- Radar System Improvement Program (RSIP)

Subsequently, beginning in 1994, a study was conducted for the
mid-term objectives, which was finalized in 1997. Many of the changes
requested in the mid-term upgrade came from experiences learned
while flying more than 10,000 sorties in support of Balkan operations.
Priced at $1 billion, work began in 2000, with the entire fleet complet-
ing the upgrade by January 2002. Also called MAGIC 2000, these
upgrades are reversing the general trend of creating a technology gap
between Europe and the United States. NATO AWACS mid-term
upgrades will include:

- Improved Man-Machine Interface
- Multi-Sensor Integration

- Automated Digital Comm Switching
- Additional Display Consoles (from 9 to 14)
- Wide-Spectrum VHF Radios
- Satellite Communications
- IFF Transponder (Mode S)
- IFF Interrogator
- Navigation System Improvements

NATO is not content with the mid-term modernization program and preliminary plans are underway for a long-term enhancement program. There are a number of current high-priority unfunded items for the NATO AWACS fleet which may be included in their long-term upgrade program. These programs, if funded, would continue the AWACS upgrade through 2010 and enable the NATO fleet to stay interoperable with not only the other E-3 aircraft but the ground C3 sites as well. Potential NATO long-term upgrades include:
- Airborne Collision Avoidance System
- Defensive Countermeasures (IRCM)
- Civil Aviation Requirements (CNS/GATM)
- Potential Re-Engining
- Additional UHF Radios
- Radar Enhancement (Low-Slow Targets)

## NATO Air-Ground Surveillance (AGS) Program

The success of the AWACS program with NATO as well as the awareness of the capabilities of the JSTARS aircraft has led to the requirement for an advanced AGS system. NATO has had a staff requirement for a ground surveillance capability since 1988, and a concept definition study was conducted using a multi-national task group from June 1998 to April 1999. Unrest in the Balkans gave an air of urgency to the NATO requirement and the selection process actually began in October 1999. Possible JOSTARS platforms include:
- Joint Stars (U.S. Air Force)
- Global Hawk (U.S. Air Force)
- ASTOR (Royal Air Force)
- HORIZON (French Army)
- CRESO (Italian Air Force)
- SOSTAR (Belgium)

This will not be a quick decision. The current U. S. offer as of the summer of 2001 emphasizes that selection of the JSTARS over the other platforms will expedite the delivery of an aircraft to NATO. The U.S. Air Force had proposed to actually divert airframes from their fleet starting in December 2000, with a second platform delivered a year later, but that offer was never accepted. The United States would have also included upgrades of the radar and communications suites, cooperative production, and a retrofit of the first two aircraft.

While the United States has lobbied hard for the E-8C as a "fast track" solution to the NATO AGS requirement, the high price tag ($225 million per aircraft) and the large crew complement (21) has led the NATO nations to balk at the U.S. Air Force proposal. In addition, the dated technology of the JSTARS has also led to claims for different platforms. Subsequently, Northrup-Grumman has re-evaluated this proposal and initiated offers to install the radar technology including RTIP on a variety of different platforms such as the Airbus A320 or the Gulfstream V. These changes for the JOSTAR competition could also have implications for the U.S. Air Force JSTARS program. The proposed upgrades to the JSTARS airframe include a high-range resolution MTI and an inverse synthetic aperture radar system to give future JSTARS operators much higher confidence in their tracking capability. However, the costs for a JSTARS aircraft are high. Other options, including business jets such as the British ASTOR demonstrator, give NATO many choices for this large, multiyear defense purchase.

### Spain/Turkey/Greece/Italy

Spain has developed an organic AEW capability in the form of six Sikorsky SH-9 (modified SH-3 AEW) helicopters. Operating off of their aircraft carrier *Principe de Austurias*, these AEW platforms are the primary sea-borne surveillance assets of the *Arma Aerea de la Armada Espanola* with *Escuadrilia* 005. The typical deployment schedule has two aircraft onboard the ship and the third back at Rota, undergoing maintenance. It is expected that these helicopters will be upgraded to the Mk.7 status in the near future.

The Turkish Defense Agency has developed a program to acquire four AEW aircraft, which may result in a huge new contract worth between $900 million and $1.4 billion. The decision has been delayed because of financial difficulties following Turkey's deadly 1999 earthquake, but final offers were delivered on 10 February 2000. A decision was expected in late 2001, with potential competitors including the Boeing 737-700 IGW Multi-Role Electronically Scanned Array (MESA) and Airbus 310 Phalcon systems. Lockheed Martin and Northrup-Grumman have already been eliminated from this lucrative contract. It is unknown at this time if Turkey will continue to attempt to purchase new AEW aircraft, but in the end, the Turkish government may opt for an EMB-145 with the Erieye system. However, the fact that the Hellenic (Greek) Air Force bought the same model may preclude this option. Turkey, however, still is covered under the NATO AWACS umbrella and routinely sends aircrew to fly with NATO.

The Greek Air Force has long been interested in acquiring their own organic AEW fleet even though they belong to NATO and receive use of those AWACS aircraft. In 1998, bids were offered by a number of manufacturers, including Northrup-Grumman, for a sale of four Hawkeye 2000s, but the Swedish Erieye design won out. In July 1999, it was announced that a Brazilian, Swedish, and French team had won a contract to supply the Greek Air Force with four EMB-145 aircraft to be outfitted with the Erieye radar system. This is the same platform recently purchased by the Brazilian Air Force. A regional jetliner, the EMB-145 AEW aircraft will have a crew of five mission specialists onboard, with a possibility of flying relief aircrew as well. The contract is valued at up to $500 million for the installation and delivery of the four AEW systems. A proposal configuration showed five operator consoles, an ESM package, NATO communications interoperability, IFF, and possibly a Link-16 datalink system. The sale of the Erieye to the Hellenic Air Force makes Greece the third major nation to buy this low-cost AEW platform, and it signals another victory for Ericsson Microwave.

As with the French Army, the Italian ground service has also developed an organic battlefield surveillance platform. Mounted on a helicopter, CRESO is an MTI radar that is linked to the Italian surveillance system SORAO. It is capable of detecting targets out to 60 miles. Operational since 1995, CRESO is very comparable to the French HORIZON system, and is under consideration for the NATO JOSTAR competition as well.

# CHAPTER NINE

# AEW Development in the Middle East and Asia

T he Middle East, with its many recent conflicts, has not, surprisingly, seen extensive use of AEW assets by interested parties. Some of the first wartime uses of AEW in the region were conducted during the 1956 Suez Crisis. Britain and France both used carrier-based AEW units (AEW.1s operating off the RN carriers *Eagle* and *Albion* and TBM-3Ws off the French, Navy's carrier *Arromanches*) in this conflict. In addition, the United States used its AEW assets to monitor the 1967 and 1973 wars, but no military aircraft directly participated in combat action.

## Israel

Born out of conflict, Israel is surrounded on all sides by nations that for many years officially denied its very existence. In that environment, it is only natural that this country would develop an early warning method of detecting attacks. Although proven in support of small aerial engagements over Lebanon in 1979 and 1981, it was in 1982 during the air battles over Lebanon's Bekaa Valley that the Hawkeye and Israeli Air Force (IAF) would gain distinction. Beginning on 2 June, several Israeli E-2Cs orbited off the Mediterranean coast monitoring activities as part of the preliminary surveillance for the air campaign of Operation Peace for Galilee. The Hawkeyes were part of an integrated force that included ELINT, jamming, suppression of enemy air defenses (SEAD), attack aircraft, and air superiority fighters; throughout, the E-2Cs used both radar and their passive detection capabilities for surveillance and battle management. Once the initial attacks began on 5 June, the IAF destroyed a number of Syrian radars and SAMs that were stationed in the Bekaa Valley. Although Syrian MiGs rose to challenge the Israeli fighters, heavy Israeli jamming deprived the MiGs of ground-controlled intercept, while the E-2Cs monitored their takeoff frequencies and quickly vectored F-15s and F-16s into ambush positions, often using beam attacks. At its peak, the battle reportedly involved 90 Israeli and 60 Syrian aircraft. Superior training and the excellent use of command and control systems by the IAF resulted in 23 Syrian losses. The debacle for the Syrian Air Force continued for several weeks, so that by the end of July this exchange ratio was 85 to Ø!

What Operation Peace for Galilee demonstrates is the awesome combat multiplier potential of AEW in general and, in this case, electronic warfare in particular. The IAF was able to pinpoint every SAM battery position through the use of dedicated ESM platforms and indiscriminate use of these assets by the Syrians. When the time came to attack the SAM sites, the IAF knew just where to go and what to do, and the Syrians never knew what hit them. Likewise, the proven and judicious use of airborne radar systems in the E-2C and the F-15 was able quickly to overwhelm the limited use of ground control radar systems by the Syrians. This rout by the IAF is still regarded, almost 20 years later, as the supreme example of how a properly used electronic warfare campaign can truly enhance combat operations.

This victory by the *Tsvah Haganah Le Israeli – Heyl Ha'avir* (Israeli Air Force) might not have been possible if the IAF had not heeded the lessons learned from the October and the Yom Kippur Wars. Israel desperately desired an indigenous AEW capability and in 1978 became the first nation outside the United States to acquire four E-2Cs (Group Ø). This new platform of course inspired a desire for a similar capability by Israel's Arab neighbors, and both Saudi Arabia and Egypt quickly acquired AEW aircraft in 1986 and 1987, respectively.

The IAF was not content with just using E-2Cs delivered from Grumman. Over time, they modified these aircraft with organic electronics from Iisraeli Aircraft Industries (IAI) and ELTA as they enhanced the performance of these systems. However, the Hawkeye is still constrained by range, and the IAF desired an aircraft with longer legs and the ability to operate as part of their overall air defense system. Therefore, an effort was begun to field a larger AEW aircraft that could serve as a theater platform. This led to the eventual purchase by the IAF of the Phalcon. Developed by IAI, it features a phased array radar system fitted on a modified Boeing 707. The Phalcon uses an electronically scanned ELTA EL/M-2075 L-band conformal radar consisting of 768 elements, each individually controlled by a transmit/receive module. Phalcon was made public at the 1993 Paris Air Show, and several countries have reportedly expressed interest in the technology, with one modified 707 already delivered to Chile. Conversions on other aircraft have also been made using the Y-8 Cub by the People's Air Force of China, but one drawback for the Phalcon radar is that it does require a large airframe to support the components. This may limit its applications in the medium- or low-cost categories. However, there are many advantages to the phased array technology. These mainly include better ECM protection and faster target refresh rates than a rotating antenna. More discussion on the Phalcon and its exportability will be covered in the section on China.

### Egypt/Saudi Arabia/Iraq/Iran/Kuwait/United Arab Emirates

The *Al Quwwat Al Jawiya Il Misriya* (Egyptian Air Force) acquired four Hawkeyes (Group Ø) in 1986. Many analysts saw this as a response to the overwhelming successful use of the Hawkeye by the IAF in their 1982 Bekaa Valley campaign. Although fear and controversy were rampant in the U. S. Congress over the sale of the four E-2Cs and F-16s to Egypt in 1984, eventually the deal was struck. Operated by their 222 Fighter Regiment, the aircraft are based at the Cairo West Air Base and have been used in numerous interoperability exercises with U.S. military forces.

In 1991, the Egyptian Air Force acquired one E-2C Group II to test for possible future upgrades and follow-on purchases. In late 1999, Northrup-Grumman announced that they were upgrading the rest of the Egyptian E-2Cs to a Hawkeye 2000 status. This $138 million contract involved replacing the APS-138 radars with APS-145, as well as adding the mission computer upgrade and the new workstations. This contract would make the Egyptian Hawkeyes on par with the U.S. Navy fleet and enable them to continue to operate in joint exercises.

Saudi Arabia was the second country in the region to obtain AEW capability. Sales of the E-3 Sentry were begun by the Carter administration and completed by President Reagan in 1982, with the Saudi AWACS deal becoming one of the most controversial in the history of arms sales. Providing E-3s and F-15s to the Saudis was meant to counter possible Soviet or Iranian aggression. However, fears were raised that the sales posed a threat to Israel. The sale was eventually approved and the five E-3As to the Royal Saudi Air Force (RSAF) (Alquwwat Al Jawwiya Al Malakiya As Sa'udiya) were developed as part of the "Peace Sentinel" program with all aircraft delivered between June 1986 and September 1987. Currently operated by the 18th Squadron at Riyadh AFB, these AWACS played an important role during the Gulf War, with one crew responsible for the shootdown of two Iraqi Mirages. These aircraft use the CFM-56 turbofan engines, the same used by the FAF E-3Fs, but they lack the JTIDS capability.

Probably spurred by the poor performance of her air defenses in the early 1980s, Iraq undertook a number of initiatives, among them the conversion of an IL-76 into an AEW configuration sometime prior to 1989. Installing a Thompson-CSF Tiger radar under the tail, this aircraft was called "Baghdad 1" and was reportedly used in the Iran-Iraq War by the Al Quwwat Al Iraqiya (Iraqi Air Force). The radar theoretically has a 180-degree scan and 350-kilometer detection range. A second IL-76 AEW variant, "Adnan 1," was reported to have undergone testing in 1990. Equipped with a more conventional rotodome, Iraq reportedly had three such aircraft at the start of the Gulf War, of which one was later modified into the "Adnan II" using an updated radar. Claims of enhanced performance by the Iraqis have not been substantiated. If nothing else, these aircraft were intended as symbols of Iraqi military might, although the aircraft undoubtedly had far less capability than the popular press indicated. Their effectiveness during the Gulf War was minimal and the only reason that two aircraft survived that conflict is that they fled to Iran.

Therefore, the Iranians (Islamic Republic of Iran Air Force) now possess the Iraqi Adnan system with no apparent intent to return it. While the status of these aircraft is unknown, they may have resparked Iranian interest in AEW as the Iranian Air Force have reportedly ordered two A-50s from Russia. This would not be the first time that Iran has expressed interest in the purchase of large AEW aircraft to project power beyond its borders. Throughout the 1970s, the Imperial Iranian Air Force (IIAF) under the Shah attempted to purchase an AEW aircraft to upgrade its warfighting capability.

Pushed hard by the Department of Defense, the U.S. Air Force, and Boeing toward the E-3 AWACS, eventually politics overruled any decision, with the fall of the Shah in 1979.

What is very interesting, however, are the charges that arose from this potential aircraft sale. With the majority of interest conducted between 1974 and 1977, there was an intense amount of pressure to diversify sales of the E-3 to spread the development costs to other nations. Some of these charges were relatively innocuous, such as inaccurate reporting or comparison of the parameters between the E-2C and E-3A. However, there were also reports of direct interference of the DOD into the competition. According to internal Pentagon documents, E-2Cs were not allowed to be flight-tested or demonstrated to the Shah during his visit to the United States on two occasions in May of 1975. In addition, pricing information requested by the Chief U.S. Military Mission with the Imperial Iranian Army for the E-2C was also denied, thereby forcing the IIAF into accepting offers for only the E-3. While all of these charges were eventually overcome by the aforementioned political constraints, the hard push for an outside sale of the AWACS aircraft was only relieved by the purchase of 18 AWACS by NATO in 1978.

In 1995, TCOM and MidEast LTA Logistics Supplies & Services was formed to support the sale of aerostats to the Middle East. This joint U.S.-Kuwaiti company provides support, services, and supplies to the operational aerostat systems in the region. TCOM has made a similar sale of aerostats to the United Arab Emirates (UAE), allowing this Middle East nation to upgrade its surveillance capabilities. Utilizing the TPS-63 2-D radar installed within an aerostat has given the UAE Air Force a good look-down system into the southern Arabian Gulf. This setup with a TPS-63 and an aerostat is very similar to what the U.S. Air Force is using to counter drug smuggling aircraft along the southern border of the United States. This system is very useful to the UAE Air Force because of its relatively low cost, easy maintainability, and the fact that all personnel are ground-based at the receiver station. A sign of things to come, the use of aerostats may gain much more popularity in the future because of their low cost and versatility.

## AEW Development in Asia

As was the case in the Middle East, the initial use of AEW in Asia was by the United States, in support of its Pacific Fleet and operations during the Vietnam War. Such presence probably promoted the desire of countries in this region to acquire their own AEW capability. While this originally involved purchasing off-the-shelf equipment, principally from the United States, the development of aircraft industries in some countries including India and China, coupled with availability of British, French, and Israeli electronics systems, have led to the fielding of indigenous AEW capability by the region's powers. Therefore, at the present time there is a mix of AEW capabilities spread across the region. Some countries, such as Singapore and Taiwan, have AEW assets while others in the area, such as Indonesia, South Korea, and Thailand, already have assets devoted to sea surveillance, and the addition of an AEW capability to include air surveillance is likely in the near future. However, the largest and most unpredictable player in the region still remains the People's Republic of China.

### Japan/India/Singapore/Taiwan/Korea/China

The Japanese Self Defense Force (JSDF) has always maintained a robust early warning capability with 28 fixed ground radar sites located around the island nation. Obviously recognizing the inherent limitations associated with a ground-based system, they sought very early on to acquire an organic AEW aircraft fleet. Japan acquired 13 E-2Cs (Group Ø) in 1982 and deployed them to Misawa Air Base in northern Honshu during 1987. The *Nihon Koku Jieitai* (Japanese Air Force) and the United States recently signed a $200 million contract to upgrade the aircraft to the Hawkeye 2000 status.

Japan's desire to improve its reaction to the threat posed by Soviet forces deployed in the Far East region prompted the nation to seek a more permanent AEW capability. In December 1992, Japan ordered four E-767 aircraft, and on 11 March 1998 it received the first two AWACS versions of Boeing's 767 aircraft. The third and fourth aircraft were delivered to the JSDF on 29 January 1999. Valued at $840 million, these new AWACS are the most expensive AEW aircraft in the world. Built from modified 767-200ERs, these new AWACS platforms, called the E-767, use the larger platform and newer airframe vice the traditional 707 version. Major differences include a smaller flight deck crew, two engines, and an increase in mission consoles.

India, as has already been discussed, benefitted from the use of a MOSS aircraft during her 1971 war with Pakistan. This led to an indigenous program, Airborne Surveillance Warning and Control (ASWAC),

**E-767 Interior**
Notice the immense difference in interior space between an E-767 and the traditional AWACS platform. The E-767 can fit four operators across (as shown in the pit area) and still have a larger walkway than a normal 707 airframe. This is one reason many analysts believe that the U.S. Air Force should switch to this fuselage for their next AWACS platform, but at $210 million an aircraft, that is a very expensive option. *Boeing*

begun in 1984. Progress was slow on the initial design, reportedly due to a lack of advanced software. The program reached a milestone in November of 1990 when the *Bharatiya Vayu Sena* (Indian Air Force), using an HAL-748 aircraft equipped with a mix of Indian, French, German, British, and Swedish electronics, made its initial test flight. The HAL-748 is a medium-range turboprop transport, originally designed by Hawker Siddeley in 1959.

The original program called for six aircraft. Progress has been slow but steady throughout the 1990s. Without the use of American or Russian technology, Hindustan Aeronautics had attempted to develop an indigenous AEW aircraft, but unfortunately on 11 January 2000 they suffered a tragic setback. On that date, their primary test aircraft crashed near Madras, India, killing all eight aircrew and scientists onboard the AEW platform. This incident dealt a severe blow to the Indian project and it has only recently begun to recover.

If the Indians do now decide to try to field a fixed-wing AEW system, they will probably use a larger aircraft such as an IL-76 Candid to build a system like the A-50 Mainstay. In July 2000, India began talks with IAI about the purchase of two Phalcon AEW systems for $500 million. Coming after the cancellation of the sale of these components to China, the deal also fell into difficulty because of the export of advanced technology. At the time, India was under a series of economic sanctions from the United States after their nuclear tests in 1998. In February 2001, India signed a deal with Russia to buy four Kamov KA-31 AEW helicopters, and in May they increased that order by another five, for a total of nine. Altogether these two sales are worth over $201 million.

The South China Sea has become an increasingly active arena for AEW. Singapore acquired four Group Ø Hawkeyes in 1987 and has been upgrading them ever since. The Republic of Singapore Air Force flies their E-2Cs in the 111th Squadron from their main base at Tengah. Operating in the central South China Sea area, these Hawkeyes are designed to give early warning to Singapore and are tied into their ground-based air defense system. In 1998, Singapore was cleared to begin installing Link-16 systems onto their fighters and Hawkeye aircraft, which has kept these older aircraft compatible with U.S. Navy and Air Force systems.

Taiwan ordered four Group II Hawkeyes from the United States in 1994. These aircraft were delivered in 1995 and were used to augment the Republic of China's Air Force surveillance systems. One of the aircraft suffered major damage in an emergency landing in 1997 and required extensive repairs through 1999. In July 1999, the *Chung-Kuo K'ung Chun* (Chinese Air Force) ordered two more Hawkeyes, this time labeled E-2Ts, with the Hawkeye 2000 capabilities as opposed to their older Group Ø models. The sale, worth $400 million, will help Taiwan maintain its early warning capability.

The Republic of Korea Air Force (South Korea) has been negotiating with both the United States and Israel on the purchase of AEW aircraft since 1996. Funds totaling $416 million were authorized for two aircraft at that time, but to date no decision has been made. The plan is to acquire six to eight aircraft total and platforms under consideration include the Boeing E-767, the C-130 AEW aircraft, the Hawkeye 2000, or a Boeing 747 with the Israeli Phalcon system. In addition, in 1994 the Republic of Korea Air Force was briefed on the possibility of acquiring four JSTARS aircraft, but nothing further came from that proposal.

China's recent assertions of sovereignty over areas such as the disputed Spratley Islands and acquisition of systems such as the long-range Su-27s are likely indicators of an accompanying desire for AEW capability. Though accelerated by current events, the desire for such capabilities is not new. In 1991 the Aviation Museum in Beijing displayed an aircraft designated the AP-1. This was a converted TU-4 (itself a Russian derivative of the B-29) fitted with a rotodome. This pubic display probably indicates a project long abandoned, since rumors at that time concerned an AEW program involving the Shaanxi Y-8 (a license-built AN-12).

Most recently, the Chinese have reportedly concluded two separate agreements to acquire AEW technology. In 1998, at an Asian air show, a model of the Y-8 was displayed with the Skymaster radar. An interim design, this project is a development that uses the RACAL Skymaster radar, a Searchwater derivative that maintains its overwater/maritime capability. A total of six to eight radars worth $66 million have been sold since 1996 by RACAL, which has installed the system in the nose of the aircraft. Although the aviation branch of the People's Liberation Navy (PLAN) claims 360-degree coverage from the radar, with only one operator, the aircraft is supposed to be used to patrol coastal waters. Taiwan, on the other hand, has claimed that these AEW aircraft can conduct long-range targeting of anti-ship missiles. The true mission is still undetermined at this time.

A third possibility that has arisen recently involves the use of the Israeli Phalcon system on the IL-76. This was thought to be questionable, since the Russians may be reluctant to sell the IL-76 in preference to their own A-50. And that, in fact, seems to have been the case. In October 1999, the Beriev aircraft company completed modification of an A-50 to accommodate the Phalcon radar. Flight-testing of the aircraft was conducted and the Israelis were preparing to install the radar components into the airframe. With a requirement of four aircraft and the possibility of a billion dollar sale, *Zhongkuo Shenmin Taifang Tsunputai* signed a contract with ELTA for one aircraft to conduct research and development testing.

But controversy trailed the Israeli plan to sell AEW technology to China. The United States has a unique relationship with China—it's not a strategic threat nor a rogue state nor a moral pariah, yet U.S. policies seem to reflect a belief that it combines elements of all three. Therefore, as the proposed sale of the Phalcon radar system to China progressed, opposition within different U. S. organizations, including Congress, the administration, and American Jewish groups, grew to the point that Israel could not continue with the sale. The White House, Pentagon, and State Department expressed serious reservations over this transfer of new technology and attempted in many different ways to cancel the sale. The Clinton administration looked at this $250 million arms transfer as destabilizing and a threat to Taiwan. The sale was viewed as just the latest in a 10-year struggle to limit and cut the amount of high-tech arms sold to China.

Thus, throughout 1999, Clinton administration officials worked to cancel the delivery of these aircraft. While the pressure may have escaped public scrutiny, the IAF and Israeli officials complained of the heavy-handed tactics. A variety of other defense-related programs have met resistance in Washington, and there was talk of sanctions against Israel if the deal went through. Although both State and Defense Department officials denied an orchestrated campaign, by the summer of 2000 the pressure was so intense that Israel decided to back out of the deal, officially announcing on 12 July that they would not sell the Phalcon technology to China. Since the Chinese government had already paid $240 million for their first installment of the Phalcon system, the Israelis fully expect to have to pay back not only all that money but the rest of the $500 million contract as well. It is expected that the Israeli government will cover the charges, although some observers suggested Washington should contribute as well. This denial of a sale to China by Israel of a sophisticated AEW platform is a good example of how these aircraft increase a country's presence and prestige. As a component of its national strategy, the United States made a long-term concerted effort to deny China access to these advanced radar systems.

## Australia

Australia has unique airspace surveillance problems due to its extremely long coastlines, widely dispersed population centers and military bases, and the lack of a direct, threatening enemy. These and other factors have tended to force the Royal Australian Air Force (RAAF) to look at AEW aircraft that can cover wide areas for long periods of time. This has pushed the options for the service to the larger airframes. However, with a relatively limited budget, the Australians have been very cautious and detailed in their study of AEW platforms. In addition, the Royal Australian Navy has no fleet AEW capability; therefore they were looking for a platform that could provide maritime surveillance, air defense, and strike support as well.

The RAAF considered an AEW aircraft to be a natural fit with its current power projection capabilities using its F-111s, F-18s, P-3Cs, and C-130s. The proposed AEW airframe would also integrate with the Jindalee Over-the-Horizon Radar Network (JORN) to complement this ground-based radar system by adding low-altitude coverage. The RAAF AEW program is called Project Wedgetail or AIR 5077 and is the most expensive aircraft contract to be decided over the next few years for an Asian nation. Investigating different systems since the mid-1980s, the RAAF has even stationed exchange officers at VAW-120 in NAS Norfolk since 1990 in their quest for the best platform. Systems studied include the Nimrod, P-3C AEW, E-3, E-2C, the C-130 AEW version, 767 AWACS, Phalcon AEW aircraft, and aerostats.

In 1996, after 10 years of debate, the Australian Defence Force (ADF) acted to complete Project Wedgetail, the acquisition of an AEW aircraft. The procurement of an organic fleet was considered a key part of its defense policy. The three primary contenders were the Boeing 737-700 aircraft with a FASS multi-scanned array (developed by Northrup-Grumman), an Airbus 310-300 aircraft with the Phalcon radar mounted in a non-rotating dome, and a Lockheed Martin C-130J-30 with the APS-145 radar system. In September 1999, Australia announced that it was purchasing the Boeing 737 airframe with a Grumman radar system. This package for a seven-aircraft fleet was estimated to cost $3.4 billion (U.S. $2.2 billion) and will use a substantial portion of the ADF budget in the future. The purchase of a new AEW aircraft by Australia will go a long way toward adding to that nation's air defense and power projection capability.

Seven aircraft were to have been contracted for by the Royal Australian Air Force. The actual AEW aircraft acquired by the RAAF could be "the" future for this technology. Combining the well-proven airframe Boeing 737, of which over 3,400 are currently in service, with the MESA

**Boeing 737 with MESA Radar**
This is an artist's rendition of the Boeing 737 with the MESA radar flying with Royal Australian Air Force (RAAF) markings. Notice the refueling track above the cockpit windows and the exterior modification where the MESA antenna assembly is bolted onto the fuselage. When these aircraft are delivered, they will bring the RAAF into the twenty-first century as far as AEW systems are concerned. *Boeing*

radar as a state-of-the-art system makes this platform very attractive to the export market as well. Developed by Northrup-Grumman, this 360-degree steerable radar is distinct in its appearance with a top hat–type shape. The MESA radar is a technologically innovative system that uses a unique antenna design. It provides two 120-degree side-looking sectors with its dorsal antenna, and nose/tail coverage via 60-degree sectors from the electronically steered "top-hat" end-fire array mounted on top of the dorsal fin. There are 288 transmit/receive modules in the active-array radar, which will not only power the side-facing arrays but the top-hat end-fire arrays as well. Because the antenna does not rotate, it uses an active, electronically scanned radar technology to provide 360-degree coverage with a 10-second update out to a range of 200 miles. It is this advanced technology that allows the three different arrays to combine to give the total 360-degree coverage. Similar in concept to the FASS system proposed on the Nimrod AEW aircraft 15 years earlier, this technology has improved to the point that this option is now economically feasible.

The reason that the Boeing 737 costs substantially less than a traditional 707 AWACS is the manner in which the "top hat" antenna is attached to the airframe simply using 22 bolts, with no major changes to the 737. A few skin panels, frames, and stringers will have to be modified, but not to the extent of installing a heavy rotodome like on the 707 or 767 AWACS. In addition, with over 3,400 737 aircraft sold around the world, there are plenty of airframes available to modify. Because the RAAF platform is a large aircraft, it could quite easily be put into the large or top-end systems, but because it will have fewer consoles than an AWACS, it may be much closer in capability to the Hawkeye. In fact, since most of the RAAF leadership involved in the future training at Williamtown were exchange officers with the U.S. Navy, the current concept is for the aircrew to work as a single team, not in the surveillance and weapons tracks like the AWACS crews. The Wedgetail platform is proposed to have six consoles with a possible growth capability up to 10 workstations. The intensity of aircraft operations will obviously drive the number of aircrew as will training and total manning for the wing. However, as mentioned earlier, the RAF E-3D suffered in its conduct during the Kosovo campaign, and while more expensive in the acquisition process, usually it's better to have a greater number of consoles available than just those needed for a surveillance mission.

The basing concept for the ADF is to keep the majority of aircraft at Williamtown, with deployments primarily to Tindal, the forward base, but there are also bare bases at Learmonth, Curtin, and Schurger. The home base of Williamtown will host the reactivated No. 2 Squadron as well as the wing headquarters, operational maintenance, logistic and mission support, and the operational and flight simulators. The forward base at Tindal will host a detached headquarters, with operational, logistic, and mission support. It is proposed that two aircraft will be stationed forward semi-permanently at RAAF Tindal to support operations in the Northern Territory. These platforms will rotate back to RAAF Williamtown for depot-level maintenance. In comparison, the bare bases will have no maintenance or logistic support, with only limited ground support or facilities.

Yet there are still a few hurdles for the final agreement on the Wedgetail program. The first is the issue of the releasability of the technology by the United States to Australia. The new generation radar transmit and receive modules in the MESA system will substantially boost performance and thus are subject to review. In fact, as recently as September 1999, the U. S. Defense Threat Reduction Agency was tasking Boeing, Lockheed-Martin, and Raytheon to provide all briefing materials that they had given out in foreign nation sales proposals specific to AEW aircraft. The DOD is investigating Boeing for possibly giving out classified information on low-observable and counter low-observable technology (LO/CLO) to the ADF in their attempt to win the contract. What is also surprising is the huge amount of emphasis on stealth technology by both the RAAF and Boeing, since many observers do not see a big threat from stealth platforms in that geographic region. However, the real reason for the investigation may have been to ensure that Boeing did not pass on any LO/CLO technology to not Australia, but to other nations that are looking at purchasing the 737 AEW aircraft, specifically South Korea and Turkey.

The biggest problem for the procurement of the Boeing 737 AEW aircraft by the ADF, however, is the cost. That reluctance was evident by the Australian Defence Minister's decision on 21 August 2000 to postpone the acquisition process. Totally unexpected by Boeing middle management and RAAF officers, the decision to delay the decision to better assess the "costs" of the program may have serious implications for potential sales of the 737 AEW to other nations, most notably Turkey, who was expected to make a decision soon. The Australian government's decision sent a shock to the ADF, RAAF, and Boeing, and it was only in February 2001 that the eventual outcome of Project Wedgetail became known. At that time the RAAF announced plans to buy four 737 aircraft with the MESA radar system for $300 million. An option for three more aircraft exists as well. Although the Australian procurement cycle did send a ripple through the AEW market, once the decision was made to go ahead, the RAAF seems to be moving along smartly. In June 2001, the DOD requested to sell 16 JTIDS Class-2 terminals to Australia to use not only on the Wedgetail aircraft, but on shore- and sea-based platforms as well. At an estimated cost of $64 million, these advanced communications systems will greatly facilitate future interoperability between the RAAF AEW aircraft and its U.S. Navy and Air Force counterparts.

# CHAPTER TEN

# AEW Use in the Gulf War/ Bosnia/Kosovo

Operation Desert Shield and Desert Storm are recent examples of large-scale warfare conducted by the United States. They are also excellent showcases of the ability of AEW aircraft, in this case the E-2C Hawkeye and E-3 Sentry, to exploit and overcome surveillance deficiencies to effectively conduct a successful operation. Much has been said and written about how technology won this war for the United States, and the proper use of AEW was one of the outstanding factors in that victory. Likewise, the continued use of both of these radar platforms in the operations in former Yugoslavia has proved their worth over and over.

## Sentries in the Storm

Like its EC-121 predecessor, the E-3 excelled during a time of conflict. Operations Desert Shield and Desert Storm demonstrated the inherent strengths of the E-3 as a C3 platform. Coincidentally, Desert Shield began at the same time as a scheduled mobility exercise at Tinker AFB. As E-3 crews reported in for simulated mobility processing, news of the Iraqi invasion of Kuwait added a sense of urgency to the exercise. Several E-3 crews found themselves departing for Riyadh within 48 hours of the invasion. During the following months, the three operational squadrons at Tinker AFB contributed the bulk of their resources to Operation Desert Shield and, subsequently, Desert Storm. Already a veteran of numerous conflicts in southwest Asia, the E-3 was in familiar territory when employed during Desert Storm. Prior knowledge of theater terrain, geography, order of battle, and associated considerations contributed to the need for only minimal local orientation for many AWACS crews. The formation of a dedicated mission planning staff and tactics cell also ensured the success of AWACS operations.

Operation Desert Shield afforded the E-3 community time to resolve operational limitations between U.S. and foreign systems, thereby enhancing coalition employment capabilities. For example, E-3 technicians solved Air Force and Navy radio incompatibility problems, thus facilitating joint communications. Also, RSAF E-3s underwent Have Quick modifications to support interoperability with U.S. Air Force and U.S. Navy aircraft. Operating from Riyadh Air Base, the 552d AWAC Wing (Deployed) provided uninterrupted surveillance of Iraqi airspace and aircraft movements. Air refueling capabilities enabled E-3s to remain aloft for 15 to 17 hours, maximizing surveillance and control. Many E-3 crew members who flew missions during earlier deployments found themselves returning to familiar duty, with imminent hostilities a daily threat. A contingent of 552d AWACW crews and aircraft also operated from Incirlik, Turkey, supporting Operation Proven Force.

From the outset, AWACS involvement in Operation Desert Storm contributed significantly to the success of the coalition air campaign. During Desert Shield, U.S. military aircraft operating near the Iraqi border effectively desensitized the Iraqi Air Force (IQAF) to coalition air operations. The presence of E-3s was not a "new" element when the war began, and the Iraqis were unaware of the impending offensive, since these aircraft appeared to be performing routine operations on 17 January 1991. Functioning as key C3 nodes, U.S. Air Force E-3s flew in three primary orbits along the Iraqi border. During the first and last weeks of the air campaign, a fourth aircraft flew in a "Backstop" orbit, filling in when other E-3s refueled with KC-135s. The "Backstop" E-3 also served as a radio relay between E-3s and the Tactical Air Control Center (TACC) at Riyadh. RSAF E-3s flew sorties in support of the air campaign, with crew members from the 552d AWACW augmenting RSAF crews to provide assistance with language and employment problems.

The presence of AWACS in Desert Storm served to coalesce force employment throughout the air campaign. E-3 weapons controllers provided CAP, strike, refueling, escort, and surveillance control to more than

171

**AWACS 30/35**
Like the Hawkeye, the AWACS is truly a model of adaptability. The modern E-3 is a symbol of intent by the United States. The movement of these aircraft can send a signal worldwide, much as a battleship or aircraft carrier would. These AEW aircraft are a part of our national strategy in more ways than one. *Boeing*

110,000 sorties. Surveillance operators provided high- and low-altitude surveillance of Iraq, Iran, and Kuwait, while maintaining a comprehensive datalink picture of the theater from the Persian Gulf to the Red Sea. Datalinks provided essential information to E-2Cs, E-8s, RC-135s, AEGIS cruisers, CVBGs, Patriot missile batteries, and the TACC in Riyadh. E-3s flew a combined total of 845 sorties during Desert Shield, Desert Storm, and Proven Force, achieving 96.17 percent sortie effectiveness and 100 percent mission effectiveness rates. Total E-3 hours flown were 10,598 with AWACS controllers directly responsible for assisting with 39 of the 41 air-to-air engagements between U. S. and IQAF aircraft. Pilots achieving air-to-air kills generally cite AWACS as the key to providing early threat detection, and overall as a superb builder of their situational awareness.

Operation Desert Storm served as a showcase for the battle management and C3 capabilities of the E-3 system. Deploying E-3s to the southwest Asian theater in August 1990, the 552d AWACW provided immediate surveillance to augment RSAF ground and airborne radar systems, and support the massive influx of coalition air, ground, and naval forces. At the initiation of hostilities, AWACS became a key focal point for the Desert Storm air campaign, providing surveillance and communications for coalition assets throughout the entire theater. Employment of E-3s included integration of airborne command element (ACE) teams to serve as airborne representatives of the Joint Forces Air Component Commander (JFACC). As a result, AWACS could autonomously employ forces on a real-time basis. As many air power enthusiasts have noted, it was the AWACS and their total control of the coalition air effort that led to the overwhelming success of Operation Desert Storm.

**VAW Operations in Desert Shield and Desert Storm**

Carrier-based AEW also played a major role in the U.S. Navy's operations during Operation Desert Shield and Desert Storm. With six carrier battle groups deployed simultaneously at the onset of the ground war, VAW squadrons were efficiently used by naval commanders to influence the outcome of these operations. Over half of the Navy's 15 deployable AEW squadrons saw service in the Middle East during Operations Desert Shield and Desert Storm, with six squadrons actually engaged in combat operations that began at 0238 Gulf time, 17 January 1991. Additionally, several other E-2C Hawkeye squadrons were prepared to deploy if needed, and the fleet replacement squadrons, VAW-110/120, supplied maintenance personnel as well as parts to support the war.

The 34 aircraft that served in the Gulf were a mix of relatively new Hawkeyes and those that had flown with the fleet since the early 1970s. The West Coast squadrons were beginning a transition to Group I aircraft (APS-139 radar) and a few of these newer systems saw action in the immediate aftermath of the war. During the Gulf War, E-2Cs regularly monitored traffic throughout Iraq and adjacent regions and frequently functioned in support of U.S. Air Force E-3B/C AWACS detachments.

Despite the demanding operational environment, night operations, weather conditions, and ever-present hostile air threats, no VAW aircraft or aircrew were lost during the eight squadron deployments.

Early Desert Shield experiences shattered the myth that the Hawkeye was a purely defensive air wing component. The decision to enforce the Iraqi embargo would have been far more difficult, perhaps impossible, had it not been for the reliability of mobile, carrier-based early warning and C3 capability available simultaneously from as many as six flight decks. It quickly became apparent that in addition to its principal function of force defense, a major Hawkeye contribution was to be its effectiveness in over-the-beach strikes by sea-based squadrons. In fact, the preponderance of E-2C Desert Shield/Desert Storm missions proved to be offensive rather than defensive.

The Black Eagles of VAW-113 were on station in the Indian Ocean when Iraq invaded Kuwait on 2 August 1990. Operating onboard the USS *Independence* (CV-62), they moved at best speed to take station in the northern Arabian Sea. Within five days, the battle group arrived on station and began flight operations. Later sorties into the Gulf of Oman and the Persian Gulf in October and November 1990 were especially critical as a safeguard against possible Iraqi air attacks upon vulnerable logistic ships that were arriving in increasingly large numbers at Bahrain, Oman, the United Arab Emirates, and Saudi Arabia.

Operating in the eastern Mediterranean, the USS *Dwight D. Eisenhower* (CVN-69) was completing a routine Sixth Fleet deployment when Kuwait was invaded. Alerted at the onset of fighting, VAW-121 flew its four aircraft in continuous surveillance and C3 missions while *Eisenhower* transited the Suez Canal on 8 August 1990, en route to the Red Sea. At the time, VAW-121 was the only AEW squadron deployed in the Red Sea, and it assumed responsibility for monitoring the entire western side of Saudi Arabia.

With the arrival of the USS *Saratoga* (CV-60) in late August, the *Eisenhower* Battle Group completed its Red Sea deployment, passing through to the Mediterranean and arriving back in the United States on 12 September 1990. As with VAW-113, the Bluetails had logged an unusually high number of flight hours during the buildup for what was to become Desert Shield. VAW-121 was also the first VAW squadron to be directly involved in maritime interdiction during the prewar embargo against Iraq.

Sea-based air surveillance was essential, and the E-2Cs were soon supporting U.S. Air Force E-3 AWACS missions flown by the 552d AWACS Wing (Deployed) from Riyadh, Saudi Arabia. The presence of the reliable Hawkeyes permitted the Air Force crews to concentrate their efforts on Iraqi air activity inland. By assuming the critical and complex shipping surveillance role from the Air Force, the Hawkeyes contributed significantly to the success of the AWACS mission and ensured the safety of naval and merchant shipping in the region.

The foray of the *Independence* Battle Group through the Straits of Hormuz on 2 October 1990 created considerable apprehension in the Pentagon and at Pacific Fleet headquarters over the safety of the group. Of particular concern during this "trial deployment" was the vulnerability of the battle group to Iranian and other Silkworm cruise missile sites positioned within range of essential shipping channels. This concern placed intense pressure on VAW-113 for full, accurate C3 and early warning services while the battle group operated in the narrow confines of the Gulf. One of the first priorities VAW-113 had upon its arrival in the Gulf of Oman was to establish link communications between the CVBG and a mobile operations center (MOC) set up in the UAE. From the outset of hostilities, it was critical to the UAE to be able to "see" what was happening in the Gulf as well as to the north and the east. In early August there was much concern over the outcome of the war had Saddam Hussein elected to continue south into Saudi Arabia. The ability of the E-2Cs to fly into the Gulf and supply this critical picture to the UAE brought calm to a tense situation. It allowed our allies in the region to see for themselves what the situation was, in real-time terms.

By October 1990, VAW-115 was in the Indian Ocean aboard the USS *Midway* (CV-41). Air Wing Five had hurriedly completed its work-ups, loadouts, and last-minute training before deploying to Yokosuka, Japan, a few weeks earlier. By November, the *Midway* had relieved the *Independence*, and thereafter the Liberty Bells (VAW-115) flew continuous, around-the-clock airborne patrols with special attention given to Iraqi and Iranian aircraft. The expansion of operations in the Gulf, together with the refinement of coordination and tactics with the *Midway*, produced more efficient battle management. VAW-115 operated from November to early January 1991 in the Arabian Sea and Gulf of Oman to monitor surface and air traffic as well as to train with *Midway*'s air wing. Until the arrival of the USS *Ranger* (CV-61) in early December 1990, VAW-115 was the source of the area's only sea-based, all-weather surveillance capability in the Gulf of Oman and the north Arabian Sea.

Reacting to an obvious gap in AWACS coverage in the northern Arabian Gulf, the Commander U.S. Naval Forces Central Command (CUSNC) requested a detachment of E-2Cs to be based at Bahrain to supplement the area maritime AEW coverage. To meet this new requirement, the VAW-123 Screwtops and the VAW-124 Bear Aces each provided aircraft, aircrew, and maintenance personnel to the CVW-8 Detachment Bahrain. The detachment, adopting the name "ScrewBears," filled in for U.S. Air Force AWACS E-3s during their refueling cycles. The two-aircraft detachment began operations 15 December 1990 and flew up to three sorties daily until 19 January 1991, when carrier-based VAW aircraft began to operate continuously in the north Arabian Gulf. In a Herculean effort, the Detachment racked up over 395 flight hours under challenging field conditions.

The *Saratoga* and the *John F. Kennedy* Battle Groups cleared east coast ports in early August 1990. Transiting the Mediterranean in late August, these two CVBGs were to operate in the Red Sea and eastern Mediterranean throughout their deployments. The alternating Red Sea and Mediterranean on-station periods from August to January were especially demanding for the *Saratoga*'s VAW-125 and *Kennedy*'s VAW-126. On station between the Gulf of Aquaba and south to Djibouti, these two squadrons were responsible for more than 1,500 miles of the Red Sea and the protection of the massive sealift that by now poured shiploads of military supplies into Saudi Arabian ports. Additionally, the VAW squadrons covered the sea lanes and denied Iraq critical raw and manufactured materials, food, and other supplies via the Gulf of Aquaba. The various Red Sea AEW squadrons monitored seaborne traffic continually within this region. Owing to the presence of these battle groups, no ships were seriously threatened during the Gulf War.

During Operation Desert Shield, massive numbers of ships and aircraft were arriving daily in the potential war zone. Adding to the difficulties was the fact that many wing, squadron, and unit commanders were new and operating in a strange environment, and as many as 30 or 40 different models of modern, high-performance combat aircraft were continuously airborne. Keeping the confusing air picture sorted out was a challenge for the hardworking Hawkeyes. Alerts were frequent and continuous as Hawkeye aircrew received their toughest challenge to date.

The USS *Ranger* (CV-59), departed San Diego on 8 December 1990 to arrive in the Gulf of Oman on 13 January 1991, loaded and ready for combat. *Ranger* entered the Straits of Hormuz the next day, the third CVBG in Desert Shield operations to do so. Her stay was not a quick, nervous "overnighter," but one of considerable length and importance. She was to remain in the Arabian Gulf until 19 April, for a record-breaking 93 consecutive days until relieved by the USS *Nimitz* (CVN-68). As one of the first Coalition carriers to launch offensive strikes into Iraq during the predawn hours of 17 January 1991, Air Wing Two on the *Ranger* flew throughout the war, mostly at night. Following the cessation of hostilities on 27 February, the air wing continued operations over Iraq well into March to enforce the cease-fire agreement. The Sun Kings of VAW-116 flew weeks of intensive training, including war-at-sea operations, overland strike monitoring, SAR coordination, and over-the-horizon targeting. These training flights brought the Sun Kings and the *Ranger* to their highest state of combat readiness since the squadron's establishment on 20 April 1967.

The stakes were high considering the battle group's vulnerability to shore-based cruise missiles. In addition, the reduced sea room available for carrier operations and the looming Iraqi mine threat were all considerations in the use of a carrier in the Arabian Gulf. As Comdr. Paul Hauser, Commanding Officer VAW-116, stated after the conflict: "We had concerns initially about the E-2C's ability to remain mission-capable under severe, extended deployment conditions. The intensive, high-tempo operations, multiplied over six carrier battle groups, was bound to strain the heretofore excellent maintenance and parts pipeline which had been established over the years. However, following an unprecedented 93 days of continuous Arabian Gulf operations, the lion's share of which were at night, we demonstrated that the E-2C could successfully meet its battle group commitments."

Also involved in Arabian Gulf Operations were two CVBGs from the Atlantic fleet. The USS *Theodore Roosevelt* (CVN-71), the USS *America* (CV-66), and their battle groups departed on 28 December 1990 from the East Coast ports. After passing Gibraltar, they transited the central Mediterranean to the Suez Canal before taking temporary station in the Red Sea on 15 January 1991. VAW-123 and VAW-124 were the fifth and sixth E-2C squadrons to reach assigned positions on the eve of the air offensive. With their arrival, the Navy was prepared to attack Iraq from three sides: the Mediterranean, the Red Sea, and the Arabian Gulf.

VAW-123 supported combat strikes against a variety of Iraqi military and industrial targets in southwestern and central Iraq. The majority of its missions, beginning on 19 January, were flown over western Iraq and the Saudi border region. After two weeks of intensive combat, the *America* steamed from the Red Sea, passed through the Gulf of Aden, and on 15 February 1991 entered the Straits of Hormuz. Once in position, Air Wing One resumed combat air operations from its position deep within the Arabian Gulf, with the Screwtops supporting CVW-1's A-6E Intruders, FA-18C Hornets, and F-14A Tomcats. The Screwtops continued combat operations from the Arabian Gulf until the 27 February cease-fire.

VAW-124 onboard the *Theodore Roosevelt* monitored Red Sea air and surface traffic while its battle group raced southward, departing the Red Sea at Bab el Mandeb on 19 January and entering the Straits of Hormuz on 25 January. CVW-8 conducted combat operations from the Persian Gulf until the cease-fire. Along with the *Midway* and the *Ranger*, the four battle groups in the Arabian Gulf represented the heaviest concentration of deployed, carrier-based air power since World War II.

Diversity in Hawkeye missions was common in the Gulf War. Some E-2C sorties supported U.S. Air Force and allied strikes against Iraq and aided in maintaining the airborne radar net over the region. E-2Cs regularly worked with Tomcats and Hornets to protect strike elements and tankers that were operating at times hundreds of miles inside Iraq as well as assisting High-Speed Anti-Radiation Missile (HARM)–equipped EA-6B Prowlers in neutralizing enemy radar and missile sites, because SEAD was an ongoing requirement. Hawkeyes also vectored strike formations to tankers orbiting at various points, often well within Iraq. The E-2C's radar was also particularly adept at countering the "low-slow flyer" threat frequently confronting battle group commanders. Routine, daily commercial helicopter traffic from the beach to offshore oil platforms in the Arabian Gulf was a chronic concern. Equally troublesome was the practice of news reporters attempting unauthorized flights in leased helicopters and light fixed-wing aircraft over and near the battle groups. Another area in which the Hawkeye excelled was in identifying large formations of friendly aircraft returning southward from raids against Iraqi targets. Compounding the problem were the numbers of similar aircraft (Iranian F-14s, P-3s, and Omani F-1s) operated by friendly, hostile, and neutral forces.

The Hawkeye's C3 capability was also especially useful in support of F-14 Tomcat Tactical Airborne Reconnaissance Pod System (TARPS) pre-strike and bomb damage assessment (BDA) missions, where the threat from hostile fighters and SAM batteries is always high. E-2Cs also vec-tored bomb-carrying Navy S-3Bs to assigned targets where, for the first time in combat, the Vikings delivered Mk-82 general-purpose bombs. Several other successes stand out. When VAW-125 returned to NAS Norfolk on 27 May 1991, their lead Hawkeye, Tigertail 600, carried two MiG-21 Fitter silhouettes on its nose, clear evidence of the aircraft's suc-cess in its primary mission in the Gulf War. That particular strike consisted of a self-contained/self-protected Navy strike package from a CVW-17 that embarked from the USS *Saratoga* (CV-60), and targeted the H3 airfield in western Iraq on 17 January 1991, the first day of the war. When MiG air-craft launched from H3, two VAW NFOs (Lt. Jim Durfer and Lt. John Joyce) controlled the FA-18s to intercept and destroy the Iraqi aircraft. Tigertail 600's early identification of enemy fighters over Iraq prompted the diversion of an FA-18 strike section from VFA-83, already briefed, loaded, and airborne for a bombing attack, to shoot down the two MiG-21s. After this brief engagement, the Hornets resumed their planned bombing missions against Iraqi targets.

The Gulf War was a tremendous proving ground for both the E-3 Sentry and the E-2C Hawkeye. Operating in a hostile environment, the aircrew and aircraft met all of the expectations that were placed on them. The battle management and C3 capabilities that these AEW aircraft pro-vided to not only the battle staffs but also to the many strike elements allowed, in the span of a few short, violent months, the crews of the AWACS and VAW community to prove conclusively the ability of these air-craft to operate as command and control platforms, an ability that had been sought for the past 50 years.

## Royal Navy—Sea Kings in Action

The invasion of Kuwait by Iraq in the late summer of 1990 found Britain with the best capability to provide its forces with AEW assets in its history. At that time the Royal Navy had a total of 10 AEW Sea King platforms as well as the newly acquired Boeing E-3D AWACS aircraft that were coming on line. Once again, however, the Royal Air Force and Royal Navy found themselves under the radar umbrella provided by the U. S. forces whilst their capability remained on alert in Europe. Thus, the

British contingent deployed without their hard-won AEW capability, but were able to operate with U. S. support throughout the conflict. These forces have continued to serve in Operation Southern Watch and in the northern no-fly zones without support from their own AEW assets. The assets are nevertheless available should Britain find itself in need of an autonomous AEW capability in a future conflict whereby support from the United States is considered improbable.

## Bosnia

The use of AEW aircraft in coalition operations over Bosnia and the former Republic of Yugoslavia is just the latest chapter in the history of the program. NATO AWACS first began to evolve from a strategic defense asset to a more tactical role in Operation Desert Storm. Flying from their Forward Operating Bases in Greece and Turkey during the period from 7 August 1990 to 16 March 1991, NATO AWACS aircrews flew 740 sorties for more than 7,000 hours in Operation Anchor Guard. Acting mainly as a deterrent against any Iraqi aggression toward Turkey, this "out-of-area" mission helped the program begin its evolution toward a peacetime support focus.

A year later, on 16 July 1992, NATO began what has been a near continuous flying patrol in support of the Bosnia contingencies. Starting with Operation Maritime Monitor and then evolving to Sky Monitor, Deny Flight, Deliberate Force, Decisive Endeavor, and Deliberate Guard, the NATO AWACS logged hundreds of thousands of hours tracking coalition aircraft and watching for flight violations. The crews of the NATO AWACS are the most experienced AEW operators in the world today. Together with U.S. Navy E-2Cs and French Air Force E-3Fs, they have provided a constant aerial surveillance picture to allied forces.

The main mission throughout these operations of the NATO AWACS has been to enforce the no-fly zone and protect the United Nations relief flights. In addition, the E-3As also attempted to prevent Serbian aircraft from flying ground attack missions. The two primary stations used for orbits were over Hungary and the Adriatic. From these vantage points they could observe all of the low-flying aircraft in the former Republic of Yugoslavia.

The operations in Bosnia have changed the mission of the NATO AWACS. Although some evolution had begun as early as the Rome Summit in 1991, it was the development of a new NATO strategy in 1994 and new force structures that are making the biggest difference. Yet these aircraft are also experiencing growing pains as they transition from a Cold War role to one of a multi-faceted command and control platform. The emphasis on flexibility, mobility, and multinational forces is tailor-made for the NATO AWACS, and as they receive all of their planned upgrades, they can be expected to be called on to operate in this manner and play a more major role in all future NATO operational commitments. The latest such mission has been Kosovo.

## Kosovo

If there has been any one mission or one operation that has truly defined the overall utility of the NATO AWACS fleet, the air operations over Kosovo were it. During Operation Allied Force, which lasted from 24 March to 9 June 1999, the alliance AEW fleet was stretched to the limit as they flew around the clock for that entire period. Utilizing 14 aircraft full-time, the force flew 656 sorties and over 4,500 hours in support of coalition operations.

The NATO AWACS fleet conducted the lion's share of the missions, typically flying eight sorties per day, covering three stations. In addition, more aircraft were needed to cover alert periods. Yet there were shortages in the air, and they weren't necessarily reflective of the number of aircraft, but more often were related to the number of controllers on the coalition aircraft. The NATO E-3As and RAF E-3Ds only have nine consoles onboard, so they could only have two controllers airborne at any one time in an aircraft. The typical U.S. Air Force AWACS has 14 consoles with five consoles for use by controllers. This can be expanded to eight controllers' consoles if needed. One has to wonder if cutbacks in the original pur-chase agreement of NATO AWACS two decades earlier came back to haunt the platform in this operation, especially during this conflict.

# CHAPTER ELEVEN

# Future AEW Markets

All of the nations and organizations discussed so far have either solicited proposals, written requirements, or conducted feasibility studies into the acquisition of AEW systems. Whether they actually acquire them depends on the economy and politics, but as of the summer of 2001, this chapter represents most if not all of the potential sales of AEW aircraft and components over the next five years.

An old idea that still continues to provoke interest within the U.S. Navy and other services involves the use of airships or aerostats as AEW platforms. From initial experiments involving the ZPG-2W and ZPG-3W in the 1950s, there was nearly a 30-year gap until 1987, when a new program was awarded to Westinghouse for airship development. However, this contract was never received due to lack of funding. Instead, Westinghouse built a demonstration model, entitled "Sentinel 1000," which first flew in June 1991. Logging 300 test hours in 80 flights, the Sentinel 1000 is a forerunner of a much larger airship proposal by Westinghouse.

In 1996, an aerostat was used in the Roving Sands exercise to detect contacts out to 200 miles. This aerostat passed information to Patriot batteries as well as command/control sites, and it proved to be a good source of long-range radar data. TCOM has developed aerostats that can be sea-based, as well as a transportable, land-based system that has operated north of the Arctic Circle as well as continuously for 30 days at altitudes up to 20,000 feet. These platforms can send their information via fiber optics or microwave links to rapidly transmit critical data to command units. Aerostats and towed array radar systems are the future of AEW, especially for the low-end market. This is mainly because these platforms are so versatile. Overall, over the past decade, the use of aerostats for not only counter-narcotics operations but AEW operations has increased dramatically.

An issue that will also need to be addressed in the future involves the use of a common datalink within U. S. military platforms. Right now the common ground station used by JSTARS and U-2 aircraft is not interoperable with any of the tactical datalinks used by other AEW aircraft. Likewise, some non-U. S. AWACS aircraft are still not Class 2 Link-16 capable and must use Link-11 to integrate with U.S. Navy aircraft and ships. The U.S. Air Force under the Aerospace C2&ISR Center is investigating a fully integrated common data environment that can basically provide a common datalink for all to use.

When originally developed, AEW aircraft were solely thought to be surveillance platforms. In fact, to this day, the most important selling points for these aircraft are their time on-station and the number of aircraft needed to cover a geographical area for 24 hours a day, seven days a week. Yet, as these platforms become more common, nations and operators are beginning to realize that their true value lies in the airborne battle management role. If you want a surveillance asset, an aerostat will work. But if you want an aircrew to analyze the situation, make decisions, and communicate to ground and airborne personnel in real-time, then you need an AEW aircraft. That is precisely the reason why, in an era of downsizing and austere budgets, these expensive aircraft are being sold around the world. It is because they can perform, and they have proven that very well in combat over the past 50 years.

In addition, AEW platforms are expanding the missions they currently perform. The air-ground surveillance operations conducted by JSTARS, the counter-narcotics missions performed by the U. S. Customs Service, and the helicopter support and control experimented with by the U. S. Marine Corps are all examples of "new" missions that have involved AEW aircraft. Because these systems are so versatile, more and more they are being called on to conduct all different kinds of tasking that their designers never planned for in their development. But as with many military airframes, the AEW platforms seem to be adapting to this new environment, thus making them even more desirous by other nations.

There are a number of countries that are currently actively involved in the purchase of AEW aircraft. The most commonly listed nations include Australia, Brazil, Chile, China, Mexico, South Korea, and Turkey. These countries have all entertained proposals from the AEW manufacturers about specific airframes and systems, and as mentioned elsewhere, some have delayed their acquisition process at this time because of financial constraints. However, that could change rather quickly, and if so, the sale of AEW platforms to these nations may occur very soon.

The following section deals in detail with the current upgrade or AEW acquisition programs around the world. As you can see, there is a great deal of activity at the current time, and this is projected to continue through at least the next five years. So while the world seeks to acquire AEW aircraft and systems, the different military services of the United States have also been developing new upgrades to their current platforms—specifically the E-2C Hawkeye and the E-3 Sentry. The next several paragraphs will examine modifications to these aircraft as well as proposals for other systems.

### Future Hawkeye Upgrades

The U.S. Navy is continuing to invest money into AEW systems more than 50 years after it began to develop this kind of aircraft. In fact in 2001, the E-2C is one of only two types of carrier-based aircraft currently being purchased by the U.S. Navy. The plan has been to upgrade all VAW squadrons to the Group II (APS-145) standard by the end of 2000, with more improvements in store for the venerable E-2C. Named the Hawkeye 2000, this is an umbrella term that encompasses the latest version of this aircraft. With fleet testing begun in 1999, variants of this new Hawkeye could continue to serve in the U.S. Navy until at least 2020. As of October 2001, the Hawkeye 2000 has completed flight testing, and 21 production models were under contract to be built.

The fact that the E-2C Hawkeye is in such a strong position within the U.S. Navy is in no small part due to a recognized need for its continued capability, as well as long-range planning by the VAW community. This is evidenced by the 1997 multi-year buy of 36 new E-2C aircraft for over $1 billion. This purchase was unique in that the particular model that was actually bought will change over time. Since the actual production of these aircraft started in 1999, the initial 15 models built were Group IIs. Starting in fiscal year 2001, the production line will shift to building the Hawkeye 2000. In fact, the last Group II was delivered to the Navy on 25 January 2001. The Navy is expected to save $375 million alone from this multi-year buy. Thus, the final 21 aircraft of the multi-year buy should all be built to the Hawkeye 2000 standard between fiscal year 2001 and fiscal year 2006, with the first production aircraft due for delivery in October 2001. At that time, Northrup-Grumman is hoping not only to upgrade the 45 remaining E-2C Group IIs to the Hawkeye 2000 model, but also to begin production for another 15 to 20 new Hawkeye 2005 aircraft to supplement the fleet.

The Hawkeye is evolving to meet a number of changes driven by the tactical environment, including a push toward more littoral operations vice blue-water missions, theater ballistic missile defense, network-centric warfare, and land target surveillance and targeting. The U.S. Navy is working on adapting the Hawkeye into an air-to-ground surveillance system. With these changes has also come increased funding. The Office of the Secretary of Defense's 1999 report proposed that the entire Hawkeye fleet of 75 aircraft be updated and eventually replaced for $2.4 billion. The planned HE2000 upgrades include:

- Navigation Upgrade (NU)
- Changes in Flight Controls
- Mission Computer Upgrade (MCU)
- New CIC Displays (ACIS)
- Upgraded Vapor Cycle (VC)
- SATCOM
- Cooperative Engagement Capability (CEC)

The first and key upgrade to the Hawkeye 2000 will be the Cooperative Engagement Capability (CEC). This system will extend sensor detection of the carrier battle group. It links together the different radar systems and correlates their data to provide a more precise picture of the environment. In fiscal year 1999, 51 flight missions were conducted to test CEC. Operations during calendar year 2000 involving both the E-2C and land- and ship-based sites demonstrated the viability of these concepts. VAW-117 will be the first squadron outfitted with the CEC system to further test the system, which will undergo its final Operational Test and Evaluation in 2003. This program has taken more time than originally planned because the Hawkeye 2000 is upgrading multiple systems concurrently. Flight tests for the CEC have been delayed due to software integration of multiple new systems, including the new computer, scopes, and cooling system. Current planning is for CEC-equipped E-2Cs to begin operating in the fleet by fiscal year 2004.

The Radar Modernization Program (RMP) is similar to the RSIP and RTIP upgrades proposed for the AWACS and JSTARS. Specific proposals include:

- Two-generation leap in radar detection over land and in clutter
- Two-generation leap in radar performance against casual and intentional EMI
- Look-back and dwell for special interest targets and zones (120-degree sector)
- Order of magnitude increase in accuracy
- Advanced tracking techniques
- Numerous NCID techniques
- Overland height finding

This two-generation leap means a 20-decibel performance enhancement in just about every important radar parameter. But that performance does not come cheap. The RMP is very expensive, and there is no guarantee that this program will be approved. However, that has not stopped testing of the RMP technology. The first of these tests were conducted in 1997 and 1999 using the mountain-top antenna in Hawaii, with aircraft demonstrations scheduled for a C-130 platform in fiscal year 2002 and fiscal year 2004. Initial Operation Capability (IOC) for RMP technology into the Hawkeye airframe is planned for fiscal year 2008. In addition to the radar component improvements, the U.S. Navy is also upgrading the antenna to the Hawkeye 2000. Called the ADS-18S, this antenna will host the RMP and is also called the UHF Electronically Steerable Array (UESA). Although the antenna will still rotate, it also has the ability to stop and focus on a high-interest track if needed. The first prototype array was tested in 1998 at the Hawaii mountain-top facility, with more tests scheduled for fiscal year 2001. A C-130 airframe will be used to conduct airborne tests in fiscal year 2002–2004 with IOC scheduled concurrently with the RMP in fiscal year 2008. In fact, this is the same C-130 that was formerly used by the USCG as an AEW platform.

As mentioned earlier, the U.S. Navy is trying to improve not only the radar system of the Hawkeye but also its components. The multisource integration effort by Northrup-Grumman uses the seven different input components of the E-2C (radar, IFF, PDS, CEC, L-4, L-11, and L-16) to build a database that helps the system identify contacts. A huge effort by the U.S. Navy, the road map for this program started with lab demonstrations in fiscal year 2000 with the Hawkeye 2000, with aircraft integration to occur in fiscal year 2002. This will be followed by a lab demonstration in fiscal year 2004 for the Hawkeye 2005 and flight integration in fiscal year 2006 using the C-130 test bed. This road map calls for the identification process to eventually use inputs from the Hawkeye 2005 to include the RMP radar improvements, PDS, infrared search tracker, non-coherent tracking radar, the advanced tracker, combat identification, SATCOM, L-16, and CEC. The eventual result of all this effort will hopefully provide the war fighter with the information needed in a timely manner.

To counter the theater ballistic missile threat, the E-2C is being upgraded with an infrared search and track system. Because the carrier battle group is often located closer to the threat nations than perhaps a CONUS-based system, the Hawkeye may be the first system to detect a missile launch. Therefore, the concept is to detect the missile in its boost phase, thereby giving Navy AEGIS cruisers targeting data in time. The IRST designed for the E-2C has already been installed in a prototype on the Hawkeye using a dual-band, single target tracker that could predict launch and splash locations. The planned upgrade will be able to track multiple targets with a wide/narrow field of view and longer range, and should be introduced to the E-2C in fiscal year 2003.

There is also a plan to upgrade the Hawkeye to track slow and non-moving ground targets. The Precision Surveillance and Targeting (PS&T) system is an enhancement to add a JSTARS-like capability to the venerable E-2C. A new multi-mode radar system would be added to the airframe with an antenna array attached to the side of the aircraft. If funded and approved, the PS&T system would add incredible flexibility with its capability to land on short airfields or, of course, aircraft carriers. The PS&T data would eventually use the future common datalink proposed for the U.S. military.

The Navy is not, however, content with its modernization plan for the E-2C with the Hawkeye 2000. Because the Navy has downsized the number of different types of aircraft on the aircraft carrier, follow-on variants to the E-2C have been proposed to conduct different missions. These CVW support aircraft (ES-3, S-3B, EA-6B, and C-2A) will eventually need a platform, and variants of the Hawkeye 2000 may be the answer. Therefore, the Navy is planning on building the Hawkeye 2005 and 2010 as follow-on models with the emerging technology as noted earlier. One possible lucrative market for AEW sales will be if the Hawkeye 2010 evolves into a common support aircraft; if that happens, then obviously 75 aircraft currently in the inventory will not be enough to conduct all of these missions. Proposals have been forwarded to host 6 to 8 aircraft per carrier, with eventually a total fleet of 112 to 150 platforms. The final proposed evolution for the E-2C is the Hawkeye 2010. The system would include all of the aforementioned system upgrades and would be the primary surveillance system for the U.S. Navy until 2040. As the testing of these parallel research developments is completed, it is proposed that the force in the future eventually will transition to an all–Hawkeye 2010 configuration. Proposed HE2005 and HE2010 upgrades include:

- Radar Modernization Program (RMP)—Littoral/P3I
- Tactical Cockpit
- Multi-Sensor Integration (MSI)
- ESM Upgrades
- Precision Surveillance and Targeting (PS&T)
- Infrared Search and Track (IRST)

Although it would seem that for the long-range future the U.S. Navy is locked into the E-2C Hawkeye airframe, that hasn't stopped aircraft manufacturers from submitting other proposals for medium-size AEW platforms. Prior to 1992, before there was concrete agreement with the U.S. Navy on the Hawkeye 2000, Lockheed Corporation made a number of unique designs all based on the S-3 Viking as a possible new AEW aircraft. These included a triangular dome, large billboard antennas hung from wing pylons, and phased array antennas embedded into the aerodynamic surfaces of the aircraft itself. None of these designs was accepted, but that hasn't stopped other ideas from being proposed as well. In July 2000, Northrup-Grumman suggested an AEW version of the Fairchild 728 Jet A regional aircraft. This new platform would give longer range and more onboard space than the Hawkeye, which is a major selling point for any new AEW aircraft. This type of platform could possibly give Northrup-Grumman a portion of the market that Ericsson has captured with its Erieye. As you can see from the proceeding discussions on the Hawkeye 2000 upgrades, there are numerous separate programs that are all proceeding in parallel to bring tremendous improvements to the E-

2C over the next eight years. Whether all of these changes actually occur on time, only time and budget will tell, but it shows how important the E-2C and the Hawkeye are to the U.S. Navy.

## Future AWACS Upgrades

The future of a successor to the U.S. Air Force AWACS fleet is very unclear at this time. With RSIP upgrades underway and a proposal for a series of computer and display upgrades incorporated into the 40/45 proposals, the 707 airframe is planned to last at least until 2025, perhaps as late as 2035. That's a long time, up to 58 years, for some of these very heavily used airframes to continue in service. One of the problems the Air Force is grappling with is which airframe is going to be their workhorse of the twenty-first century. Although the Boeing 707 is a wonderful aircraft, it was essentially designed in the early 1950s, and a new platform using modern technology is needed. The Air Force has commissioned the RAND Corporation to complete a study for a Common Replacement Aircraft (CRA). Whatever platform is eventually selected will serve a variety of purposes including AEW, intelligence, surveillance, reconnaissance, and tanking.

Until that time, however, the E-3B/Cs will continue to be upgraded. The 40/45 upgrade will mainly affect the following areas:

- Common displays for all controller positions
- Multi-Source Integration of display to include radar, IFF, ESM, L-16, PPLI, CID, and other data inputs into a single target/single track
- Datalink Integration, which is essentially an L-16 software enhancement
- Intelligence Broadcast System to convey real-time and near real-time intelligence to shooters. This would include TIBS, TRAP, and TADIXS-B information

Currently the planned IOC for the 40/45 upgrades is from fiscal year 2008 to fiscal year 2010 and an FOC from fiscal year 2012 to fiscal year 2014, but that could shift to out years depending on funding. In June 2001, Boeing won a $7 billion contract for modernizing and sustaining the current AWACS fleet, and these changes will be conducted prior to any 40/45 upgrades. Yet there are also other ideas concerning what the

U.S. Air Force should do about the future of its AEW fleet. The U.S. Air Force AWACS are some of the most used platforms in its inventory, and as such, there are many people who believe that the service cannot wait for a common aircraft 25 years in the future. The general argument is that the U.S. Air Force should acquire other AEW aircraft to augment or perhaps replace their aging Boeing 707 fleet. Some of the aircraft most frequently mentioned are:

- Boeing 767 AWACS version that is currently being bought
   by the JSDF
- Boeing 737-700 IGW with a MESA antenna similar to the
   RAAF AEW aircraft
- C-130 AEW aircraft

While some of these aircraft, especially the C-130 AEW platform, are less capable than the E-3, the idea is that this aircraft could supplement the AWACS on missions and exercises where a full crew or longer on-station time was not required.

In fact, until 21 August 2000, Northrup-Grumman and Boeing officials were optimistically talking about a potential sales market of up to 50 Boeing 737 AEW aircraft over the next decade. In addition to the proposed sale to Australia, there were early discussions with a number of countries including Turkey, Israel, Italy, Spain, Malaysia, Singapore, South Korea, Taiwan, and Thailand. Notwithstanding the fact that only 72 AWACS platforms have been sold over the past 25 years, many analysts believe that there is still a huge market for the right-priced AEW system. While Ericsson and TCOM may argue about what is the best platform, at $150 to $190 million an airframe, the Boeing 737 compares very favorably to the JSDF E-767, which costs about $400 million a copy.

An alternative approach to an airborne platform for AEW is a space-based system. Placing a radar on a satellite is not a new technology; in fact, the Soviet Union had the RORSAT in use for a number of years throughout the 1980s. While at first glance a space-based system may seem to be ideal, there are a number of drawbacks, which became evident with the use of the RORSAT by the Soviets. First, a blip is a blip is a blip. Therefore, this radar could only tell the operator that something was out there. Without corresponding corollary evidence from other sensors, it is hard to determine the identity of a particular contact. The second major problem is the lack of operators to conduct battle management, which, as anyone knowledgeable about AEW systems knows, is the real value of these platforms. And this may be the number one reason why a space-based system may not be realized in the near future.

A new proposal to extend the range for the AWACS would be to use the Global Hawk UAV as a receive-only platform in a bistatic configuration. The radar returns from targets that are beyond the detection range could be received by the UAV and then relayed back to the Sentry. If conducted properly, this configuration could possibly double the range of the AWACS. A test platform modified by Northrup-Grumman has been funded by the U.S. Air Force and was tested in early 2000, but to date, no official program has been initiated.

**Potential U.S. Marine Corps AEW Platforms**

The U.S. Marine Corps has also examined the C-130 AEW airframe for use in their Marine Air Command and Control System. Fiercely independent, the "Corps" has had to rely on U.S. Air Force and U.S. Navy AEW aircraft to augment their land-based systems. Although the Marines possessed AD-4Ws during Korea, they have not kept or maintained an AEW capability since that time. Interest in acquiring an AEW aircraft has been ongoing for the past 15 years with several important documents including a Tentative Operational Requirement and a Mission Need Statement released as the USMC decided on what kind of platform it needed. However, with the harsh realities of the drawdown and military cutbacks, no monies have been appropriated for a Marine Corps AEW aircraft. Thus, if the money were to become available, possible platforms include the C-130 and V-22 aircraft as candidates for an AEW system, but as of 2001, without funding, prospects are bleak for an organic U.S. Marine Corps AEW capability.

**Other Potential AEW Markets**

A new entry into the AEW market could be the Mexican government. Advanced discussion with Ericsson has led to proposals for a fleet of up to 11 Embraer EMB-145SA AEW aircraft. However, to date Mexico has only signed up to purchase one EMB-145 (AEW&C) airframe and two maritime patrol platforms. While more orders may eventually come, for now the Mexican government is expected to spend up to $250 million on these new aircraft. This sale, if completed, would be the third foreign venture for the Erieye system after Greece and Brazil. It appears from this latest sale that the Swedish platform has a lock as the pro forma choice for the low end of the market. The EMB-145 being sought by Mexico may also be modified with winglets to increase endurance.

The United Kingdom has initiated a number of studies to build a future organic airborne early warning platform for its proposed conventional aircraft carrier. Whether this is a helicopter or a fixed-wing aircraft is obviously dependent on the ship configuration. Westland and Bell Boeing have proposed AEW variants of the EH-101 Merlin and V-22 Osprey to support this requirement, which could have an in-service date of fiscal year 2012.

The NATO decision for the JOSTAR platform also carries real-world operational concerns. In November 1995 when the U.S. Army attempted to deploy Ground Station Modules to Bosnia to support the U.S. Air Force E-8C JSTARS, these U. S. military forces were met with resistance and indifference from the allied nations. Some of this may have been due to the fact that France, Italy, and the United Kingdom all have systems that are competing with the JSTARS for the NATO JOSTAR bid.

The Turkish decision to purchase an AEW system was leaning heavily in favor of the Boeing 737 with a MESA radar until the recent announcement of deferral by the RAAF. The lack of a proven sale by Boeing and the problems associated with the IAF's Phalcon commitment to China has led to a definite slowdown in the decision cycle by the Turkish government. The original requirement was for six aircraft, but only four have been funded so far. As of the summer of 2001, preliminary negotiations began moving forward rapidly with respect to Turkey and it is expected that a contract will be signed in the near future.

The entire Southeast Asian AEW market, including Singapore and South Korea, as well as Pakistan, Taiwan, Thailand, Indonesia, and Malaysia, will depend on the ADF procurement cycle. Since the RAAF purchased the 737 MESA system, the market is now wide-open, with competition for AEW sales at the medium end of the market between the MESA platform and the Erieye. Specifically, South Korea announced in March 2001 that they plan to acquire four AEW aircraft for $1.6 billion between 2002 and 2008. A bidding competition will undoubtedly commence with the deadline of 1 February 2002.

Likewise, Malaysia has also expressed interest in acquiring AEW platforms to augment its long-range surveillance and ground-based radars. No particular aircraft has been identified for this requirement, nor has any funding been set aside. The proposed use for these aircraft would be as defense assets protecting the Malaysian peninsula and territories in Borneo. Both Thailand and Indonesia also have clearly defined needs and requirements for an AEW system but have faced funding deficits. And, finally, Pakistan has also expressed interest in acquiring an AEW capability and is reportedly negotiating with Embraer for up to six EMB-145s.

A proposal for an AEW system for the South African National Defense Force (SANDF) has been developed. As a regional power in Southern Africa, the SANDF is looking into purchasing an AEW platform to use in a multitude of missions, including border patrol and fishery rights protection. However, cost is a huge factor and that may drive the SANDF to using the UAV platform to host an AEW radar. The type of system that South Africa could possibly afford might include the Global Hawk. This type of data could give the SANDF real-time information on the enemy as well as its own forces. The other option for these forces may be the Erieye radar system mounted on an indigenous platform. Although more expensive than a UAV, this aircraft option will give South Africa much more capability in the future. Whether or not the SANDF can afford a manned airborne platform is the ultimate question.

# CHAPTER TWELVE

# The Future of AEW

A irborne Early Warning has become a desirable and, with advances in electronics, an increasingly practical capability worldwide. The number of developers and variety of systems have increased the probability that astute users will be able to find an AEW capability suited to their needs. However, even with the progress noted above, AEW remains among the most expensive and sophisticated of defense technologies, so proliferation is likely to continue at a slow pace.

## The Importance of AEW

The evolution of the AEW aircraft has been a succession of small improvements in the basic designs of the original TBM-3W aircraft and its APS-20 radar. The first AEW programs, Cadillac I and II, were developed to allow the task force commanders to detect incoming hostile air and surface tracks. It was quickly realized that AEW aircraft could be used for a number of other missions that necessitated more capable platforms. The result was an evolutionary succession of aircraft employing a version of the APS-20 radar that included the PB-1W, AF-2W, AD-3W, AD-4W, AD-5W, WV-1/2, and the EC-121. All of these aircraft tried to overcome inherent deficiencies with the radar by increasing the speed of the aircraft and adding more operators. However, the radar picture was not substantially changed until the introduction of the E-1B and the E-2A, when a series of new radar systems was developed. With the advent of the Hawkeye, and in particular the E-2C, bloodlines of naval ship– and shore-based AEW finally merged. The E-2C represents a revolutionary milestone not only in the history of naval AEW, but in the history of air warfare in general. For the first time in more than 30 years of development, the Navy possessed a truly reliable, all-weather, carrier-based AEW aircraft that could operate autonomously or with a CVBG.

The E-2C Hawkeye was the epitome of what all the other naval AEW aircraft had aspired to from the beginning. At the time of its introduction in 1973, this latest version of the Hawkeye was the supreme AEW aircraft in the world. The success of the E-2A and its successors (the E-2B/C) sounded the death knell for land-based naval AEW. The Hawkeye was able to accomplish the mission of the *"Willie Victors"* and still remain with the fleet, combining the missions of the E-1B and the WV-2. Able to operate as an airborne CIC from the confines of the carrier deck, the Hawkeye combined technological sophistication with the inherent flexibility and capability of a carrier-based aircraft.

That is a lot of praise for one aircraft, but one must understand just how far ahead of its time the Hawkeye was when it was introduced. It was literally the grease that made the air wing work. Providing AEW coverage to the fleet, the Hawkeye served as fighter control for the F-4J Phantoms and the new F-14A Tomcats. The E-2C controlled the air wing strikes with the venerable A-7B/E Corsairs and A-6E Intruders, in addition to performing a myriad of other duties. Task force commanders would not launch an attack without an AEW aircraft airborne, and these aircraft participated in all phases of carrier air wing training. The Hawkeye aptly became known as the "Eyes of the Fleet."

The concept of Air Force AEW also evolved through the flexibility, mobility, and survivability of airborne C3 platforms. The need for early threat detection in World War II provided the impetus for a technological revolution in airborne radar and IFF systems. The development of an airborne CIC became a key element of the Air Force's EC-121 and E-3 systems. The EC-121 began service in the Air Force as a strategic surveillance platform, yet emerged from the conflict in Southeast Asia as a mature C3 node. The success of the Connie validated the use of a large-platform AEW while providing the foundation for E-3 design and capabilities. Like the EC-121, the E-3 initially served in a strategic air defense role. However, the all-terrain, all-altitude surveillance capabilities of the E-3 enhanced its potential as a force multiplier. Pulse Doppler technology provided the Air Force with an immense advantage in the area of overland surveillance and detection.

Operation Desert Storm secured the future of Air Force AEW as a key component of joint C3 warfare. AWACS continues to meet the challenges of providing airborne surveillance and forward presence, despite an aging fleet of aircraft. PACOM and Air Combat Command (ACC) AWAC squadrons also continue to play a major role in counter-drug operations. The proven capabilities of the E-3 system make it an attractive asset to foreign Air Forces. France, Great Britain, and Saudi Arabia maintain E-3s in their respective inventories, while the NATO E-3 fleet based in Geilenkirchen, Germany, is proving a valuable asset to operations throughout Europe. Likewise, Japan is also procuring four E-767 aircraft, providing a replacement for the out-of-production 707 airframe. In addition, South Korea and Italy are investigating the feasibility of E-3 purchases as well. So, for the foreseeable future, AWACS will continue to play major roles in a number of Air Forces throughout the world.

**Advantages Inherent in AEW**

Although the concept of AEW was easy to conceptualize, its development was not. Aspirations and expectations often exceeded performance of the earlier aircraft, and one, the E-2A, in fact was canceled during its production run. The unknown quality of naval AEW was severely tested throughout much of the post–World War II era. Yet it was this evolution of aircraft and avionics systems that was to prove its worth over 50 years of operational use. Able to detect and track contacts well beyond the normal limits of ship-based radars, AEW aircraft have vastly expanded the area of influence of the CVBG. The radar coverage provided by AEW aircraft allows an enormous amount of flexibility and capability that was not previously available in a task force that only possessed ship-mounted radars. This feature gives the battle group commander a much better picture of his surrounding environment and enables him to defend his fleet from surprise attack.

From an Air Force perspective, AWACS exploits the three-dimensional nature of aerial warfare by providing speed, range, and versatility within the realm of C3 employment. Given the dynamic, complex environment of low-intensity and conventional theater conflicts, AWACS provides the ideal show of force with minimum risk of escalation. However, AWACS can also respond to short-notice contingencies and facilitate the projection of power abroad. E-3s support operations in conjunction with, or separately from, other military forces by deploying throughout the world. The long-range surveillance, communications, and control capabilities of AWACS sustain the Air Force concept of Global Engagement.

## Were the Military Services Correct in Their Approach?

Could the Navy have continued a two-track system? Perhaps, but probably not. The VW aircraft were expensive to operate, hard to maintain, and probably seen as in direct conflict with VAW assets available to the fleet. Therefore, the Navy decided to operate its AEW forces solely from the decks of aircraft carriers. The Navy chose to protect and justify its AEW aircraft by judiciously concentrating on missions normally associated with the sea-going service. What started out as two separate pipelines with Cadillac I and II aircraft have over the years merged into a single platform, the E-2C Hawkeye. This aircraft epitomizes the evolution of the naval AEW aircraft throughout 50 years of development.

Likewise, Air Force AEW supports strategic and tactical commanders at all echelons by centralizing the air battle and providing a responsive air control system. Commanders can deploy, adjust, concentrate, and maneuver forces to meet the dynamic needs of modern warfare. Technology, combined with effective training, operational experience, and tactical awareness, contributed to the success of AEW systems during Vietnam and the Gulf War. In its short history, Air Force AEW has been and remains an invaluable asset in the arsenal of modern aircraft systems.

The United States continues to place a high value on AEW, and the evolution of the Hawkeye and AWACS will continue for the foreseeable future. The Hawkeye 2000 and the 40/45 upgrade are the next generation of these venerable aircraft and, as this book goes to print, are continuing testing and are beginning their production runs.

The U. S. Navy realizes that accurate sensors are a key to its future success, and the AEW communities of the Navy and U. S. Air Force will continue to play a major role as their aircraft evolve. Follow-on variants to the HE2000, including the HE2005, HE2010, and the CSA, as well as the 40/45 upgrade, will help the Navy and the Air Force keep abreast of technological threats. In addition, with the recent emphasis on littoral warfare, the AWACS and VAW communities are moving toward a supporting role in fire support, close air support, and the ability to work with a variety of forces in maneuver warfare. The increasing value commanders place on modern command, control, communications, and intelligence technology in particular, places "AWACS-like" platforms high on the list of desired capabilities for countries with significant air or naval forces. Improved electronics have also resulted in lighter, more reliable systems that can more easily be tailored to specific applications. When combined with the number of avionics suppliers worldwide, this has increased the potential for new or unique integration efforts. Electronic advances have also somewhat lowered the cost to acquire and operate a variety of AEW platforms. These include smaller aircraft, helicopters, and even aerostats. Yet, as support aircraft, AEW aircraft have not received the attention that they properly deserve. They literally are the centerpiece of an operation, and it is only when the AEW aircraft are not airborne or break down that people truly begin to realize their value to the mission. Quiet efficiency is their trademark, and more often than not, a successful operation hinges on the actions of the AEW operators. This book is a tribute to all of the men and women who made Airborne Early Warning what it is today, the cornerstone of any military evolution, a platform that daily provides for the security of our nation.

# APPENDIX A

# AEW Capabilities by Country

**AUSTRALIA**  ROYAL AUSTRALIAN AIR FORCE
Project Wedgetail: The RAAF selected the Boeing 737-700 aircraft with a
Northrup-Grumman Multi-Role Electronically Scanned Array (MESA) system
over the following other contenders.

**BRAZIL**  BRAZILIAN AIR FORCE
EMB-145 (5)  Eight Embraer 145 aircraft have been ordered, of which five are scheduled
to be fitted with the Ericsson Erieye radar.

**CHILE**  FUERZA AEREA DE CHILE (CHILEAN AIR FORCE)
Phalcon 707 (2)  One of two aircraft originally ordered from Israel has been (1995)
delivered. Primarily used for testing, this aircraft is also called CONDOR.
Aerostats (2)  Two aerostats are in use to test their capability.

**CHINA**  ZHONGKUO SHENMIN TAIFANG TSUNPUTAI
(AIR FORCE PEOPLE'S LIBERATION ARMY)
The proposed prototype was a Russian Il-76 or 707 modified with the Israeli
Phalcon radar. Project on hold as of July 2000.

AVIATION OF THE PEOPLE'S NAVY
Six to eight four-engine land-based (possibly Y-8) AEW aircraft to be equipped
with British Searchwater Radars (RACAL)

**EGYPT**  AL QUWWAT AL JAWWIYA IL MISRIYA
(ARAB REPUBLIC OF EGYPT AIR FORCE)
E-2C (5)  Four Group Øs and One Group II aircraft operating under (1987/1991) the 222
Fighter Regiment, Cairo West Air Base

**FRANCE**  ARMEE DE L'AIR (AIR FORCE)
E-3F (4)  Delivered in 1991, these aircraft are operated by No. 36 AEW Wing, Avord AB

AERONAUTIQUE NAVALE (NAVAL AIR ARM)
E-2C (4)  Intended for the air wing of the new carrier Charles de -Gaulle - four required,
two Group IIs, two HE2000s

FRENCH ARMY
HORIZON  SAR system mounted on a Super-Puma helicopter for AGS

**GREECE**  HELLENIC AIR FORCE
EMB-145 (4)  Four Embraer 145 aircraft fitted with the Ericsson Erieye radar were sold in 1999.

| | |
|---|---|
| **INDIA** | BHARATIYA VAYU SENA (INDIAN AIR FORCE)<br>Airborne Surveillance Warning and Control (ASWAC) aircraft (modified HS-748 carrying French and Indian electronics). Up to six aircraft were initially required. Due to crash of main test aircraft, current project status is unknown. |
| **IRAN**<br>Ilyushin Il-76 (2)<br>Beriev A-50 (2) | ISLAMIC REPUBLIC OF IRAN AIR FORCE<br>"Adnan" - Impounded Iraqi aircraft (1991)–current status unknown<br>"Mainstay" - Reportedly two aircraft were ordered in 1992 – status unknown |
| **IRAQ**<br>Ilyushin Il-76 (3) | AL QUWWAT AL IRAQIYA (IRAQI AIR FORCE)<br>"Adnan" (1989) |
| **ISRAEL**<br><br>E-2C (4)<br>Boeing 707 (2)<br>Aerostat (2) | TSVAH HAGANAH LE ISRAELI - HEYL HA'AVIR<br>(ISRAEL DEFENSE FORCE - AIR FORCE)<br>Group Øs operated by the 192nd Squadron out of (1978)<br>Aircraft modified with the Phalcon radar (1993)<br>Reportedly two aerostats are in use by the IAF. |
| **JAPAN**<br>E-2C (13)<br><br>E-767 (4) | NIHON KOKU JIEITAI (JAPANESE AIR SELF-DEFENSE FORCE)<br>All Group Øs operated by the 601 Hikotai, Misawa Air Base, originally purchased in 1982.<br>Four aircraft on order, first delivery in 1998, still in testing and fit-out phase. |
| **KUWAIT**<br>Aerostat (4) | KUWAITI AIR FORCE<br>TCOM-manufactured aerostats equipped with the TPS-63 2-D radar |
| **NATO AEW FORCE**<br>E-3A (17) | Based in Geilenkirchen, Germany, with operating locations (1982) in Italy, Norway, Greece, and Turkey. Aircraft are nominally registeredin Luxembourg. In addition, E-3Ds (7) of the RAF also fulfill NATO commitments. |
| **RUSSIA**<br><br>Tu-126 (8)<br>A-50 (15)<br><br><br>Kamov Ka-31 (3) | VOYSKA PROTIVO-VOZDUSHNOY OBORONY<br>(TROOPS OF AIR DEFENSE)<br>Status unknown<br>Unit unknown. Assigned to Pechora Air Base<br><br>AVIATSIYA VOYENNO-MORSKOYO FLOTA<br>(AVIATION OF THE NAVAL DEFENSE FLEET)<br>Three to five helicopters reportedly exist. Intended for carrier use. In addition, versions of the AN-72 and YAK-44 have also been tested for AEW use. |
| **SAUDI ARABI**<br><br>E-3A (5) | ALQUWWAT AL JAWWIYA AL MALAKIYA AS SA'UDIYA<br>(ROYAL SAUDI AIR FORCE)<br>Purchased in 1986, these aircraft are operated by the 18th Squadron, King Faisal Air Base, Riyadh |

| **SINGAPORE** | REPUBLIC OF SINGAPORE AIR FORCE |
| E-2C (4) | Purchased in 1987, these Group Øs are flown by the 111 Squadron, Tengah AB |

| **SPAIN** | ARMA AEREA DE LA ARMADA ESPANOLA (SPANISH NAVAL AIR ARM) |
| Sikorsky SH.9 (6) | Operated off the carrier Principe de Austurias (H-3 Sea King AEW) |

| **SWEDEN** | SVENSKA FLYGVAPNET (SWEDISH AIR FORCE) |
| SAAB 340 (5) | Original test platform for Ericsson Erieye Aircraft |
| S100B (6) | Delivered in 1997, these aircraft are used by the Swedish Air Force as a key component of their IADS. |

| **TAIWAN** | CHUNG-KUO KUNG CHUAN (REPUBLIC OF CHINA AIR FORCE) |
| E-2T/2000 (6) | Four Group IIs were ordered in 1994. Two more HE 2000 were ordered in 2000. |

**UNITED ARAB EMIRATES**
Aerostat (4)     TCOM-manufactured using TPD-63 2-D radar

**UNITED KINGDOM** ROYAL AIR FORCE
E-2D (7)     AEW.Mk 1 Delivered in 1991, these aircraft are operated by the 8th and 23rd Squadrons out of Royal Air Force Waddington.

ROYAL NAVY
Sea King (11)     AEW. Mk.2A. All Sea King AEWs operated by 849th Squadron, Culdrose
Sea King (3)     AEW. Mk 5. A Flt assigned HMS Invincible; B Flt, HMS Illustrious
Sea King (3)     AEW. Mk 7. Expected upgrade of existing AEW. Mk 2As
Defender     Using a similar Thorn-EMI radar, the Pilatus Britten-Norman Defender has also been modified to an AEW configuration. Although this aircraft is used by many countries for maritime patrol, no sales of this AEW variant have been reported. One Multi-Sensor Surveillance Aircraft (MSSA), modified with an APG-66 radar has been sold to Turkey.

**USA**     U.S. AIR FORCE
E-3B/C (33)     Operated by the 552nd Air Control Wing, Tinker AFB (1977). One E-3 accidentally lost in 1995.

U.S. NAVY
E-2C (78)     Procurement continuing (1973). Mixture of Group Øs and Group IIs with the whole fleet upgraded by 2000.
C-130 AEW (1)     Currently used as a testing platform for UESA antenna.

U.S. COAST GUARD/CUSTOMS
UP-3As     U.S. Coast Guard/Customs have also used AEW assets to combat drug smuggling, including P-3 AEW&Cs and tethered aerostats equipped with radar.

# APPENDIX B

# Evolution of AEW Aircraft: A Timeline

| | 1945 | 1955 | 1965 | 1975 | 1985 | 1995 | 2005 |
|---|---|---|---|---|---|---|---|
| TBM-3W | ——— | | | | | | |
| PB-1W | ——— | | | | | | |
| AF-2W | —— | | | | | | |
| AD-3W | | —— | | | | | |
| AD-4W | | —— | | | | | |
| AD-5W | | —— | | | | | |
| GANNET | | | —————— | | | | |
| WV-1 | —— | | | | | | |
| WV-2 | | —————————— | | | | | |
| WV-2E | | — | | | | | |
| E-1B | | | —————— | | | | |
| E-2A | | —— | | | | | |
| E-2B | | | —————— | | | | |
| E-2C(0) | | | | ——————————— | | | |
| E-2C(I) | | | | | | — | |
| E-2C(II) | | | | | | —— | |
| HE2000 | | | | | | —— | |
| MOSS | | | | ——— | | | |
| MAINSTAY | | | | | ——————— | | |
| EC-121 | | —————————— | | | | | |
| E-3A | | | | ——— | | | |
| E-3B | | | | | ——————— | | |
| E-3C | | | | | ——————— | | |
| E-3D | | | | | | —— | |
| E-3F | | | | | | —— | |
| E-3A NATO | | | | | ——————— | | |
| EC-130 | | | | | — | — | — |
| ERIEYE | | | | | | —— | |

202

# APPENDIX C

# AEW Aircraft Matrix

| | AWACS | Hawkeye | Helicopter | Erieye | Aerostats | Other |
|---|---|---|---|---|---|---|
| Brazil | | | | EMB-145 (4) | | |
| Chilean Air Force | | | | | 2 | Phalcon (2) |
| Egyptian Air Force | | E-2C 0/II (5) | | | | |
| French Air Force | E-3F (4) | | | | | |
| French Army | | | HORIZON | | | |
| French Navy | | E-2F (4) | | | | |
| Greek Air Force | | | | EMB-145 (4) | | |
| Indian Air Force | | | | | | |
| Iranian Air Force | | | | | | |
| Iraqi Air Force | | | | | | |
| Israeli Air Force | | E-2C 0 (4) | | | 2 | Phalcon (2) |
| Italian Air Force | | | CRESO | | | |
| JSDF | | E-2C 0 (13) | | | | |
| Kuwaiti Air Force | | | | | 4 | |
| People's Liberation Air Force | | | | | | |
| People's Liberation Navy | | | | | | |
| Peru | | | | | | |
| Poland | | | | | | |
| Republic of Korea Air Force | | | | | | |
| Royal Air Force | E-3D (7) | | | | | |
| Royal Australian Air Force | | | | | | 737/MESA (7) |
| Royal Navy | | | SH-3 (10) | | | |
| Royal Saudi Air Force | E-3A (5) | | | | | |
| Russian Air Force | | | | | | |
| Russian Navy | | | | | | |
| Singaporean Air Force | | E-2C 0 (4) | | | | |
| Spanish Navy | | | SH-9 (6) | | | |
| Swedish Air Force | | | | S100B (6) | | |
| Taiwanese Air Force | | E-2C 0/II (6) | | | | |
| Turkish Air Force | | | | | | |
| UAE Air Force | | | | | 4 | |
| US Air Force | E-3B/C (33) | | | | 12 | |
| US Coast Guard | | | | | | C-130 (1) |
| US Customs Service | | | | | 4 | UP-3A (4) |
| US Navy | | E-2C II (78) | | | | |
| | AWACS | Hawkeye | Helicopter | Erieye | Aerostat | Other |

# APPENDIX D

# AWACs Variants

|  | E-3A | E-B/C | E-3D | E-3F |
|---|---|---|---|---|
| Numbers | 17 | 33 | 7 | 4 |
| Engines | Pratt&Whitney | Pratt&Whitney | CFM-56 | CFM-56 |
| AAR | Boom | Boom | Boom/Drag | Boom/Drag |
| Consoles | 9 | 14 | 9 | 9 |
| UHF Radios | 12 | 15 | 9 | 10 |
| HQ/SAT Comms | 4+1 | 6+2 | 4+1 | 4+1 |
| VHF Radios | 2 | 4 (1 FM) | 2 | 3 (1 FM) |
| ESM Suite | Boeing | 30/35 | Yellowgate | 2001 |
| Maritime | Basic | Basic | MSSP | Basic |
| Crew Numbers | 17 | 23 | 17 | 17 |

# APPENDIX E

# Hawkeye Variants

|  | Group O | Group II | HE2000 |
|---|---|---|---|
| Egypt | 4 | 1 | |
| France | | 2 | 2 |
| Israel | 4 | | |
| Israel | 4 | | |
| JSDF | 13 | | |
| Singapore | 4 | | |
| Taiwan | | 4 | 2 |
| United States | 10 (USNR) | 62 | 6 |

# APPENDIX F

# Erieye Variants

|        | SAAB 340 | EMB-145 | S100B |
|--------|----------|---------|-------|
| Brazil |          | 5       |       |
| Greece |          | 4       |       |
| Sweden | 5        |         | 6     |

# APPENDIX G

# Class "A" Accidents— E-2/E-3 Aircraft

| Type A/C | Date | Fatalities | Cause |
|----------|------|------------|-------|
| E-2A | 09 April 1970 | 5 | Electrical fire in FEC |
| E-2B | 08 August 1972 | 2 | Uncontrollable elevator control problems |
| E-2B | 19 June 1973 | 5 | Pilot error: disoriented in weather |
| TE-2A | 31 July 1974 | 4 | Pilot error: abnormal power levels |
| E-2B | 02 November 1975 | 0 | Pilot error: fuel starvation |
| E-2C | 14 January 1978 | 5 | Elevator control pushrod became disengaged/loss of elevator control |
| E-2B | 13 November 1979 | 1 | Pilot error: fuel exhaustion (one aircrew parachuted to safety) |
| E-2C | 17 August 1985 | 2 | Pilot error: failed to use power lever lock and was unable to move power levers past flight idle detent on waveoff from aircraft carrier |
| E-2C | 20 August 1990 | 4 | Electrical fire in FEC (USCG) |
| E-2C | 08 July 1991 | 0 | Starboard engine fire (bailout) |
| E-2C | 31 July 1992 | 5 | Electrical fire in FEC |
| E-2C | 26 March 1993 | 5 | Pilot error: crew rest and disorientation |
| E-3C | 22 Sept ember 1995 | 24 | Dual engine failure: flew into a flock of geese |
| E-3B | 14 July 1996 | 0 | Bird strike on takeoff: aborted ground roll (NATO) |

# Index

KA-31 "Helix B", 126
Kadena Air Base, 75, 80, 109
King, Adm. Ernest J., 3
Kirkland Air Force Base, 73
Kuhn, Ens. Joe, 34
Lakenheath Air Base, England, 96
Langley Air Force Base, 75
Libyan Air Force (LAAF), 93
Lockheed C-130 AEW, 166, 190
Lockheed C-130, 102
Lockheed EC-121, 33, 49–51, 55, 56, 59, 69, 76, 121, 125, 170, 195
Lockheed ES-3 Viking, 187
Lockheed P2V-5/P2V-7, 12
Lockheed P-3 Orion, 137, 138, 166
Lockheed RC-121, 28, 31
Lockheed S-3B, 187
Lockheed U-2, 117
LTV A-7B/E Corsair, 195
MAGIC 2000, 152
McChord Air Force Base, 74
McClellan Air Force Base, 27, 28, 31, 35
McCoy Air Force Base, 53
McDonnell Douglas DC-8, 70
McDonnell Douglas F-4A Phantom II, 19
Ministry of Defense, 141
Multi-Mission Aircraft, 120
Multi-Sensor Surveillance Aircraft, 140
Mutual Defense Assistance Program (MDAP), 17
NAF Naha, Okinawa, 52
NAS Atlanta, 101, 109
NAS Atsugi, 64, 109
NAS Cubi Point, 52
NAS Miramar, 66, 88
NAS Norfolk, 14, 62, 88, 99, 103, 109, 179
NAS North Island, 62
NAS Oceana, 62
NAS Paxtuxent River, 14, 30
NAS Pt. Mugu, 109
NAS Quonset Point, 14, 62
NAS Roosevelt Roads,100
NATO Air-Ground Surveillance (AGS) Program, 121
Naval Air Facility Glynco, 19
Naval Air Weapons Station (MCAS), 88
Nelson, Lt. Commander Robert, 34
North American Aerospace Defense Command (NORAD), 73
North Atlantic Barrier, 40
North Vietnamese Air Force (NVAF), 55
North, Lt. Col. Oliver, 94
Operation Allied Forces, 181
Operation Blue Straw, 51
Operation Decisive Endeavor, 180
Operation Deliberate Force, 139, 180
Operation Deliberate Guard, 180
Operation Deny Flight, 1, 139, 180
Operation Desert Shield, 170–177
Operation Desert Storm, 1, 80, 188, 170–174, 180, 196
Operation Enduring Freedom, 123

Operation Joint Endeavor, 119
Operation Just Cause, 80
Operation Maritime Monitor, 180
Operation Noble Anvil, 119, 143
Operation Peace for Galilee, 123, 125, 156, 157
Operation Proven Force, 171, 172
Operation Provide Comfort, 84
Operation Sky Monitor, 139, 180
Operation Southern Watch, 110, 180
Operation Sowrball, 122
Operation Thunderbolt, 98
Operation Vigilant Overview, 74
Operational Development Force (OPDEVFOR), 11
Operations in the Vicinity of Libya (OVL), 93
Otis Air Force Base, 27, 28, 36, 53
Pacific Barrier, 33
Panavia F-3 Tornado, 139
Passive Detection System (PDS), 67
People's Air Force of China, 158
People's Liberation Navy, 164
Phalcon, 155
Positive Identification Radar Advisory Zone (PIRAZ), 58
Precision Surveillance and Targeting (PS&T), 187
Project LAST (Low-Altitude Surveillance Task), 131
Project Mercury, 50
Project NA-112, 4
Project NA-178, 5
Project Wedgetail, 166, 169
Radar Modernization Program (RMP), 186
Radar Sensitivity Improvement Program (RSIP), 112
Radar Technology Insertion Plan, 119
RAF Waddington, 139, 141
Ramstein Air Base, 72
Reagan, President Ronald, 94, 98, 99, 159
Republic of Korea Air Force, 163
Republic of Singapore Air Force, 163
Ritchie, Capt. Steve, 58
Royal Air Force (RAF), 129, 139, 140, 179
Royal Australian Air Force (RAAF), 166, 167
Royal Canadian Air Force (RCAF), 78
Royal Navy, 129, 133, 179
Royal Saudi Air Force (RSAF), 159
Royal Swedish Air Force, 143, 144
RVAW-120, 63
Saab S100B Argus, 144
*Saratoga* Battle Group, 176
Schaffel, Kenneth, 21
Schreivogel, T. Sgt. Gene, 37
Search and rescue (SAR), 18
Semi-Automatic Ground Environment, 33
Seventh Air Force, 59
Sikorsky HR2S-1W, 12

Sikorsky SH-3 AEW, 132–134, 142
Sikorsky UH-60 Blackhawk helicopters, 84
SOSTAR (Belgium), 153
South African National Defense Force (SANDF), 193
Strategic Air Command, 21
Tactical Action Officer (TAO), 89–91
Tactical Air Control Center (TACC), 171
Tactical Airborne Reconnaissance Pod System (TARPS), 179
Tactical Defense Systems (TDS), 123
Tan Son Nhut Air Base, South Vietnam, 55
Tinker Air Force Base, 76, 77, 80, 84, 109, 170
Tupolev Tu -114, 127
Tupolev-126, 127
Tyndall Air Force Base, 80
U.S. Air Force Electronic Systems Division (ESD), 69
U.S. Air Force Theater Air Control System (TACS), 79
U.S. Defense Threat Reduction Agency, 169
U.S. Navy Carrier Airborne Early Warning Wing Twelve (CAEWW-12), 99
UHF Electronically Steerable Array (UESA), 186
Unmanned Aerial Vehicles (UAVs), 117
USS *America* (CV-66), 96, 177
USS *Bon Homme Richard* (CV-31), 46
USS *Coral Sea* (CV-43), 96
USS *Dwight D. Eisenhower* (CVN-69), 174
USS *Enterprise* (CVN-65), 48
USS *Forrestal* (CV-59), 104
USS *Franklin D. Roosevelt* CV-42), 51, 63
USS *Independence* (CV-62), 64, 94, 174
USS *John F. Kennedy* (CV-67), 94
USS *Kitty Hawk* (CV-63), 64, 65
USS *Midway* (CVA-41), 64, 103, 175
USS *Nimitz* (CVN-68), 177
USS *Ranger* (CV-61), 175, 177
USS *Saratoga* (CV-60), 87, 94, 96, 174, 179
USS *Theodore Roosevelt* (CVN-71), 105, 177, 178
USS *Yorktown* (CVS-10), 17
VAW Squadrons, 62–65
VPB-101, 9, 13
VPW (Patrol Search), 13
Westland Sea King, 131
Wiesner, J.B., 5
WV-2, 26, 42
WV-2E, 43
XAD-1W, 17
XBT2D-1, 16
Y-8 Cub, 158
Yurchak, Comdr. John, 104
Zia, Comdr. Ralph K., 95
ZPG-2W, 42, 182
ZPG-3W, 12, 42, 43, 182